LOST and FOUND

Also by Betty Jean Lifton

I'm Still Me
Twice Born: Memoirs of an Adopted Daughter
Children of Vietnam (with Thomas C. Fox)
Return to Hiroshima (photographs by Eikoh Hosoe)
Contemporary Children's Theater (editor)

FOR CHILDREN

The Orange Monster
The Silver Crane
The Dwarf Pine Tree
Kap the Kappa
Mogo the Mynah
Joji and the Dragon
The Secret Seller
Jaguar, My Twin

Betty Jean Lifton

LOST
and
FOUND

The Adoption
Experience

The Dial Press
New York

Published by
The Dial Press
1 Dag Hammarskjold Plaza
New York, New York 10017

Grateful acknowledgment is made for the use of portions of the following:

The American Dream by Edward Albee, copyright © 1960, 1961 by Edward Albee. Reprinted by permission of Coward, McCann and Geoghegan, Inc.

"Breaking Open" by Muriel Rukeyser, copyright © 1973 by Muriel Rukeyser. "Speed of Darkness" by Muriel Rukeyser, copyright © 1968 by Muriel Rukeyser. Reprinted by permission of the author.

"Pavanne for the Passing of a Child," first printed in *Primagravida,* copyright © 1974 by Laura Chester, published by Christopher's Books, Santa Barbara, California. Reprinted by permission of the author.

The Gates by Muriel Rukeyser, copyright © 1976 by Muriel Rukeyser. Reprinted by permission of McGraw-Hill Book Company.

"The Puzzle" from *How To Save Your Own Life* by Erica Jong, copyright © 1977 by Erica Mann Jong. Reprinted by permission of Holt, Rinehart and Winston, Publishers.

Library of Congress Cataloging in Publication Data

Lifton, Betty Jean.
  Lost and found.

  Includes bibliographical references.
  1. Adoptions—United States. 2. Children, Adopted—United States. 3. Children, Adopted—United States—Family relationships. I. Title.
HV875.L458 1979b   929′.1   78-21526
ISBN 0-385-27901-9

For Karen and Ken—roots and wings

Contents

PART THREE—ROOTS AND WINGS

LOST and FOUND

Part One

LOST

In this world
There is
No perfect drop of dew—
Not even on the lotus.
ISSA

1

On Being Adopted

I am sitting in a small New York café in the late afternoon with Judith, an actress and writer. We have gone there rather than to either of our apartments because it is quieter. A telephone won't ring, a child won't wander in. Here, with the roar of traffic swirling about us, we are alone, free to disconnect ourselves from our present families and talk about the "other" us, the child in us.

Judith is the first friend I have scheduled to talk with about what the adopted and nonadopted have in common as people, as marriage partners, as parents. She is not adopted, I am. I want to explore how much being adopted influences who we are. I grew up thinking it meant everything. Although I never spoke of it to anyone, it permeated my being like a fungus spreading slowly through the various stages of my development. Since it was invisible contamination, I passed as being nonadopted. It was a secret. I am not proud of that now.

Judith is not saying the things I expected to hear. "The pain in growing up is not too different whether you are adopted or not," she informs me. "In fact, I hated my mother. I was afraid of her. She was a killer. I got out at sixteen, as soon as I could."

She speaks rapidly now, passionately. She has told this mother-daughter story before to many analysts over the years as she sought release from her anxiety. I listen as a woman, but being adopted I am an impostor. I am one of those animations that keeps shifting in size and shape. At times I am a helpless change-ling, at others an omnipotent creature from another planet. I am not real, and so I do not have a receiving set that will pick up everything Judith is trying to tell me.

I will miss some things.

She does not understand this. She keeps seeing me as someone like herself and her other friends. I forgive her. That's the mistake all nonadopted people make.

"I think the obsession to find out who you are is universal," she is saying. "It is an obsession to re-create yourself. To give birth to yourself under another set of circumstances." She pauses, and then adds: "I always thought adoptive parents must be better than natural ones, because at least those people wanted a child."

Does she understand what she is saying? She speaks as if the mere *wanting* makes one into a good parent.

I know that not too many people have thought about adoption. Why should they? They have accepted society's myth that the adoptive family is no different from the biological one. I remember a friend who was raised by her grandmother telling me that she never realized adopted people were displaced persons like herself. We decided that it was because everyone is so busy pretending there is no displacement in adoption that the Adoptee's feelings are not allowed to radiate out into the community. Even Judith, who understood so much, having been sensitized to others through confronting her own pain, could not grasp what it meant to grow up separated from one's own blood kin.

"It doesn't matter if the person is your real or adoptive parent," she insists. "What matters is if they are truly loving. Otherwise you think there is something the matter with *you*. You take the blame on yourself. If a person cannot keep the illusion of being loved, she might commit suicide."

"But even if you are rejected by your parents, at least the blood knot holds you," I argue. "You don't blow away. You are rooted on this earth."

It was not roots we were talking about, but being rooted.

"Still at some stage of your life you have to give birth to yourself," she counters. "You have to recover and rewrite your own history."

But histories must have a beginning, I tell myself. Judith knows where she began.

Over the next year I had many conversations like this with nonadopted men and women. At times they sounded like a broken record, and so did I. At times we seemed to have a lot in common, and then we would be worlds apart. But we got a lot of insights into each other, and ourselves, in the process.

I came to understand that all people, if they dare to think at all, think of themselves in some sense as orphans—foundlings—who are struggling with problems around alienation. Everyone has some feeling of having been deprived, of playing the impostor because they're not supposed to be here. Everyone is in some kind of pain. Everyone, as Loren Eiseley observed, contains within himself a ghost continent.

And yet—everyone but the adopted has caught a glimpse, however fleeting, of his own ghosts. Unlike the *real* orphan who still carries his family name, the Adoptee is cut off completely from his past. And though he has "psychological" parenting in the adoptive home, he suffers a severe physical deprivation in being cut off from anyone whose body might serve as a model for both the wondrous and fearsome possibilities of his own. To explain this to the nonadopted is like asking the sighted to see into the dark isolation of the blind. Even the adopted, themselves, do not always perceive the peril of the darkness within them.

It was to try to purge myself of that darkness that I wrote *Twice Born,*[1] my own memoir of what it was like to grow up adopted and then set out on the forbidden search for origins. But I remained haunted by the complexity of this subject even afterward. Rather than freeing me as a writer to go on to other things, it seemed to plunge me deeper into the mysteries around what it means to be adopted. I was inundated with letters from men and women telling me I had told the story of *their* lives, that my experience was a mirror image of what they had been through. It made me realize that I had plumbed the depths of my own personal journey, but not its universality. What did I share in common with those who recognized a kindred spirit in me, a voice that seemed to come from within themselves?

It was with this kind of question in mind that I set out to collect and collate the experiences of other Adoptees. I limited my subjects to those who had been separated from their birth parents at an early age and were raised by non–blood-related people. I refer to them as the Adoptee, which I use in an androgynous sense, since the adopted come in both sexes.

The Adoptees you will find in this book—some lost, some

found, some still in limbo—represent the hundreds of adopted men and women I have been in touch with over the past few years. Their names, and in some cases their professions, have been changed to protect the privacy of their adoptive and birth parents, but their stories are as they told them—and they wanted them to be told. They have all faced the questions I am raising, though they have not necessarily answered them. We have communicated through individual interviews, in weekly rap sessions, and by mail and questionnaires when distance separated us. Many of them sought me out by phone or letter because they thought I had the answers to what was troubling them; others I myself sought out because I hoped something in their situation would illuminate the questions I was pondering.

Among other things, I wanted to understand if there is such a thing as an adoption syndrome—a series of traits that are peculiar to adopted people. What are the inner factors that make some people preoccupied with knowing about their lost origins, while others are able to turn off this need? Why does one take that final step of contacting the birth parent, while another dares not? What happens after reunion? Did those who were lost consider themselves found?

And something more.

What importance is there to the blood tie? How profound is the folk saying "blood is thicker than water"? What happens to people when they are cut off from their blood connections?

Is our need to return to our roots related to Jung's archetypal urge to reconnect the severed tie? To the biological homing instincts of birds, or to the migratory instinct of lemmings, who seem driven to seek out the land of their ancestors, now covered by sea?

One summer when I had an opportunity to meet Edward Wilson, the father of sociobiology, at a conference, I asked him if it is "the secret wisdom of our genes" that propels the adopted to seek their blood kin. I expected a ready answer from this advocate of genetic influence on social behavior, but even he had not thought about this question.

"Perhaps it is not mere happenstance that people speak of 'blood of my blood,' 'flesh of my flesh,' " he said with caution. "Perhaps there is a genetic tendency to seek physical bonding and to feel deprived when it is missing. It seems plausible. We would need to study this."

Stephen Jay Gould, the paleontologist, whom I also consulted, was vague on the subject, too. "A study should be made to see if those who feel the need to search were imprinted on their mothers in those first hours after birth," he suggested.

Data are the life line of science.

"There is no one who knows these answers yet," Erik Erikson told me. "That data must be gathered by the adopted themselves. Since they are the ones who have been deprived of genetic bonding, they are the ones who can furnish insight into this condition."

That is what I have tried to do. But I am aware that in my description of the Adoptee's life cycle—from passively being chosen to actively making choices—I concentrate only on those moments of intense awareness when Adoptees are tapping their pain, when they are trying to dredge up the repressed feelings that until now they had not dared to bring to the surface. I know that the adopted are not always suffering, that like everyone else they laugh, they love, they have moments of incredible happiness.

What I am dwelling on—the pain, the feeling of emptiness, of being outsiders—is the neglected dimension of the adoption experience. I want to evoke that part not looked at before, so that the reader's imagination can be stirred, so that he or she may come to think "Ah, so that's what it's like to be adopted." And in the process gain some insight into the frailties inherent in all relationships, whether by blood or social bonding.

This book is only a beginning. I have tried to look at the psychological meaning of adoption from all sides—from the point of view of the adoptive parents and birth parents, as well as of the Adoptees—which has meant uncovering the paradoxes and conflicts embedded in what psychiatrists have called "an experiment in our society."

Many of the parents had gotten in touch with me after reading *Twice Born*. They too had questions and doubts. The adoptive parents were obsessed with knowing the best way to tell their children they were adopted, and how to handle those who wanted to search. The birth mothers were obsessed with knowing how they could help get the records updated and open, and if they had a right to search for their children.

Both groups had experienced a lot of pain. In their own ways, they wanted what was best for the child.

I began to realize that to exclude these two seemingly op-

posed groups would be to write about Adoptees in the very
vacuum I was trying to remove them from. We were all in this
together, acting and being acted upon, in a social arrangement
whose forces we could not fully understand or control. We were
our own unique family, held together and separated by our
unique secrets, which were, in effect, forcing each of us to lead
a double life.

What do I mean by this? Consider.

The Adoption Game—as I call it—requires Adoptees to lead
a split existence. Cut off as they are from knowledge of their
origins, they go underground emotionally. While seeming to live
entirely in the "real" world with their adoptive parents and
friends, they are inhabiting a subterranean world of fantasies and
fears governed by demons, which they can share with no one.

The adoptive parents, meanwhile, are leading another kind
of double life. Having spent years trying to conceive a baby of
their own, they now pretend that adoption is the superior way
of parenting: "Other people had to take what they got, but we
were able to choose you." And while believing themselves to be
doing everything for their children's well-being, they are actually
withholding from them the very knowledge they need for their
development into healthy adults. This double role of savior/with-
holder eventually works against the adoptive parents, estranging
them from the very children they want to hold close.

So, too, the birth mother, from the moment she surrenders
her baby, is forced into this double life. Advised by the "experts"
to pretend it never happened, she never tells anyone what was
probably the most important and traumatic event of her life—her
first baby, gone, in a relinquishment as irrevocable as death. She
has her next child as if it is her first. On the surface she is a
virtuous, often religious, woman, but deep inside she knows she
is, and always will be, an impostor.

Because of the human capacity to repress, most Adoptees,
adoptive parents, and birth parents do not understand that they
are leading double lives, that the Adoption Game has made impostors of them all. They know that something is wrong with their
relationships, or inside them, but they cannot pinpoint the source.

We will try to pinpoint it in the course of this book.

2

Messages from the Underground

1920s
Today is the day we give babies away,
With a half of pint of tea.
You open the lid, and there is a kid,
As healthy as it can be.

CHICAGO TRIBUNE PERSONALS
Wanted to adopt Baby Girl up to 4 years. Will furnish
ideal home and best refs. Address M 476, Tribune.

Wanted for adoption by wealthy Chicago couple, infant
boy or girl. Address KH 386, Tribune.

Want home. 7 year old boy, adoption.
Call 2932 Indiana Ave., Chicago.

1970s
Today is the day the baby grew up,
Drank the tea, ate the cup.
She gave a loud sigh, and said, "Who am I?"
And went on a search to see.

NEW YORK TIMES PERSONALS
Adopted? Searching for a male born Nov. 1943, a female
born July 1957, & a male born Aug. 1955. All born &
adopted in Chgo. area. Write: G.L.F., Box 2199, Chgo.

Reward info on all adoptees accepted for search register
(Confidential).

Judy Horton—born 9-20-48—is searching for her mother
Shirley Mae Horton. Call collect.

Will the former Mary Priveterre or anyone knowing her
whereabouts please contact her natural son, Bruce
Stevens. . . . Ms. Priveterre was known to have been in
Coral Gables, Florida, or vicinity in the years 1947–49.
Important and urgent.

9

Today I open my *New York Times* and check the Personal columns. There is a notice asking if anyone has knowledge of a baby girl abandoned at 540 Southern Boulevard, the Bronx, on February 22, 1935. And a phone number. I try to imagine how many years this woman has been searching, if this is her last desperate attempt to make contact with someone out there. And if she will be found.

I see my friend Maxine's ad further down the column. "ADOPTEE FEMALE Esther born 10/3/37 Crown Heights Hospital, seeks Ruth Green or anyone who knows her whereabouts." And a box number.

Maxine has been searching for five years. Today on her fortieth birthday she is giving herself this present—a three-day special. If nothing happens—then what? Until now her life has been stalled in this quest. Unmarried, she has been unable to move either backward or forward in time. The only way to exorcise the baby and free the woman is to find the port of entry through which she came into the world. The harbor is sealed.

It is hard to remember that only in the last few years have the adopted dared to use this method. For, just as it became taboo after the 1920s for couples to advertise for children in the newspapers—adoption agencies were founded to handle such solemn matters—so did it become taboo for adopted children, whatever age, to seek out those parents from whom they had been separated.

It is still taboo, but things are changing—slowly. The very landscape of adoption, as we once knew it, has been defoliated by the Pill, the legalization of abortion, and the determination of young unwed mothers to hold on to their offspring. Few healthy, white babies are left to fertilize the barren adoptive soil. We see infants being imported like precious saplings from Korea, Thailand, Latin America—harvested by the ingenious rich in the fields of the demoralized poor. We see these children's roots being severed just like ours before them—this has not changed—and we wonder in what manner, what code, they will someday seek what is lost to them.

The Lost-and-Found columns we read now are filled with the broken taboos, the fragmented lives of yesterday's children. They are sending messages from the underground, from the underbelly of a Puritan society. The lost call out to each other in code that may or may not be picked up. The message is always different, and yet always the same—Is anyone out there? Is anyone looking for me?

But—some readers will protest here—not all Adoptees feel a need to know their heritage. You can't speak for all of them.

And they are right.

The majority of Adoptees (and I count myself among them) manage to make some kind of accommodation to their existential condition while they are growing up. Many thrive, being able to channel their heightened sensibilities into some creative expression. However, there are always the less hardy who become permanently lost. Most we'll never hear of, but a few make the headlines:

Karen Ann Quinlan, the girl in the coma, sleeping out the last stages of her search for self after an overdose of drugs and liquor, her rage turned inward, her body in the fetal position in which she began; David Berkowitz, the infamous "Son of Sam," the impostor who did not know whose son he was, venting his crazed rage on women victims who may or may not have symbolized the mother he felt rejected by.

A few months before she went into her coma, Karen Ann wrote in her journal: "I wish to curl myself into a Fetal rose/and rest in the eternal womb awhile."[1]

Who can say why Karen Ann chose to sleep, while David chose to kill? Society becomes preoccupied with legalisms—Does she have a right "to die with dignity"? Is he sane enough to stand trial? The law does not concern itself with the inner turmoil that led each of these young people to their tragic destiny. Here were two who did not succeed in mastering the distorted reality of their lives. Their apparatus was too fragile to make it over the mined roadbed that the adoption system lays for us all. A defect in the genes perhaps? Or in the system?

It is this system and what it does to those who grow up in it that we must examine here. And in the process we will unfreeze time, explore the path not taken, wander through what might have been, and re-create what is.

3

The Adoption Game

Few Adoptees know the history of adoption while they are growing up adopted. I, who hid my special status from everyone, certainly did not. But when I came to understand that it was *my* history, and how it had influenced my fate, I went back to its origins—which I found as entwined with mythology as my own.[1]

In the beginning, we are told by the social historians, there was the word—adoption. It was rare in the animal world, but not in ours. There were guidelines for it in the Babylonian Code of Hammurabi, the oldest written set of laws. There was Moses, adopted by the Pharaoh's daughter who found him abandoned in the bullrushes; and Oedipus, adopted by the King and Queen of Corinth after he was left to die on the mountain.

Moses and Oedipus are the Adoptee's forefathers, the beginning of a long chain down through time; a chain that snaked through the Holy Roman Empire, through the modern kingdoms of Europe and Asia, until it eventually made its way to the United States of America. We do not know if Moses ever asked, "Who am I?" We do know what happened when Oedipus asked that question, and what were the consequences of his not knowing—until it was too late. By that time he had committed murder and incest, and put out his own eyes.

12

We have no record of what happened to the millions of other Adoptees from ancient times until now: whether those children in Babylonian times who persisted in searching for their fathers and mothers were returned to them, as the Code of Hammurabi decreed, or if those adopted by courtiers, a special group forbidden to search, had their eyes and tongues torn out when they defied the law.

We have no testaments of the experiences of Adoptees separated from their blood kin in any period: we have neither songs of joy, nor cries of rage.

After adoption the rest was silence.

Until recently in this country—until the ferment of the 1960s spawned the various liberation movements—the Adoptee was in the closet. If he was adopted, he didn't tell others. If she wanted to know about her past, she didn't ask questions. If they felt rootless and alienated, they endured it. If they were afraid of unknowingly committing incest, with a brother or sister, they didn't marry.

They were the true silent minority. They were playing the Adoption Game.

Rules of the Game

Without intending to, R. D. Laing has given us a perfect description of what the world looks like through the eyes of the Adoptee in his book *Knots*. Here we have a series of human interactions—tangles, impasses, binds, dysfunctions, knots—that make up the game of life as people play it with each other:

> They are playing a game. They are playing at not playing a game. If I show them I see they are, I shall break the rules and they will punish me. I must play their game, of not seeing I see the game.

Until now the players of the Adoption Game were said to make up a triangle—adoptive parents, birth parents, and the child. But actually there are many more people involved—the social workers who place the child, the lawyers and doctors who arrange private adoptions, the judges who seal the records, and the clerks who guard the records like lion dogs protecting the sacred temples wherein lies the godhead.

I see the game as a circle. The Adoption Circle. Sometimes the baby is in the center of the circle, and the other players are outside. In that case, the baby is enclosed, encapsulated, shut off from everyone else, while those outside form a homogeneous group. As one man put it, "I always felt like the boy in the plastic bubble—you know, the one who was born without resistance to disease. The bubble was like an invisible shield. I could see, I could even come close to others, but I could not be touched."

However, the game can also be played with the baby outside the circle and everyone else within. A woman expressed it this way: "My parents said I was the best thing that ever happened to them. But I always felt they were inside the circle, and I was on the outside looking in, never feeling a part of them."

As If

Another name for the Adoption Game, be it circle or triangle, is the Game of As If. Everyone pretends *as if* the Adoptee belongs to the family raising him or her, belongs on all levels, not just the social-psychological one. This version is not unlike the emperor who has no clothes, in that everyone must pretend the Adoptee never had any other parents. The adoptive parents embrace the child *as if* it were of their own blood and ask the child to live *as if* this were true. To share the illusion.

Inherent in the adoption process is the expectation that the child is to regard the birth parents *as if* dead—if not literally, then certainly symbolically. They are, in other words, taboo.

We find words to support this in some of our state adoption statutes:

> Custody may be awarded for a temporary duration but a decree of adoption severs forever every part of the parent and child relationship; severs the child entirely from its own family tree and engrafts it upon that of another. For all legal and practical purposes a child is the same as dead to its parents.[2]

Such statutes have the effect of bequeathing death as a legacy to the adopted child, who will internalize it as a taboo as fearsome as those that primitive societies placed around their dead.

The Veil between the Living and the Dead

The English, always articulate, went right to the heart of this death-tainted matter in a court ruling before their records were unsealed:

> In general it is the policy of the law to make the veil between the past and present lives of adopted people as opaque and impenetrable as possible, like the veil which God has placed between the living and the dead.[3]

A veil. Reading these words is like an epiphany.

I recognize it as the veil which beckons the Adoptee in his dreams, strangles her in her nightmares. It drapes the coffins of his ancestors. It masks the face of her mother and her father. It conceals his past, cloaks her reality. It hides the beast that must be slain in the labyrinth.

In moments of acquiescence, the Adoptee salutes this veil like a flag. In moments of wild abandon he waves it like a matador's cloak in front of the demons. In moments of despair she dons it like a garment of mourning.

The veil is a patchwork quilt that comes down to us through the ages, a work of folk art with no signature. Where did the design for it originate? Why did it have to be opaque? Perhaps, as lawyer C. L. Gaylord tells us:

> The ancient and traditional concept of adoption is that as of the moment of the adoption, the child is literally born again. It has, *by law*, been given a second birth. Its past life is cancelled out. The child is a new person. . . .
>
> Historically, adoption could probably not have survived without a willingness on the part of the members of early societies to believe, or at least pretend to believe, that adoption could make the adopted child something the child was not: the blood relation of the adoptive parents. It apparently was crucial that people accept that religious and legal rituals could emulate nature. To the extent that members of archaic societies were willing to so believe, adoption was accepted.[4]

The veil was a necessity, then, making it possible for earlier societies to imagine adoption. It enabled people to indulge in a "willing suspension of disbelief" in order to ensure continuity for their clan and heirs who would perform the ancestral rites.

Of course, the risks were not too great: one usually adopted children whose blood lines were known. It was *good* blood. Some societies actually had ceremonial rituals where the birth parents handed the child over to the adoptive parents.

We have no such rituals here, and it may be because in this country adoption grew out of very different needs—societal ones around relocating children of destitute immigrant families who overran the Eastern seaboard in the great migrations. It began with the rescuing of "unfortunate," "unwanted," and "unwashed" children from almshouses and asylums, first by apprenticing them out, and then by shipping tens of thousands of them out on "orphan trains" to farm families in the Middle West as free labor.[5] But it was not until after the turn of the century, when it was found to be cheaper to maintain surplus children in foster homes rather than in large orphanages, that adoption, as we know it, was on its way.[6]

In adoption, American-style, there has always been the taint of "bad blood" seeping down from those earlier days. Although the majority of children placed in the last fifty years were products of illegitimacy rather than poverty—their pedigrees cutting across class lines and sometimes a cut above those of their adopters— their origins were still considered dubious. Even today, when adoptable babies are at a premium, adoptive parents are considered the benefactors, rather than the benefitted.[7]

Those well-meaning "experts," who set up the institution of adoption as a convenience to serve children who needed families and families who needed children, never questioned the psychological validity of the veil that would cover the past like a shroud. In a nation of immigrants it was assumed that anyone could begin again under any conditions; that, if necessary, one could dispense with one's genetic and historical roots as easily as man had dispensed with his tail. It was an Age of Optimism, preceding Auden's Age of Anxiety, and Haley's Age of Roots.

Social damage could be repaired by social welfare.

We recognize this same "can do" philosophy in the caseworkers trying to match the physical traits of their charges to the adoptive family, as if the Adoptee were little more than a faceless artifact produced by social engineering. Perhaps it was hoped that the surface appearances would cover everyone's inner doubts that synthetic ties could hold as well as the blood knot.

The doubts were there, even then.

In the late 1930s we have the psychiatrist Florence Clothier speaking out like a modern-day Cassandra:

> The child who does not grow up with his own biological parents, who does not even know them or anyone of his own blood, is an individual who has lost the thread of family continuity. A deep identification with our forebears, as experienced originally in the mother-child relationship, gives us our most fundamental security. Every adopted child, at some point in his development, has been deprived of this primitive mother. This trauma and the severing of the individual from his racial antecedents lie at the core of what is peculiar to the psychology of the adopted child.[8]

Clothier was saying what her colleagues in the social-welfare field were not ready to accept—that the blood tie is of importance to the human psyche, and without it, the Adoptee was programmed for a difficult future.

It is Margaret Mead's belief that the extreme denial that has always operated in the adoption field covers up everyone's uncertainty that the process can work. For while Americans may not be concerned with their distant ancestors, the cultural norm is to know who one's parents are—unlike cultures where people believe they are related through the spirit world or even through reincarnation. We have, then, the incredible situation of a people who value heredity having to suppress their real feelings in order to treat children of ambiguous background as their own kin.[9]

If anyone questions this, let them read through the old adoption catalogues put out by prestigious agencies such as The Willows in Kansas City, which professed, in 1923, to deal in "Superior Babies" from "clean American stock."

> Taken as a class, they are recognized as being far brighter than the average child offered for adoption. They are far more affectionate, have better dispositions and temperaments and have clearer heads and brighter intellects. The risks usual with adoption are decreased, and their attendant consequences diminished. . . . Often the child of the slums—the offspring of depravity—is transplanted early into desirable surroundings and surprises the world with its ability. When this is true of the offspring of natural degenerates, what may not be expected of the exceptional class of babies of The Willows?

Adoption was a gamble then, no matter how safe one tried to make the Game. If you could deceive yourself otherwise, so much the better for you.

The Fraudulent Birth Certificate

Where did you come from, baby dear?
Out of the everywhere, into here.[10]

The stage is set for deception right from the beginning when the adoptive parents' names are substituted on the birth certificate for those of the original parents. *As if* the child were born to them. It makes little difference that the idea behind this amending was a noble one—to delete the word *illegitimate*—for by deleting the child's original name as well, it became a case of throwing the baby out with the bathwater.

As the Game is played now, the child's original birth certificate is put under seal, along with all papers pertaining to the proceedings, as soon as the adoption is finalized. These sealed records are the mainstay of the Adoption Game. Everything is guarded like the gold at Fort Knox. When Adoptees request a birth certificate, they are sent the fraudulent one. When they request their adoption records, they are informed that everything is sealed.

In the following sections we will examine the negative psychological effects that losing their heritage has had on Adoptees. We will see how the fictitious stories that their adoptive parents wove around their past became a determining force in shaping their psyches, preoccupying their thoughts, and hampering their emotional development.

4

The Chosen Baby

You called me a "chosen child"
And have the papers and memories to prove it.
AN ADOPTEE

A game that controls reality must control language. Adoptive parents insist that the woman who gives birth to their child must be called the biological, the genetic, or the birth mother; to refer to her as the natural mother would be to imply that they are *un*natural.[1] Adoptive parents call themselves the "psychological" or the "real" parents.

The child is "chosen."

What does it mean to be chosen? This is what the Adoptee must keep asking himself. It is like a Zen koan. It is like the riddle the Sphinx put to Oedipus. Saints are chosen. And so are untouchables.

To be chosen is to be acted upon—to be passive. It is not to choose.

When society sets any group of people apart as chosen, or special, it both exalts and dehumanizes them. In neither case does it allow them to be like others.

Although Adoptees are always being told by relatives and friends that it must be wonderful to be adopted—to be special— they view it quite differently. "I always felt it was a bad thing," a young woman told me. "Everyone made a point of saying how great it was. They did this in such a deliberate way, I knew they didn't mean it."

It is a burden to be chosen. Its very specialness isolates one.

19

"I would rather have my adoptive parents come to terms with their feelings of having a 'godsend' or a 'godchild,'" said another woman. "It can be a very lonely and awesome responsibility being someone else's answer."

She could have been referring to the adoptive mother of an eight-year-old who wrote to me recently: "We didn't consider our son someone else's baby—he was ours from the beginning. Most children brought into this world aren't really wanted—but an adopted child is wanted right from the start—he is chosen, and believe me, he is special—a gift from God."

Where do you connect with the human condition when you are chosen and everyone else is born?

I Never Was Born

I could not imagine anything to do with
my birth. I never knew the location of
the place until I was twenty-nine.

I thought God planted a seed in your body and it
grew into a baby.

I felt like I came from a book, like the
one that told me I was chosen.

I always believed adopted children weren't born.
That a stork brought them, just as my adoptive
mother said.

Dad always said, "We found Jane under
a rock."

FROM CONVERSATIONS WITH ADOPTEES

Sometimes when I'm with nonadopted friends, I will spring the question, "Did you ever think you weren't born?" I get quizzical looks as to my seriousness or sanity, but always the reply, "Of course, I was born." For without knowing it, while they were growing up, they heard random fragments about how they kicked in the womb, how Mama almost didn't make it to the hospital, and without understanding it, they were receiving direct confirmation about their entrance into the universe and their place in the flow of generations.

But the Adoptee says: "I'm not sure I ever was born." Because the womb is a forbidden, lost place, the condition of having been born becomes lost to him too. Without the original birth certificate, he has no proof.

John Brown, the psychologist who founded Browndale, a residential treatment center in Canada, tells of his surprise when a sixteen-year-old girl informed him that she had somehow been "hatched" or just sprung spontaneously into a crib at the Children's Aid Society. "And it really blew her mind when I said 'You had a father and a mother even if you don't know anything about them. Everyone is born in the same way. It can't happen any other way.' "[2]

But for the Adoptee it does.

Life does not begin for the Adoptee at conception, nor at the moment he emerges from the womb and gives his first outraged cry, but at the moment he is told of his adoption. It is the birth of consciousness, the consciousness of being different from the people around him. Unlike others, who get their evolutionary messages in their mother's milk, the Adoptee gets his message in the chosen baby story he is told. If we want to understand his behavior, we must decode that first story.

The Chosen Baby Story

It came in many versions, but the best known were *The Chosen Baby* by Valentina Wasson and *The Family That Grew* by Florence Rondell and Ruth Michaels.[3] These books read as if they were composed in a psychological vacuum, but they reflect the professional bias of their time: that a child who is given sufficient assurance of love will not need to know about his heritage. Cheerful in tone, deliberately vague about detail, they focused on how the baby came into the family, not how he came into the world. The word *chosen* was meant to act magically on the child's psyche, dispelling all curiosity about the missing parts of the story.

Not all adoptive parents went by the book. Some preferred to make up their own tales which they could edit as they wished. But permeated with denial as they are, all chosen-baby stories sound alike. Give or take a few details, they might have been delivered by the same stork. There is the standard plot: the happily married couple who need a child call on a special woman whose job it is to find babies who need a mother and father. Like a true sorceress, this woman manages to locate a perfect baby whom they love at first sight. There is no explanation as to where the baby came from—it is as if it just appeared on earth for the sole purpose of being *chosen* by them.

The following story, sent to me by an adoptive mother, is a typical example of the genre:

> When Mama and Daddy got married we thought we would soon have a baby, but time went by and time went by and we didn't have one. And so after a long time we decided that maybe God didn't want us to have one, so that when a baby was born who didn't have a Mama and Daddy to keep him, we would be ready to take him and adopt him. So we started going around and asking people if they knew of a baby we could have or, if they didn't know of one, we told them to remember that we wanted one if they ever found one.
>
> Well, time went by and one day Grandad Harry (our pastor) brought us a letter saying that if we could come to Cleveland on Thursday and talk to a lawyer we could get a baby boy the next day. So we went up and talked to the lawyer and stayed in a hotel that night, and the next day we went to a big hospital and got the baby boy and that baby was Mark.

We see here that as usual the central character, the woman who gave birth to Mark, is missing. Since it was a private adoption, the omnipotent social worker has been replaced by the pastor and the lawyer, while God has been busy in the wings keeping the parents sterile so that they would be available for Mark in his moment of need. By a process as miraculous as their birth, chosen babies never seem to ask why God didn't help their real parents keep them in the first place, or help the adoptive parents have a baby of their own.

Chosen babies choose to be gullible, as if innately sensing the wisdom of Robert Browning's philosophy: "Where the apple reddens/ Never pry—/ Lest we lose our Edens,/ Eve and I."

Beginnings of Befuddlement

Chosen-baby stories may have some fragments of truth, but we cannot call them true stories. I see in them the source of the Adoptee's distortion of reality, the seeds of a confusion that will grow in him as he grapples for some sense of authenticity over the years. Their lack of credibility can not help but affect his inner fantasies and self-image, his sense of pride or shame. For unlike those familiar fairy tales of our Western culture, which are woven through time with truths of the human condition, the chosen-baby story is filled with errors of fact, improbable details, implied horrors, as well as gaping omissions. Even when the story is seemingly benign, it has menacing undertones. The child cannot gain the catharsis from it that the true folktale gives. In fact, many Adoptees have told me that the stories made them feel twice rejected: by the natural parents who didn't keep them, and by the adoptive parents who couldn't have a baby of their own. Being *chosen* meant being second best.

When Adoptees get together, they like to compare their chosen-baby stories. No matter how different the details, it seems as if everyone was chosen from a cast of thousands.

Grace remembers her parents describing how they chose her over all the babies they saw. "I had visions of Mom and Dad walking down a very sterile room with a lady dressed in white, and two hundred bawling babies in their tiny cribs. I imagined they stopped and took one glance at me and decided I looked like I needed the most help. I probably looked like a drowned rat."

Grace was to learn later that her birth mother was an aunt, and her favorite cousins were really her brothers and sisters. "I was looking for someone who looked like me, and all my life they were right under my nose."

Jackie remembers being told when she was four that although all babies come from their mother's stomach, she didn't. She came from the hospital.

"When we got there we saw the babies lined up in their cribs. I saw you and went to the crib and picked you up. Your whole body was covered with eczema. Your father said: 'No, let's get a healthy one.' But you clung to me and smiled. 'I want this one,' I told your father. 'If that's what you want, all right. But at least put her down and look at the others,' he said.

"As soon as I put you down, you started to scream. 'I have to pick her up again,' I told your father, 'or I'll hear that scream in my ears for the rest of my life.'

"I went back and picked you up. You stopped screaming. Then we took you home."

Jackie was not very impressed with the story at first. All she could think of was that her friend Stuart came from *his* mother's stomach, and she didn't. But from then on she would say: "Tell me the story of how you got me." "It was my nightly story," she recalls. "I was chosen. Everyone else had to take what they got."

Like so many Adoptees, Jackie managed to blot out any concrete images around being born or about those other parents. "It wasn't until my teens that I thought about them as real people. When I had my own baby, I realized I never had the sense that I was born. I was adopted. But now, looking back, I felt I had no self. When you don't know how you were born, you don't exist. It muddles everything."

Warren remembers being told by his mother what she called the "How I Got You" story. She had wanted a baby and went to the agency where she was shown a room full of boys in cribs. "I looked at them all but was caught by the way you looked at me with those large green eyes," she would say over and over. "I knew I had to have you." Still she had to go home first and wait nervously for a call from the social worker, Miss Smith. "When it came and Miss Smith said I could come down and have you, I was so happy. I sped in the car to the hospital so fast that a policeman stopped me. I said, 'I'm going to the hospital to get my baby.' And he said, 'I'll escort you there.' "

Warren did not notice that he was waiting at the hospital rather than at the agency. Since his mother was divorced twice in rapid succession, he never felt he had a father, and so did not notice that there was never a father in the story of his being chosen, not even the one to whom she was married at that time. But he remembers being worried when he had to produce a birth certificate to get a driving license, wondering: "Do I have a birth certificate? Maybe I won't be able to drive because I don't have one." As it turned out, he had three—the original one, which he has still never seen, the second one with the name of his mother's first husband, and another revised one with the name of the second.

Karla remembers three versions of her chosen-baby story.

From age two to four: "We brought you home from the hospital when you were three days old. You were very very special. We wanted you so very much."

From four to seven: "We looked for you for seven long years and one morning at 6 A.M. the family doctor called to tell us we could see you. You smiled at us when we walked into the room. The minute we held you we knew you were ours." There was also some reference to the ordeal of the social worker's visits and the day in court.

When Karla was about seven, her mother added that her *first* parents had been killed tragically in a car crash. "They were a fine Jewish married couple. My first mother prayed for me and my adoptive parents as she died. This version was accompanied by the basic facts of life—that anyone can have a baby, any animal, but not everyone wanted them."

At age nine the story remained intact, but got progressively more elaborate as Karla's questions became more sophisticated and technical. "The car crash evolved into my natural father being killed on impact, my being delivered by cesarean section (which I envisioned as being picked like a watermelon), and my natural mother dying a few hours later, aware that a family had been found for me. My adoptive mother insisted that she had not seen my natural mother but got a physical description from the physician. She had no description of the natural father. There was no information about these two people who were killed—they seemed to have been just passing through. She placed ads in the newspaper trying to locate their family members but no one replied.

"I loved the story in all of its stages, and I asked for it often," Karla said. "I was not too inquisitive about my natural parents. I trusted my adoptive parents and really believed the car crash. When I learned about biology and genes and how heredity worked, my mother began to have emotional reactions. She now always stressed environment. We would go through the *story* without incident, but the questions about where I came from biologically ultimately resulted in tears and insecurity about my love. For many years I comforted my mother at this point and reassured her. This reaction made the questioning less frequent."

Alice remembers not so much her " 'doptee story," as her parents called it, but the fact that they recorded their telling of it over the years along with her responses. They played these tapes for their friends to the accompaniment of home movies, making her adoption into a public multimedia event. The excruciating pain of this invasion of her privacy is with her still, along with rage at the insensitivity of her parents, who never spoke of her adoption to her in private and were offended if she asked questions.

Trudy was given a chosen-baby book to read when she was five, but her parents did not tell her she was adopted. "I knew I didn't want to be adopted or special. I just wanted to be ordinary like a younger sister," she recalls.

When she was seven she remembers sitting in the back seat with her sister and hearing a man say to her mother through the car window, "Which one is yours?" Her mother said, "They're both mine," closed the window and drove off quickly. Later, when she asked her mother if she was adopted, her mother denied it and wanted to know why she was asking. "I was so relieved. I told her I would hate it if I was adopted."

When Trudy was eight, her mother had twin boys. She remembers being jealous and clingy. Then when she was eleven, there came the day she stayed home from school because she wasn't feeling well. "I was talking to my mother while she was ironing, and she said to me that someday she would like to tell me a story. I wanted to hear the story *then,* so she gave in. She said that she was unable to have children and wanted them very badly. So she went to the Catholic agency and found me. I was eleven days old. She said I was special because she picked me, but she had no choice later when my sister and the twins were born. It was quite a shock to me.

"I couldn't absorb it all. I went running out to the backyard crying to my sister that I had something special to tell her. 'I'm adopted!' I blurted out. She looked up at me and said simply, 'So.' 'So,' I said, 'don't you know what that means? It means we're not sisters.' And she said, 'Of course, we're sisters. It doesn't make any difference. You're my sister no matter what.' "

This was some comfort, but Trudy remembers entering her teen years uneasily. She attributes her insecurity and depressive periods to that sudden moment of learning what she had suspected and feared most.

Trudy's parents had obviously taken half-measures, giving her the book, but pretending it didn't apply to her. Other parents give half-truths which become so familiar over the years that even they begin to believe them. Some lie outright, and hope to get away with it. Until recently, of course, adoptive parents never expected their stories to be challenged or verified. Nor did they understand the devastating psychological consequences of their seemingly innocuous fabrications.

I was told that both my parents died of illness shortly after my birth, my father of war injuries and my mother of a broken heart. I had no reason to doubt it: in fact, found it rather romantic. How could I know then that it was a common strategy for adoptive parents to marry off and then dispatch those inconvenient characters at will? It made the story much cleaner, death being irrevocable as it is, and infinite in its varieties.

A large number of Adoptees were told their mothers died in childbirth. One woman was told that her parents were killed in an automobile crash coming home from the hospital, while her younger brother's parents vanished in a plane crash. A man born in 1947 was informed that his father was killed in World War II, and even when he was old enough to know that the war ended in 1945 he did not let the discrepancy of dates enter his conscious mind. He knew intuitively that it was better to remain a little befuddled—to fail the history tests—than to see too clearly.

I myself never questioned my parents' deaths while I was growing up, but lived with ghostly shadows in my room and the conviction that I too would die young.

A woman who had been told that her mother died in childbirth expected to die when she herself gave birth. And having miraculously survived the event, she prepared herself yet again while carrying her second child. When she learned her birth mother was still alive, she was filled with rage at her adoptive parents who had so unthinkingly set her up for this torment.

The woman who was told that her parents had been killed coming home from the hospital found herself at the age of eighteen riding home from the hospital with her own baby in a snowstorm. She was terrified that they would all be killed by the same merciless providence that had removed her parents. Even now, after she has found her natural mother very much alive, the fear of cars still lingers as an irrational vestige of the past.

We see that, internalized as it is, one does not easily outgrow one's chosen-baby story.

5

The Adoptee as Mythic Hero

Does the Adoptee have a more intense fantasy life than others? I think so. But my nonadopted friends keep reminding me that fantasies are part of the human condition, even necessary to the imagination. They never fail to point out that they used to suspect they were adopted. They say things like "I felt like a stranger in my family while I was growing up" or "I thought I was just dropped there by accident." They, too, dreamed of descent from royalty, from kings and queens who would one day return to rescue them.

Anne Tyler plays with this in her novel, *Earthly Possessions*:

> These were my two main worries when I was a child: one was that I was not their true daughter, and would be sent away. The other was that I *was* their true daughter and would never, ever manage to escape to the outside world.

Freud calls the fantasy of being the child of people other than one's parents the "family romance"—the child expresses ambivalence toward the parents in order to separate herself from them and explore her own personality.

But even though the family romance reveals the universal curiosity and fundamental quest for origins that everyone shares, it is not a *romance* for the Adoptee. There really are two other parents out there. No amount of reassuring by loving adoptive parents can ever change that fact. Moreover, while Adoptees share the fantasy of royal blood along with everyone, they are also having negative fantasies—of whores, rapists, murderers; the possibilities are limitless. Back and forth they go between them, polarizing the good and bad as it suits their psychological need. But unlike the nonadopted who can eventually resolve their family romance by unifying the good and bad parents into the one set they have, there is no way for the Adoptee to resolve the polarization short of knowing about the birth parents as real people.

Still, as the character in Tyler's novel suspects, there is an advantage to being adopted. Having been encouraged to close off curiosity and go underground, Adoptees often live in a world of fantasy that may be more real or meaningful than anything happening around them. Certainly it is an escape, even a haven, allowing them to disassociate themselves from any family unpleasantness. But it can also account for the dreamy, floating quality reported in adopted children, for the lack of attention span and concentration. They live in a mythical rather than a real past. There are no limits. Their fantasies could very well be true. As Florence Clothier warned her colleagues: "Bear in mind that when we are asked to deal with problems occurring in a child who has been adopted, he may be living out his fantasy of a hero's or a revolutionary's birth."

In *The Hero with a Thousand Faces* Joseph Campbell reminds us that the birth of the hero is surrounded with difficulty. There is the oracle who prophesies that the child will bring danger to the father of the land; the child is exposed, then saved by simple people who rear him—or, as we now say, adopt him. When he grows up he goes on his Search—a terrible journey through the dark woods, with constant threats to his physical and mental well-being.

Everyone identifies with the hero who must go forth into the world alone to search out his origins, but in the Adoptee's case this is a literal quest. At times he feels that he too has a thousand faces, a thousand identities—and yet none. If he has taken up acting as a profession, he feels he can play any role because he has none of his own. Indeed, if the Adoptee can tame his fantasies, make them work for him, his acquaintance with the mythic realm may deepen him as an artist in any field.

Being something of a professional fantasist myself—having filled a number of books with folkloric tales for the young—I have always been interested in the fantasies of Adoptees—what they have in common, where they differ. And what they reveal about the condition of being adopted. I found myself collecting fantasies the way others might collect dreams. "Tell me your fantasies," I would implore all Adoptees I encountered in person or through the mail. As might be expected, there were those who fled from this invasion, for fantasies form a protective barrier around the private core of an Adoptee's deepest aspirations or fears.

However, as I accumulated them from the most intrepid among us, I began to see how they were influenced by that original chosen-baby story, as well as by the parents' openness or denial of the past. Also, I saw that they could be divided into two categories—those of childhood, blurred and dreamlike and multiple, which we will examine here; and the more concrete ones of young adulthood, which we will take up in a later section.

The Adoptee's childhood fantasies are analogous to those sprawling primitive crayon drawings of the human figure which young children are prone to create. They lack concern with mundane details such as fingers, toes, or ears. They have a whimsical, grotesque charm, but little relationship to actuality. They would never pass in a life-drawing class, but then these children never had live models to draw from.

I have noticed that women seem to have easier recall than men, who often have difficulty retrieving any fantasies—almost as if adopted boys have a fantasy-proof repression mechanism that stays operative until adulthood, when forces which we'll discuss later catapult them into contact with their unconscious.

In a longitudinal study of nineteen adopted children from birth through preadolescence, Susan Farber was struck by the fact that the girls were much more verbal and conflicted about adoption than the boys. The girls' question "Why didn't you give birth to me?" rather than "Why was I given away?" suggested to her that they have a strong need to identify with the mother.[1] However, sociological factors could also be at work in that boys are encouraged early to mask their emotions and play "macho" roles.

Norman, thirty and unmarried, is one of the <u>few</u> men I know who feels that he was always preoccupied with the fact of his adoption. He remembers being afraid to go to sleep at night for fear of being lost and never coming back—afraid that he was not really adopted, that someone would claim him. He was always looking at women in the street and wondering, Is she my mother? When he was three, and social workers came to the house to arrange for his sister's adoption, he had the fantasy that perhaps one of the women was really his mother. "They talked to me. I thought maybe my natural mother is looking for me."

In adolescence Norman had the fantasy that he might be the son of Marlon Brando, since everyone in his high school said that he looked like him. He also felt that his birth parents were like guardians out there protecting him. His father, as wealthy and elusive as Daddy Warbucks, had left instructions "to look out for the kid." But there was also the recurring fantasy that somehow he came from outer space, a locale that he still keeps in touch with through watching "Star Trek" and reading science fiction. "I am attracted to space heroes because I can understand someone cut off from Mother Earth."

Jackie fantasized that her mother was a gypsy, her father a prince. They had a romantic affair, and a child, but the prince's parents would not allow them to marry. As a punishment to that heartless royal family, the gypsy gave the child, Jackie, to a "bourgeois" family. Jackie called this the "gypsy's revenge." But this did not prevent her from ruminating on another fantasy—that she might stop in at a police station and ask if they'd take her back to where she came from.

Karla, whose mother supposedly had her by cesarean section after the car crash, said she developed a strong picture of her—a plain version of Deborah Kerr. "I would imagine the crash and see her dead. My natural father was just a body slumped behind the wheel, no face or distinguishing features. I felt they must have been just like my adoptive parents. I was the Olympic Torch that passed between the two sets of parents. I became preoccupied with death. I would provide elaborate rituals for my pets when they died."

Helene, who knew only that she came from an agency, had the fantasy that whoever had her was dead. "It was the only way I could deal with it. I thought about it constantly, but never asked questions. Sometimes I even had the fantasy I wasn't really adopted, that they were just telling me that because they were ashamed of me. Other times I would imagine that my mother came from another planet."

June said: "I had the fantasy I was the illegitimate daughter of my mother's unmarried sister. But there was another fantasy too. My mother was always dragging me off to charities to help the poor. I had the feeling that this was where I originated. Right here. My mother was rubbing my nose in it. And yet, at the same time I had the fantasy that I was the daughter of a king and queen."

Sybil had the fantasy that she would be returned, though she never understood to whom. "I was terrified I would be given back. Can a natural child ever understand that? I learned to behave in ways that would win the approval I craved."

Susan knew who she'd be given back to. Her mother was always saying: "If you aren't good, I'll give you back to the Indians." "I knew it was a common expression, but in my case, she could. I wasn't part of their family, didn't act like them, didn't do the right thing. And there was a Sioux tribe living in the area. I used to have nightmares that they would come for me."

Mark fantasized that the old couple who used to visit his music camp and listen to the children play were really his parents looking in on him. He knew that they did not approach him because they wanted it to be a secret. And so he played their game and did not speak to them either.

Lisa, who was told that her parents had been "too poor" to keep her, brooded over it throughout her childhood. In fact, she fantasized that the poor Chilean family who lived on her city block was her real family. She was the last child whom they couldn't keep, and now by chance they all happened to live near each other. She never told them that she knew she belonged to them, but she spent as much time as she could at their house, sometimes sleeping away from her home for weeks at a time.

THE ADOPTEE AS MYTHIC HERO 33

Another variation on this "poor parent" theme is the story a psychiatrist tells of a young adopted boy brought to her for stealing money and candy, which he gave to other children. After many interviews she began to get to what bothered him. While he was talking into the dictaphone that she gave her young patients, he told of parents who had to steal in order to feed the many children born to them. When she asked: "Wouldn't it be better if the parents turned over the care of the children to someone who could feed them?" he replied angrily that it was better to steal. It developed that the child had secretly fantasized that his biological parents had given him up because they were poor. When he stole and gave to other children, he was in some way becoming the parent who loved a child enough to steal for him.

Often a child can be relieved of his symptoms if he can be relieved of his negative fantasies, as happens in a good therapeutic relationship. The British psychiatrist Lydia Jackson, who made a study of forty cases of unsuccessful adoptions seen at a child-guidance clinic, was struck by the strongly ambivalent nature of the children's fantasies:

> The children pronounced judgment on their natural mother, calling her such names as "a bad lot," "a wicked one," "a stinking old thing." One little girl declared that she came "from God's belly"; a small boy talked of his mother looking down at him from heaven; another pictured his father as a monster with very large teeth and shaggy black hair; still another made up a story about a father who had run away to America after having left him alone in the forest "to die of starvation."[2]

Are adopted children easier to treat because of this abundance of fantasies? It seems not. Analysts report that they are more difficult because there are no known facts against which to test their fantasies.

We must consider that there is nowhere to go from nowhere—in life, as in therapy.

6

The Adoptee as Double

As we have seen, not being able to test his fantasies against reality, the Adoptee is forced to lead a double existence: the surface one which he shares with his adoptive family, and the secret one which is like a lost Atlantis sunken in his entrails.

Of course, the motif of the double runs in one way or another through everyone's life, and through both Eastern and Western thought. Plato proposed that all people are really twins: originally having been double what they are now—two heads, eight limbs—they spend their lives in search of the other half in order to be complete. Shakespeare played with the lighter side of the double, Dostoevsky with the darker. Otto Rank saw the double as the identical self promising personal survival in the future, or as an opposing self appearing in the form of evil, which represents the perishable and mortal part of the personality.

In his novel *The Bread of Those Early Years*, Heinrich Böll saw its lyrical possibilities:

> I see myself standing around in that life, I see myself smiling, hear myself talking, like a twin brother seen in a dream, the smiling, talking brother one has never had—the brother who, perhaps for a fraction of a second, was on the brink of being conceived before the seed carrying him perished.

The Adoptee, however, forced by circumstances to lead a double life, is haunted by a series of doubles—even the double has a double. There is the other possible self one might have been had

34

one been kept by one's birth parents. There is the self one might have been had one been chosen by a different couple. There is the child one's adoptive parents might have had, had they been fertile, or the child they did have, who died.

The Adoptee carries this cast of characters around with him, hoping to find release through numbing, through psychoanalysis, through the journey back to the original self.

The double who is the other *possible* self remains forever infantilized. It is always the abandoned baby. When the Adoptee goes back to search for it, it is still there, frozen in time, at the same age he left it to begin his other life.

My own double will always be standing in its crib at the Hebrew Home for Infants—waiting—although the home has long since disappeared. She has never evolved beyond that stage. She is the part of me that is eternally young, helpless, and alone.

We recognize Edward Albee's double in the child his parents *might have had* in his play *Who's Afraid of Virginia Woolf?* That child, never seen on stage, is as alive as a real child to his parents. Martha even speaks of his birth to the couple visiting her and her husband, George:

> Our son. Our son was born in a September night, a night not unlike tonight, though tomorrow, and twenty...one... years ago....It was an easy birth...once it had been...accepted, relaxed into....And I was young, and he was a healthy child, a red, bawling child, with slippery firm limbs...and a full head of black, fine, fine hair which, oh, later, later became blond as the sun, our son.

This imaginary child, the last bond between them, is destroyed by George at the end of the play as his final revenge against his wife. Pretending a telegram has arrived with the news, he announces:

> All right. Well, Martha...I'm afraid our boy isn't coming home for his birthday....Martha...our son is...dead. He was...killed...late in the afternoon...(*A tiny chuckle*) on a country road, with his learner's permit in his pocket, he swerved, to avoid a porcupine, and drove straight into a... large tree.

When Martha protests hysterically that George cannot do this to her, he informs her, "I can kill him, Martha, if I want to."

And the reason—"You broke our rule, baby. You mentioned him . . . you mentioned him to someone else."

Perhaps only a playwright who was adopted could so electrify a stage with the invisible presence of an unborn child.

The Adoptee who is fated to replace the dead baby his parents once had grows up side by side with the ghost of that baby. If the baby had a name, it assumes monstrous proportions over the years, taking nurture in the adoptive mother's fantasy of what might have been. This dead child is the perfect one, the *other* who would have achieved things far beyond the Adoptee's scope.

Jackie, who was adopted at nine months, replaced Louise, who had died at nine months. Told that Louise had died of "crib strangulation," Jackie often dreamed that she was being strangled and couldn't breathe. Her mother lit candles for Louise once a year and on that day looked very sad. It was as if Louise took over the house and the mother at those times. Once when her mother went up the stairs, crying hysterically and screaming, "She would have been fourteen today," Jackie wanted to follow her saying, "I am your daughter." But she couldn't. The words wouldn't come out. They were strangled in her throat.

When she was in college, Jackie told everyone that she had an older sister—named Louise. She thought of Louise as her double, her better half. Louise had all the social poise and talents Jackie lacked. If Jackie were lucky, someday she would be like Louise. But she did not consciously associate this imaginary sister with the dead infant until much later.

Nina, whose adoptive mother was a twin, was told that she too had been one, but that her twin had died at birth. Her mother, who had a love/hate relationship with her own twin, became fixated on making Nina look like herself. At sixteen Nina was taken to a plastic surgeon to have her nose and chin remodeled to match her mother's. Years later, when she went in search of her birth family, Nina took along a picture of how she used to look, so that they wouldn't think she was an impostor. Learning from them that she had indeed been a twin—her sister having died with the mother in childbirth—she wept for the baby who might have made her complete. She mourned this twin who stayed with the mother while she went out into an alien world, as if she were mourning herself.[1]

Norman always felt as if he had had a twin who died. "I've always been at war with myself, dealing on two levels as two people. Sometimes I think that if I looked into it, I would have two Social Security numbers and two car registrations, one belonging to me, the other to that twin whose identity I've picked up."

Karla was once informed by another adopted girl in her class that she was her twin. She remembers being terrified and running home to her parents, who assured her this wasn't true. Later, when they told her they had just missed adopting a baby boy, who would have been named Peter, she played with a phantom brother.

In his teens John always wondered if there was someone out there who looked like him. "When I was taking part in the senior track meet in school, warming up to run the mile, another runner came face-to-face with me. He looked exactly like me, but before I could get my thoughts together, he had disappeared. I never did see him again, but I said to myself, 'that could have been my brother.' "

When she was twenty-five, Robin looked in a TV guide and saw a face that had a strong likeness to her own. Excitedly she showed it to her friends, who agreed it was almost a perfect match. "Never had I seen a resemblance to anyone in my life except him," she told me. "I decided he could really be my twin brother. I wrote him, but of course I never got an answer. He was a very popular singer."

Over the next few weeks Robin brooded about this singer— her possible lost twin. "Given all the lies my family had told me over the years, it seemed that something deep and dark was being kept from me. Mother had thrown out hundreds of my books when I left home, and I realized that one of them had been my favorite, *Traded Twins*."

It was shortly after seeing her possible twin that Robin had her first breakdown, and was in and out of hospitals with "psychotic daydreams," as she calls them. She has since met her birth parents and knows that there was no twin, after all. "Is it usual," she asked me, "for Adoptees to imagine they have a twin?"

I would say that it is. I think all Adoptees unconsciously spend their lives in search of that missing part of themselves—call it mother, father, or twin. Lacking the physical tie to relatives who look like them, they feel a deficiency, as if their very system craves physical bonding with those blood-related kin who are lost to them for reasons they cannot understand.

7

The Adoptee as Survivor

It could be said that all Adoptees are survivors of a holocaust of one kind or another.

They get their first hint of this in the chosen-baby story, which has the implicit message: We saved you. To be saved from the perils of war or famine in a foreign land may sound more dramatic than being saved from an unnamed local disaster, but the psychological impact can be similar.

The past may be lost but not the squalid details of the terrible condition they were in when they arrived. Jackie was festering with eczema all over her body; others were "rotted under the arms," unable to walk or talk, or desperately ill. It could only make them wonder why, if they were so puny and puking, they had been "chosen."

Norman was told he was almost dead when handed to his parents in a hotel lobby by a social worker who had flown with him up from the South. "Mom said she took one look at me and went straight to the hospital where her cousin is a doctor. He said they had a right to refuse me, but I might not survive the trip back." Norman was given to understand that even though he was damaged goods, his parents had kept him because it was the only humane thing to do. He was regaled with tales of how he was in and out of hospitals, first for dehydration, then for a congenital hernia operation during which he caught a virus that made it "touch and go" for a while. He was fed intravenously and still has marks on his ankles from the needles.

We see in these rescue stories, exaggerated or not, the adoptive parents' pride in pulling the Adoptee back from the shadow of death. They have, in that sense, given life to the child and are responsible for its very existence. They do not understand the burden this places on adopted children to be grateful to their saviors. Having been reborn through adoption, they must be thankful for this second chance, this second life.

The "we saved you" story, on one level, is saying: You owe your life to us. Therefore, you must subsume your personal desires to ours. Since we gave birth to you in the only meaningful sense of the word, you belong to us.

On another level, the message is: Because of illicit circumstances, you were *as if* dead when born. Not until we adopted you were you legitimately alive with a place in society. You had no other existence before us.

Survivor of What?

When the Adoptee outgrows the chosen-baby story and tries to use the bedtime hour of togetherness to explore specific questions about his past—those parts missing from the once-beloved tale—he discovers that the parents no longer want to discuss it. He learns that there is no accepted sequel to the chosen-baby story. To press for one is only to bring tears to the parents' eyes. The subject is taboo. It is not part of the game.

Joyce recalls: "As I would persist with wanting to know more, like 'Why did they have to give me away?' Mom would get defensive and come back with, 'Well, we love you, isn't that enough?' And of course I would feel guilty and the conversation would end."

Warren, whose mother had a police escort to pick him up, remembers: "When I was too old to hear stories, I noticed there was no more talk of adoption. If I tried to bring up the subject, she would say vaguely, 'Yes, you were adopted.' Unconsciously I knew she'd feel rejected if I talked about it."

It is about this time that the Adoptee receives the full impact of that unspeakable calamity that is buried in the past. What it is he has survived, and why, he does not know. He only knows that as a result of whatever happened he became separated from his original parents and placed in this family.

It is difficult to be a survivor of any kind, but most difficult when you are kept in ignorance of what it is you have survived. For, since most adoptive parents are unable to see the child's loss of the birth parents as a psychic trauma, but rather as a felicitous event that has enriched their own lives, it is hard for the Adoptee to deal with his survivor role. Although he perceives that a piece of his world has been swept away, he also perceives that he must not attempt to retrieve it.

Lack of Mourning

The Russian poet Andrei Voznesensky says that within us we all bear our family graves. If this is so, the Adoptee is doubly deprived, for he has never been given a place to mourn. This was brought home to me not too long ago when a cousin recalled one of those possibly apocryphal stories that are whispered in families. She said that when I was small I had insisted on going to see my parents' graves. My aunt had driven me and my mother out to a cemetery where I was shown two headstones. (I was too young to read, so they did not have to worry that I would catch them in their deception.) I seem to have erased this incident, if it ever happened, from my memory—a talent that all Adoptees develop early. But the point is that adopted children, whether told their parents are literally or symbolically dead, are cut off from any way of dealing with it. There is no ritual ceremony, like lighting candles or sitting shivah, to mourn parents who are *as if* dead, while never having been *as if* legitimately alive.

Norman Paul, a psychiatrist who prefers to be called a physician interested in family problems, believes that the inability to mourn one's loss is the psychological clue to schizophrenia, as well as to the adopted person's repressed personality. "There is a need to mourn that is denied the adopted child," he told me. "I found in my practice that if you look back in time with adoptees, it is like being on the edge of a cliff—there is nothing beyond it."

John Brown also believes in the importance of allowing a child to mourn, and bringing to the process a sense of dignity and pride about the person who is gone. Consider here that the adopted child can have little pride in parents whose worth, or worthlessness, can only be inferred from the way in which they are, or are not, presented by others. The real messages about those lost parents are nonverbal. If the adoptive parents regard them as nonpeople, as lowlife, as immoral, the child perceives this, and some part of him becomes a nonperson or immoral. The child is then a survivor without honor, not understanding why he exists at all, or what it is his life must prove, justify, or vindicate. Either he is an accident or a creature of destiny. But which he does not know.

He cannot look to his adoptive parents for the answer.

8

Adolescent Baggage

It was found that the adopted child can encounter
problems in adolescence which are peculiar to such
children and do not enter into the experience of
adolescents growing up within their own biological family.
ALEXINA M. MCWHINNIE

T he adolescent Adoptee is the child now struggling to form a
mature identity, a task he or she finds difficult because there
is no way of integrating the past with the present. There is
no adolescent myth to replace the chosen-baby story. The lack
of communication that has become a way of life for them has
taken its toll. The teenager disappears even further into that
private space that "has no name." Overloaded with excess baggage
of repression, separation anxiety, denial, and guilt, he or she is
unable to cope. Trust is nonexistent when secrets are being kept,
reality-testing impossible when you are always confronted with
half-truths. Confusion about the credibility of the parents becomes compounded by the usual adolescent uncertainties. It is like
a split screen: These are my parents/but they're not. As a result
the authenticity of *any* feelings the adolescent has toward the
parents comes into question.

The adult Adoptees we've met so far were not part of a clinical
population, but they still described adolescence as an unbearable
turmoil of deep depressions, even suicide attempts. They said

things like "I felt I was an orphan, even though I had two sets of parents"; "I felt I didn't have a name, not the adopted one or the one I sneaked a look at on the adoption papers. You could have called me anything, and I'd have answered."

Many relied on liquor and drugs to get through. Some had babies out of wedlock and put them up for adoption, unconsciously acting out their birth mother's role. Many of the men had joined the military by the age of seventeen as a means of getting away, while the women had entered into early, disastrous marriages as a way of "being adopted by someone else." Their actions were not so much solutions as flight from a confusion they could not articulate.

We are reminded of Florence Clothier's warning that "no matter how lost to him his natural parents may be, the adopted child carries stamped in every cell of his body genes derived from his forebearers."[1] If, as she wrote, neither geneticists nor psychologists know enough to disentangle the mosaic weave of the personality to be able to say "this trait is hereditary" or "that is purely the result of identification," then how could adopted adolescents possibly understand the conflicting desires that were propelling their seemingly headlong rush into chaos?

They couldn't. The consequences of the Adoption Game were coming to the surface.

We shouldn't be surprised. In the early 1960s, child psychiatrist Marshall Schecter received a lot of criticism from colleagues and mental health professionals for observing that there was a disproportionate number of young Adoptees in his clinic, and that they seemed more prone to emotional difficulties than nonadopted children.[2] Social workers in particular were up in arms at him: "If I wasn't baldheaded by the time I went into one meeting with them, I would have been scalped totally," he recalls. "At least seventy-five of them shook their fists at me for daring to suggest their practice needed looking into. 'Adoptees do not have special problems!' they shouted at me. 'You are wrong.' "[3]

Schecter was struck by the emotionality in the adoption field, the inference that his observations should not have been published because they might discourage people from adopting. As a scientist, he had been recommending that the institution of adoption be reexamined, but he was being accused of trying to sabotage it.

Over the next few years Schecter gathered statistics from other clinics and residential treatment centers that corroborated his own.[4] His findings that adopted children showed a high incidence of aggression and sexual acting out was an impetus to other investigators to prove or disprove that Adoptees have special problems not experienced by those growing up in their own families. There is still no consensus on this issue. But many journal articles describe adopted children as having a tendency toward learning disability and underachievement, exhibiting a lack of self-identity, dependency, and fearfulness, and showing a propensity for stealing, running away, and destroying property.[5]

A growing number of prominent researchers like Alexina McWhinnie[6] and John Triseliotis[7] of Scotland are coming to the conclusion that Adoptees have additional problems beyond the usual ones that plague everyone in adolescence. This would seem to be common sense when we consider that it is hard to know where you are going when you don't know where you came from— and hard to become an autonomous person when your parents and society control the basic facts of your heritage. Still, it is alarming to come across findings that nonrelative adoption carries a higher risk for psychiatric illness than adoption by a relative,[8] and that children of parents with prison records often repeat this antisocial behavior.[9] One doesn't know how reassured to be by other studies which indicate that Adoptees are no more prone to psychopathology and delinquency than others.[10] Certainly the truth lies somewhere in between. Most Adoptees, like everyone else, manage to make it through adolescence intact, but it is the purpose of this book to call attention to the unnecessary suffering they experience.

The number of Adoptees in the adolescent and young-adult clinics and residential treatment centers is strikingly high. Doctors from the Yale Psychiatric Institute and other hospitals that take very sick adolescents have told me they are discovering that from one-quarter to one-third of their patients are adopted. A great many of these young people are in serious trouble with the law and are drug addicted. The girls show an added history of nymphomania and out-of-wedlock pregnancy, almost as if they were acting out the role of the "whore" mother. In fact, both sexes are experimenting with a series of identities that seem to be related to their fantasies about the biological parents.

The debate continues on the source of these maladjustments—

the strain of being adopted, the adoptive parents' unresolved conflicts about infertility, the mismatching of parents and child, genetic factors, or intrauterine disturbances—and doctors now admit the need for long-term studies.[11] It is encouraging that research is beginning to take place in various clinics around the country.

A few years ago I participated in an American Psychiatric Association panel with Barney Greenspan, a doctor at the Bellefaire Residential Treatment Center in Cleveland, Ohio. He and a colleague had decided to look into the effect that not knowing one's biological parents had on adolescent development, after they noticed that 16 percent of their patients were adopted. Singling out twenty-six boys and thirteen girls adopted in infancy, they found that although the reasons for referral did not differ markedly from others, these adolescents did show a higher incidence of stealing than the general population, that the boys characteristically showed more aggressive outbursts than the girls, while the girls tended toward sexual acting out and pathological lying. All had severe problems with the parents.

In their interviews with the caseworkers, most of the parents had shown a great deal of denial. They felt adoption played no part in the disturbance, although a few were highly rejecting of the child, blaming his heredity. Moreover, the fact that the child was adopted almost never came up spontaneously—sometimes it surfaced only accidentally. Greenspan was also aware that he had difficulty getting material from the children about their feelings about being adopted. A defensiveness, denial, and repression pervaded the whole area, although some children wondered why they did not think about it.

Greenspan said: "It appeared to us that the added piece of identity, *the state of being adopted*, had difficulty becoming integrated into the personality because of lack of factual material about the natural parents, conflicting stories about one's origins, and the knowledge of adoption as a forbidding subject, so that questions and feelings about the state of not knowing could not be raised and discussed."[12]

Since there was a reluctance on the part of the adoptive parents to think about adoption, the children's feelings about it either remained in their unspoken fantasy life, were repressed, or were acted out. Greenspan felt the major finding was that lack of material available to the kids made it difficult for them to work through their adoption fantasies.

The most active researcher on adoption in the psychiatric field is Arthur Sorosky on the West Coast. Sorosky became concerned in the early 1970s when, like Greenspan, he noticed that few of the adolescent Adoptees in his practice had received enough background material to incorporate into their developing ego and, as a result, could not build a strong sense of identity. There was a shadow over their emerging sexuality as they became aware that their adoptive parents were watching them suspiciously, as if suspecting that something of the illicit tendencies of those missing parents might turn up in them. The suggestion of "bad seed" was there, as well as an embarrassment about sex in general.

Together with two social-work colleagues, Annette Baran and Reuben Pannor, Sorosky set up the Adoption Research Project, whose first undertaking was to collate all the material in the field.[13] There was an amazing number of articles scattered throughout the Western world by now, each detailing some fragment of the problem, but it took the Sorosky team to dredge them up from obscurity.

Genealogical Bewilderment

In 1952 there appeared in *Mental Health* magazine a short letter entitled, "Children without Genealogy—A problem of adoption." It began, "May I draw attention to the observation that lack of knowledge of their real parents and ancestors can be a cause of maladjustment in children."[14] It was signed by a British psychiatrist, E. Wellisch, who went on to note that in questioning whether it matters if a child has such knowledge, it should be remembered that most people accept their own genealogy as a matter of fact, and are no more aware of it than one is of one's shadow or mirror image.

Expanding this analogy, Wellisch pointed out that the shadow and mirror image of a person have a considerable psychological significance in that they are extensions of the *body image*—a concept he borrowed from Paul Schilder to describe a picture of our own body which also extends beyond its confines. Wellisch reminded his readers that the shadow was regarded by primitive people as an actual part of the body, and the mirror was used in witchcraft—in Gothic tales heroes sold their shadows and mirror images to the devil with disastrous results.

We see Wellisch groping for that phantom part of the Adoptee, as present as the "phantom limb" is in amputees. (Reading his words took me back to a recurring childhood nightmare I had after hearing a radio drama in which a woman had her ear cut off. Every night she roamed her rooftop as a ghost, crying: "Give me back what you have taken from me," and every night I heard her wail and trembled with terror, as if her loss was connected with some part of me that had been ripped away.)

The deeper he went into his study, the more Wellisch was struck by the Adoptee's loss. He noted how everyone, including himself, took the presence of others with similar physical characteristics for granted, because they had grown up surrounded by relatives who resembled them:

> As a matter of fact persons outside ourselves are essential for the development of our complete body-image. The most important persons in this respect are our real parents and other members of our family. Knowledge of and definite relationship to his genealogy is therefore necessary for a child to build up his complete body image and world picture. It is an inalienable and entitled right of every person. There is an urge, a call in everybody to follow and fulfill the tradition of his family, race, nation, and the religious community into which he was born. The loss of this tradition is a deprivation which may result in the stunting of emotional development.

Wellisch closed his letter with the observation that being deprived of knowledge of their heritage could lead children to irrational rebellion against their adoptive parents and the world as a whole, and eventually to delinquency. "The problem deserves special studies and attention."

Adoption Stress

It was H. J. Sants, working in the same clinic with Wellisch, who suggested that adopted children have, in addition to the general causes of maladjustment, the burden of *adoption stress*—the stress to which they are subjected as a result of their particular status. He found "genealogical bewilderment" to be a large factor in their condition.[15]

According to Sants, a genealogically bewildered child is one who has no knowledge of his natural parents or only uncertain knowledge of them. It is not just Adoptees who fall into this category, but also any child who has at least one unknown parent. The resulting confusion undermines the child's security and affects his mental health and may send him on a relentless pursuit of the facts of his origins from adolescence on. But having said this, Sants found himself as puzzled as Wellisch about why these children had such a desperate need for genetic information.

Looking to literature for insights, he saw an analogy in Hans Christian Andersen's tale of the ugly duckling, who by being hatched in the nest of another was deprived of knowledge of his true genealogy as a swan:

> The swan is rejected because he cannot do what the others in his family can do as a result of his different genetic endowment. Persecution leads to depression and wandering (symptoms found so often in the genealogically bewildered child). At one time the young swan is fostered by an old woman who already had two other foster-children, a cat and a hen. The cat despises him because he cannot curve his back and purr and the hen because he cannot lay eggs. The ugly duckling's heredity at this stage of his development allows him only to claim swimming as one of his abilities. He ventures to say, as many foster-children have done, that his foster-family do not understand him and is told, by the hen, "You've got nothing to do, that's why you get these whimsies. You try laying eggs or purring, and you'll get over it. . . ." The ugly duckling then does what other foster-children have done before, he runs away "out into the wide world." One afternoon he sees some birds which strangely inspire him. They are swans but he does not know that. He has never seen such beautiful birds but is not jealous of them. . . . He fears they may kill him but he does not care; he must join them. "Please kill me," said the poor little creature, and meekly stretched his neck along the water and waited for death. But what do you suppose he saw in the clear water? He saw his own image. But it was no longer that of a clumsy, dirty, grey bird, ugly and awkward, but of a lovely swan.

One of the ugly duckling's difficulties, according to Sants, was that none of his foster parents knew that he was a swan. "They did not know his genealogy. Consequently they could not understand the significance of his skills nor envisage his potentials. The ugly duckling showed his need to identify with others in order to feel that he belonged, but he could not identify with animals differing so much from himself in appearance and performance."

Sants decided that differences in appearance can severely hamper a child's capacity to identify with his parents so that any feelings he might have of belonging as the result of loving care would fail to be reinforced. What the ugly duckling had experienced was not unlike the research results of some of Sants's colleagues who were studying how physical resemblances between fathers and sons and mothers and daughters affected their closeness. In one experiment with nine hundred male students, it was found that 70 percent of those who got on well with their fathers had physiques similar to them. In relating this to his questions around adoption, Sants concluded, "If differences in genetic structure between natural father and son hamper identifications, it seems likely that identification will be even more hampered when there is no hereditary link between father and child."

Seeking out cultural examples, Sants noted that the practice of ancestor worship in some societies revealed man's emotional need to identify with biologically linked predecessors—even if one could go back no further than grandparents. He decided that most people are more aware than they realize that they contain the germ plasm of their parents and more remote ancestors, and that intellectual and emotional characteristics are in part genetically determined. *Not* knowing, then, would appear to be incompatible with a secure self-image.

Sants concluded that although adoption was an attempt to "transplant" the child from his natural family into his substitute family, such a graft could never be carried out completely because "roots in the natural family can never be severed without a trace." In other words, children need to know their natural origins.

Hereditary Ghosts

Looking at genealogical bewilderment from another perspective and adding another dimension, Max Frisk noticed that because his patients felt they were adopted, rather than born, they did not have the "genetic ego" which was essential for the formation of identity. Rather, they had what he called a "hereditary ghost,"

similar to the ones he had found in people with mental disturbance, suicide, and the like in their family. In order to rid themselves of this ghost, they felt the need to see their real parents and
discover what their true character was.

Frisk felt that this need led to a symbolic search for the parents,
which could express itself in restless wandering: "Some sought
company in fundamentally different social groups, on a lower
social level than that of their families. Their pursuit was in some
ways instinctive and seemed to be an effort to find a group identity,
corresponding to the predestined group the child imagined he
should have belonged to."

Frisk concurred with Sants that to be able to integrate those
aspects of themselves connected with heredity, Adoptees "must get
to know their biological parents."[16]

One's Own Kind

Another way of approaching genealogical bewilderment is to see
it in Erikson's sense of feeling alienated from people who are not
one's own kind.[17] This can happen in blood-related families, too,
when, for instance, the father looks at his own son who resembles
a hated brother and feels that this child is not his own kind. But
how much more likely it is to occur in the adoptive situation
where, genetically and historically, parent and child may have
little in common.[18]

One psychiatrist, himself an adoptive father, expressed it like
this:

> When your kid is acting up, when he's demonstrating all of
> his least appealing traits, you tend to be a lot more tolerant
> and forgiving if you can recognize those traits as your own,
> if you can grin and think—just like his old man. Hell! How
> can I blame *him* if he got it from *me?* But when you're *not*
> the old man, and the faults are alien and unrecognizable,
> you're going to be a lot tougher. You're going to wonder—
> where did the little bastard pick *that* up?[19]

Conversely, he goes on to say, the adoptive parent is never
free of the fear that the child will feel you don't love him because
he's being punished, or that you'd act differently if he were your
own flesh.

Marshall Schecter, who has continued his adoption studies

over the past twenty years, is aware of this problem. He believes that the tendency for Adoptees to run away or gravitate to people on an economic level lower than that of their adoptive parents is a way of seeking *their own people*. He points out that their fantasies about those unknown parents have become so real that they actually believe their identity lies in where they came from, rather than in what they have become with the parents who are raising them. "Adoptees must learn to say: 'Yes, I may have come from that, but this is what I am now.' They have to learn that there's a difference between being related and developing a relationship."[20]

Today, when so many children are adopted from overseas, we can expect that by adolescence they will be overwhelmed by the biological feeling of being separated from their own kind. Unlike previous generations of Adoptees who were the products of illegitimacy in this country, these children are the victims of social upheavals caused by war and poverty. Their sense of mystification will be as deep as ours, but more complex, because it has the added dimension of cultural and racial dislocation.

I think of Kim, a Vietnamese teenager, who came to the United States from an orphanage when she was three. Instead of being able to pass, as Caucasian Adoptees do, she is stared at on the streets and has only to look in the mirror to be reminded that she comes from a place not only alien to her parents but also to her whole community. Like the ugly duckling, she is obsessed with those features which do not resemble the people around her—in her case "an ugly flat nose and short legs." When she was younger, she would follow Oriental children around the supermarket as if she were trailing her own body image. As a preteen she began retreating into a secret life, disappearing for hours at a time and seeking out friends from a different social and racial group than that of her adoptive family. When she is upset, her mother feels as if she brings a "bamboo curtain" down between herself and those who love her. She talks of returning to Vietnam some day to find a husband with whom she can have children who will look like her. Her parents are concerned about the constant challenge of helping her gain confidence about her appearance. It all seemed so simple when she was a cuddly toddler. No one foresaw the difficulties she would have as she developed into an adolescent searching for some sense of self.

In their psychological profile of the adopted, based on their own research as well as on the findings of their colleagues, the Sorosky team members have singled out genealogical bewilderment, compulsive pregnancy, the roaming phenomenon, and the search for biological relatives as emotional conflicts and behavior patterns whose dynamics are unique to the adoptive condition. They came to the conclusion that adolescent Adoptees have a greater difficulty working through the psychosexual, psychosocial, and psychohistorical aspects of their personality development than their nonadopted peers—that the existing block to their past might create a feeling that there was a block to their future as well.[21]

Of course, Sorosky and other researchers acknowledge that they are working with special groups of Adoptees—those who turn up at psychiatric centers or those who have surfaced in the Adoptee liberation movement. But I feel it is important to suggest that those Adoptees who are going on about their lives without the apparent need to confront these problems will not necessarily have an easier time in the long run than those who did not have the temperament or inclination to play the Adoption Game. For them, too, the rules of the Game are so internalized that their choices are likely to become increasingly limited rather than enlarged as they move through life. When you stifle curiosity about yourself, you stifle many other things in the process. You shrink your area of perception. You live in a smaller space.

9

Good Adoptee–
Bad Adoptee

We have seen that Adoptees played the Adoption Game in various ways during childhood and adolescence, depending on the chemistry of the relationship with the adoptive parents and on their own constitutional make-up. Like the girl in the nursery rhyme, "When they were good, they were very, very good, and when they were bad they were horrid." Some were aware that they were trying to be the Good Adoptee, while it seemed to others, in retrospect, that they were always trying to be the Bad Adoptee.

The Good Adoptee was placid, obedient, didn't ask too many questions, was sensitive to his parents' needs to make believe he wasn't adopted.[1] The Bad Adoptee was rebellious and continually acting out at home and in school.

The Japanese speak of the "debt that can never be paid." Obviously, no one could be perfect enough to repay the debt of having been saved from the terrible fate of orphanhood: the seemingly Good Adoptee might be miserable because of the thoughts and fantasies he is secretly withholding from the adoptive parents; he feels he cannot play the game well enough no matter how hard he tries. And the Bad Adoptee, who acted out early, sometimes reforms and becomes overly solicitous to the adoptive parents in young adulthood.

There is another Japanese saying: "Scratch a Japanese and you will find a samurai." In the same spirit, we may say that if you scratch a seemingly Good Adoptee, such as one who doesn't want to search, you will usually find a former Bad Adoptee, or a future one in the making. For in all Adoptees there resides simultaneously the responsible child along with the one who, being magical, is not accountable, the legitimate, law-abiding citizen alongside the outlaw.

The Good Adoptee

Mark, a professional man in his mid-thirties, has always thought of himself as the Good Adoptee, the model child. "I was grateful," he says. "Grateful to have been adopted, grateful not to have died in a concentration camp like my adoptive mother's relatives." Although he was born in New York in the early 1940s, he had nightmares about that, but also feelings of good fortune.

"I bought the *chosen-baby* bit. I still buy it. I considered myself special, still do. Bragged about it. Still do. Enjoyed the fact that I'm adopted."

When Mark was three, his five-year-old sister, also adopted, died of leukemia. His parents went into mourning for her, and the agency suggested a replacement—something that experts would think twice about doing today. A sister, two years younger, joined the family, but Mark feels he was still the special child. He went to an Ivy League college and now has a position in a prestigious firm.

Mark does not remember having any fantasies about his birth parents, whom he thought died in a car crash. He never said things like "You're not my real parents" when he was a teenager, or "I hate you." In fact, he showed no temper at all. He still has difficulty expressing anger and is beginning to understand that he used passive-aggressive means to achieve his ends instead.

When he was eighteen, Mark's parents succumbed to their daughter's pressure to talk about adoption. He then learned the truth about his background. His mother was an unmarried German Jewish refugee who was sixteen when she came alone to the United States during the war. She lived in a series of foster homes provided by a Jewish organization, and became pregnant with him at nineteen. His Irish Catholic father was married and could not get a divorce. His mother wanted to raise him but was persuaded that it was better to put him up for adoption with a Jewish family.

Mark remembers feeling stunned when he heard all this and closing the subject immediately. "A lucky person shouldn't push to find things out," he told himself. Now he understands that he never felt he had a right to be depressed, even to seek therapy when he was older, because he was alive and adopted by these people who cared about him.

At thirty-five, Mark is now in therapy, exploring for the first time the forces that shaped his character.

"My mother was a saint and sacrificing," he says. "I'm still her baby. But I always had a hard time feeling close to her."

His father was a large man who towered over him physically, gave him everything, but never seemed to take him seriously. His style was cynical—belittling what Mark said. Now Mark realizes that he used adoption as a way of feeling different from his parents as he was growing up. He asserted himself against his father's values in indirect ways. For instance, his father was adamant that Mark join a firm with Jewish contacts. Mark made a point of joining a WASP one. At the same time, he became more religious than his family by joining a synagogue and observing the dietary laws. "I must have felt unconsciously that Judaism was the one thing I could hold onto," he says. "The only tie with the heritage I came from."

This feeling of being grateful still permeates Mark's vocabulary, but how "good" is Mark now? This is what he is going over with his therapist. A few years ago he left his wife and the two children to whom he was extremely attached, to marry a woman he fell in love with shortly after his adoptive father died. He went into a deep depression after the marriage—which is why he sought psychiatric help. He worries that he had some need to act out his birth father's role in abandoning a child, especially after his adoptive father was no longer there to judge him. "I felt devastated when Dad died," he admits. "I kept thinking 'that's my daddy lying there.' It had nothing to do with being adopted then."

But how "good" would his father consider him if he could see him now, not only divorced, but also searching. This is the dilemma of the Good Adoptee who keeps all feelings repressed until he finally begins acting out in middle life. "Since I didn't express my true feelings to my parents while I was growing up, I am afraid I still don't know how to express my feelings," he says.

"I had so much fear of irrational behavior, and now I've been acting so irrationally. I guess there was a lot of anger I didn't understand—until now."

Mark's feelings about his birth mother are essentially positive. The agency told him that she was beautiful and intelligent. "I never had a negative fantasy," he asserts, then adds, as if thinking about it for the first time, "Well, I once worried she might not want to see me."

In spite of his outward self-assurance, Mark has always been sensitive to rejection. A few years ago, when he was being considered for a top job with a large firm on the West Coast, he received a letter explaining that the fact of his adoption—which he had himself brought up in one of the interviews—was worrisome to the organization because adopted people had many problems not yet understood. He was filled with rage at this discriminatory excuse for not giving him the job, but instead of protesting, he tore up the letter and promptly forgot about it—until now.

Today Mark fears the "biggest rejection," that his mother may not want to meet him. He realizes that he has resisted searching for her because of this fear, and because he knows that he will be giving up his status as the Good Adoptee. However, he is in the process of the Search because he can no longer fool himself.

The Bad Adoptee

Perhaps it takes an Adoptee to give us a classic portrait of the Bad Adoptee and his ultimate fate. Edward Albee does this brilliantly in his play *The American Dream.*

We learn that twenty years before, Mommy and Daddy had been informed by a "dear lady" named Mrs. Barker of the Bye Bye Adoption Service that she had a "bumble" for them. Now, senile old Grandma is telling a woman who looks very much like Mrs. Barker, and indeed is, that things didn't work out too well after they "bought" that bumble:

GRANDMA: Weeeeelllll . . . in the first place, it turned out the bumble didn't look like either one of its parents. That was enough of a blow, but things got worse. One night, it cried its heart out, if you can imagine such a thing.

MRS. BARKER: Cried its heart out! Well!

GRANDMA: But that was only the beginning. Then it turned out it had eyes only for its Daddy.

MRS. BARKER: For its Daddy! Why, any self-respecting woman would have gouged those eyes right out of its head.

GRANDMA: Well she did. That's exactly what she did. But then it kept its nose up in the air.

MRS. BARKER: Ufggh! How disgusting!

GRANDMA: That's what they thought. But *then,* it began to develop an interest in its you-know-what.

MRS. BARKER: In its you-know-what! Well! I hope they cut its hands off at the wrists!

GRANDMA: Well, yes, they did that eventually. But first, they cut off its you-know-what.

MRS. BARKER: A much better idea!

GRANDMA: That's what they thought. But after they cut off its you-know-what, it *still* put its hands under the covers, looking for its you-know-what. So finally they *had* to cut off its hands at the wrists.

MRS. BARKER: Naturally!

GRANDMA: Of course. And then as it got bigger, they found out all sorts of terrible things about it, like it didn't have a head on its shoulders, it had no guts, it was spineless, its feet were made of clay . . . just dreadful things.

MRS. BARKER: Dreadful!

GRANDMA: So you can understand how they became discouraged.

MRS. BARKER: I certainly can! And what did they do?

GRANDMA: What did they do? Well, for the last straw, it finally up and died; and you can imagine how *that* made them feel, their having paid for it and all. So, they called up the lady who sold them the bumble in the first place and told her to come right over to their apartment. They wanted satisfaction; they wanted their money back. That's what they wanted.

MRS. BARKER: My, my, my.

Bad Adoptees don't literally undergo the trials of the baby in Albee's play, but they could be said to do so metaphorically at various stages of their development.[2]

Karla remembers being told in effect that she was a bad baby. She couldn't eat for the first six months, even though she had been brought by her parents directly from the hospital. "I cried every time my mother tried to feed me. I was difficult. I made her feel bad. I wouldn't accept her mothering. When she'd tell me this, I would feel guilty. Occasionally while she was talking about all she went through with me, the word *gratitude* would come spilling out, and then later she would deny that she really expected it."

As they grow older Adoptees live in a repressed state of confusion about the strength of their bond with the adoptive parents, who, like all parents, are subject to outbreaks of uncontrolled rage. The child broods: "If I was adopted, could I be disadopted?" "Was I really adopted, or are my parents just saying this because they are ashamed of me?"

As if testing their own doubts and confusions, adopted children resort at stress times to tactics that immediately throw them into the category of the Bad Adoptee, a role they have a hard time shaking, even though they know it is one that is against the rules of the Game. For while Good Adoptees sustain themselves with the reminder that their parents' home is a shelter from a dangerous world in which they have already once been lost, Bad Adoptees resent being imprisoned in this house—like Rapunzel in the tower—and imagine that their true parents might be out looking for them.

Resentment leads to anger, anger leads to outbursts of fury at the adoptive parents, since there is no other target. They cannot win: if they express anger, they feel guilt. If they are forced to feel guilty, they become angry. Indeed, it is safe to say that at one time or another all Adoptees waver back and forth between these two conditions.

The Bad Adoptees are the ones who cannot adequately repress their sense of lack of connection. They cannot tolerate it. They act out as a way of feeling alive. To prove that they exist. *He* goes in for stealing, setting fires, smashing up the family car, taking drugs, and running away. *She* may pop pills, steal, or run away, but she also acts out sexually by becoming pregnant.

Daphne's parents often threatened to commit her to a home for girls, but the furthest they went was to put her under custody of the family court when she was in her teens. It was a shame because she had been so cuddly when she arrived as a baby from Greece, her adoption having been arranged privately through a Greek lawyer. Her parents hoped she would be company for their two-year-old daughter. That she would complete their family.

Daphne, who is now twenty-five, remembers playing the clown as a child—the blond, blue-eyed scatterbrained jester, to the dark-complexioned, disapproving parents who scolded and fretted continually with her and each other. It was a bad marriage, often verging on divorce, but she, rather than their biological child, became the focus of her parents' discontent.

Gradually the clown's role lost its innocence, became demonic. She became destructive of her clothes, deliberately tearing them, and remembers cutting up a pair of shoes, her mother screaming that she was a bad child. From the age of thirteen it was downhill all the way. She failed at school, ran away from home and hid at friends' houses, began taking drugs.

All that Daphne had been told about her background was that her mother was a farmgirl. She imagined her like a creature out of Tobacco Road—poor, uneducated, whorish—for her parents did not give her all the information they had: that her mother came from a devout family on a prosperous farm and trained as a nurse in Athens where she was born, or that her father was French, a student of architecture who was studying abroad when they met.

Daphne got pregnant at seventeen, the first time she slept with her high-school boyfriend. Her outraged family moved to another city and arranged an abortion. Daphne took an overdose of sleeping pills and slept for three days after her stomach was pumped. "I remember waking up laughing," she says. "My parents were horrible. Mother kept saying 'How could you embarrass us like this?' I hated her at that moment. She didn't care that I had almost died."

The communication lines seemed to be permanently down by then. Daphne left home without finishing high school and moved in with a working-class man she met in New York. Once again, like so many adopted women, she was seeking the level she thought she was from. Soon she was pregnant once more.

"I guess I really wanted a baby I could keep," she says now. "Of course, my mother wanted me to get an abortion again, or get married. But I didn't want to do either. She'd scream things at me like 'See, he doesn't want to marry you. You're nothing but a piece of ass to him!' Once she said 'You're just like your mother!' That's how I found out I was illegitimate."

Daphne did marry the baby's father, but the discrepancies in their backgrounds eventually defeated them. "I was scared when he left. Everything seemed impossible," she says. "My mother said I should put my daughter up for adoption—I realize now she wanted to punish me. And actually I did consider it. But I was lucky to have a wonderful social worker at the day-care center where I kept her. She said, 'Don't do it. You don't know how frightened you are. You need her desperately.' And she was right. When I finally got a job and put my life together, I realized that she was the only one related to me in the world."

Recently Daphne's adoptive father gave in to her pressure and admitted he had a sheaf of adoption papers in his office safe. As he turned them over to her, he said bitterly: "I've completed all my obligations to you now," as if her wanting to have this information about herself was the final betrayal by the Bad Adoptee.

In the packet was a picture of her mother, a beautiful young woman in a nurse's uniform, holding her tenderly. Letters to the adoptive parents revealed that because her parents had disowned her, she felt she had no choice but to give up her baby. Had Daphne known this while she was growing up, her story might have been different—she would have had a chance to have some pride in her heritage, and in herself. And had her parents known that it might enable their daughter to have some peace in her turbulent life, and that the adoptive relationship is stronger than it seems in times of crisis, they might have shared everything with her much earlier.

Of course, most Adoptees live somewhere between the Good Adoptee and the Bad Adoptee, without the complete repression that Mark employed or the complete acting out that Daphne resorted to. At some point Good Adoptees, like Mark, may find that their denial hinders rather than serves them, when depression suddenly sets in; and Bad Adoptees may lose the need to rebel once they gain some information about themselves.

10

The Adoptee as Adult

The adopted adult is the child now grown, although it is hard to know where one ends and the other begins.

Until their liberation movement, Adoptees were isolated within their adoptive families, desperately trying to pass as one of the clan. Now that they recognize their dislocation as a unique part of their existential condition, they are feeling the excitement of asserting their differences. Their lack of connectedness to others connects and holds them to each other.

"I wonder if we could speak of adopted people like a new species," Erik Erikson once mused aloud as I was describing all this to him.

"Do you mean a pseudo-species?" I asked, referring to his term for groups outside the accepted norm who take on a cosmology different from others.

"I guess I was thinking of that," he said thoughtfully, still not committing himself. "It happens when there is a new discovery. New loyalties are developed. People recognize each other. There is a newborn feeling in everyone who goes through it."

I considered this.

More than one analyst had already suggested to me that Adoptees might fall into Freud's category of the *exception,* meaning those people who because of early childhood deprivation do not feel themselves held to the same reality principles as other people. Freud's examples had included the deformed Richard III, and others who suffered congenital injuries they felt were unjust.¹

I had considered this, too, and decided that the condition of being cut off from knowledge of the blood tie is *more* exceptional than the exception—aware, of course, that the main characteristic of all exceptions is to feel just that.

Call them what you will—a pseudo-species, survivors, exceptions—adopted adults insist they feel outside the mainstream of human existence. Instead of asking "Who am I?" they ask "Who are we?" Speaking an emotional shorthand, they compare common traits in their adoptive parents as if they had emerged from a communal womb. They sound like brothers and sisters reminiscing about the family. The gravitational pull of their shared experience holds them together in their own private galaxy. Just as society has kept secrets from them, so they kept secrets from society. It is this private world of tribal secrets that binds them together in a new kind of kinship. Together they have a chance of discovering who they are.

There has been very little research on adopted adults. Perhaps this lack reflects society's difficulty in thinking of the Adoptee as someone who actually grows up. (Jackie, who became pregnant with her second child at the age of thirty-five, was warned by her doctor that she was an "old" mother, but he introduced her to his colleague as an "adopted child.")

It is only in the past few years that researchers like William Reynolds, an adoptive father as well as a psychologist at Queens College, are becoming concerned with the adopted adult. Using a battery of tests in which he compared Adoptees to norm populations, Reynolds came up with this profile:

> The adoptee is inclined to be a rather shy and personally wary individual who is ill at ease in dealing with others. Impulsive in decision making style, whose self-image tends to be remote and untrusting, who has real difficulty persisting at tasks without immediate rewards, and whose tolerance for frustration and delay is minimal.²

Reynolds concluded from his data that there may be "personally debilitating facts in the status of being adopted itself, which may be far more complex and basic than current discussions of the significance of the Search would imply."

There are, of course, great variables in Adoptees, but I've found that both men and women recognize aspects of themselves in

Reynolds's profile. Regardless of their professional or social success, they see themselves as shy and withdrawn, loners, afraid of rejection or conflict, anxious to please, submissive but filled with rage. We must keep in mind that though these basic feelings which they have about themselves may never surface in actuality, they are there. We might call them the hidden phenomenology of the Adoptee.

During interviews I was to hear from both men and women whose lives on the surface seemed stable and productive: "I feel my life is in transition." "I have the sense that everything is temporary, that I must keep moving on." "I've never felt rooted, doubt if I ever will." "Roots attract and terrify me at the same time." "I don't know if I have the capacity to feel connected to anyone."

They described experiencing a lifelong depression, feeling empty inside—empty and helpless—as if all they had was their own skin. One woman said: "We are a held-back people—inhibited, tentative, dreamers not doers. Holding back curiosity about oneself for the sake of others makes one hold back in other things too."

In our rap groups everyone spoke of a persisting guilt toward their adoptive parents; of a recurring fear of abandonment that permeates their friendships and marriages; of a sense of taint from the early secrecy around their illegitimate origins; of not being able to free themselves emotionally from overly domineering adoptive mothers; of symptoms of claustrophobia in crowded places; of fear of choking and strangulation; of problems around the issues of leadership and authority.

The Murdered Self

It is as if each Adoptee carries within him "the murdered self," which William James saw as the self one must not be. That self, the one born to another clan, with all the genetic pulls involved, must not be acknowledged. By being forced out of the natural flow of generational continuity, as others know it, it is as if one has been forced out of nature itself.

Seen in these terms, Adoptees become impotent creatures who have been denied free will. Everything has been determined either before or just after they were born. They are pawns moved by others and forced to live by the definition of reality which others give them. That deadness within them, which they call "emptiness," seems to hinder their ability to give or receive love.

Adam, the psychotherapist, spoke of sharing a low intimacy tolerance with his adoptive patients. "I think we Adoptees have trouble making and sustaining relationships. We share a vulnerability to the stresses and strains of everyday interactions, have real difficulty forming ties and connections. We need security and dependency, but try to escape from it. We seem to need freedom. We don't trust people. We suffer from what I call survival paranoia."

Intergenerational Continuity

Many Adoptees, both men and women, have ambivalence about having children—becoming parents themselves. "I don't mean to pun," a man told me, "but in society one is not apparent and substantial until one becomes a parent."

But how can the adopted child, who never fully grew up, become a parent? This is the quandary they all face, cut off as they have been from full autonomy over their lives. Writing of adopted children as well as children separated from one parent by divorce proceedings, Norman Paul observed that ignorance of their true story can lead to crucial defects in their capacity to function adequately as parents:

> The question is what are the experiences this child requires, needs, has a right to have so that he or she will not be rendered dysfunctional when both adulthood and parenthood are achieved. Because parenthood in part includes a reactivation of unresolved feelings and attitudes about oneself when one was a child, it is incumbent upon society to review and evolve more effective techniques that are not going to disable children.[3]

Sometimes when Adoptees are confiding in each other, they summon forth those repressed children they once were. "Perhaps the child in me needs to be brought to light and understood before she can grow in peace," said a woman who was in the throes of "sifting and sorting" and being "rooted and unrooted." These vulnerable children have much about them that is magical. Their specialness gives them a sense of omnipotence, makes them feel at times indestructible. But this lack of reality also has a negative, demonic force—it makes them feel unconnected, always in a fog, not alert, suffocated by emotional blankets, mere sojourners, lost in a black hole.

Norman Paul tells us that adopted children who are not able to resolve their feelings about themselves will transmit their sense of unreality to the next generation. I think of the teenager who wrote me: "When my children ask me someday about their roots, what do I say, 'You're one-half English, one-half mongrel!?'"

In his book *Wanderer's All*, Gregory Armstrong speaks as the child of two adopted parents (*secret orphans,* he calls them) who acted as if they were carriers of a deadly virus which they would pass on to him:

> Both of them lived as if they believed that other people were always better. People with parents. They took so little for themselves. The little they did take they took so apologetically. So deferentially. Despite his great talent, my father was never able to succeed in the world. It was almost as if he believed that orphans had no right to worldly success. . . . In spite of their best efforts the sense of their orphan's stigma was passed on to me. Somewhere deep inside myself, I believed that the most I could do for my children, the biggest gift that I could give to them, was to withhold myself from them. That was why I took such a small part in their lives. Why, in some sense I made orphans out of them just the same way I had been orphaned by my own parents. To protect them from myself.

Because Armstrong equated his lovelessness with the sense of rootlessness he had inherited from his birth parents, he took a "pilgrimage" to find their families, as a way of learning how to love.

Erikson has already told us that the person who does not learn intimacy in his adolescence will be isolated, a loner, unable to have a relationship that will lead to what he calls *generativity*.[4] Perhaps it is no coincidence that many Adoptees, isolated as they have been from a sense of true relatedness, choose homosexuality or bisexuality as an alternative lifestyle. We could say that not being rooted or connected to others gives one the freedom to experiment, to be many things. Not being real, one does not have to be responsible to the social norm.

Molly, an Adoptee, who chooses lesbianism in *Rubyfruit Jungle,* says it like this:

I never thought I had much in common with anybody. I had no mother, no father, no roots, no biological similarities called sisters and brothers. And for a future I didn't want a split level home with a station wagon, pastel refrigerator, and a houseful of blonde children evenly spaced through the years. I didn't even want to walk into the pages of *McCall's* magazine and become the model housewife. I didn't even want a husband or any man for that matter. I wanted to go my own way. That's all I think I ever wanted, to go my own way and maybe find some love here and there. Love, but not the now and forever kind with chains around your vagina and short circuit in your brain. I'd rather be alone.

Erica, a poet whose reunion story we will go into later, felt that her lesbianism was an affirmation of women:

This longing toward the female, I think is a part of me. When I told a friend of mine about the frustrations of my search, she said "My God, it's as if you were tracking a lover!" She may have a point. And it could be the abrupt separation from my natural mother at birth. I mean nursing for a few weeks and being wrested away. And my love for my adoptive mother, a feeling of protection toward her. She was very strong, but I think as a child I sensed that she didn't have children in the usual way, that somehow she couldn't, and I should protect her from possible accusations that she's not a true mother. So I've been closely in touch with women, and have a great empathy about the role of women.

A lot of these women speak of feeling hostile to men because they imagine their fathers deserted their mothers. Erica said: "At times I think that adoption, I mean the whole concept of the *bastard*, is really a patriarchal attitude to insure men that they know who their children are."

Another lesbian, Gail, feels she might not have been put up for adoption if her father had taken responsibility: "I always felt he was some creep after his jollies." Her adoptive mother fainted when Gail told her she was gay. "I said, 'Mother, get up.' She said, 'You didn't get that from me.'"

Many of the adopted men I've interviewed are gay. A number of those who are not described themselves as bisexual or having problems with the male role model. Brian, whose reunion story we will follow, speaks of fighting a potential for bisexuality.

"I don't want to develop it. I have to learn to make commitments, overcome my anxiety and reluctance to form close relationships." Adam has a pattern of ending marriages and affairs after two years. "I am not gay, but I don't have a need to prove my masculinity," he said. "I feel comfortable accompanying gay friends to bars and dancing, without the hangups most men would feel in those circumstances."

Both Brian and Adam happen to be psychologists. They speak of not being able to sustain a relationship, not being able to tolerate long periods of intimacy with women. In order to attract them, a woman must be independent, both professionally and emotionally. Once she is made vulnerable by love, they move away from her. They are both aware and troubled that something in them cannot give nurture, or take responsibility for another's life. I have the impression that many male Adoptees have difficulty identifying with their adoptive fathers, and they often have unacknowledged rage toward that mother who rejected them. But there needs to be much more research in this area, especially on interactions with the adoptive father, about whom almost nothing has been written.

No matter what their lifestyle—heterosexual, homosexual, or bisexual—or their occupations—artists, housewives, professionals, business people—all these Adoptees managed to reach the place where they could acknowledge their need to know their heritage.

Looking back now they all wonder how they could have so blindly and unquestioningly played the Adoption Game.

They wonder why it took them so long to wake up.

Part Two

FOUND

The world of dew
Is the world of dew,
And yet . . .
And yet . . .
ISSA

11

Waking Up from the Great Sleep

The idea of the sleeper, of somebody hidden from mortal eye, waiting until the time shall ripen has always been dear to the folkly mind—Snow White asleep in her glass coffin, Brynhild behind her wall of fire, Charlemagne in the heart of France, King Arthur in the Isle of Avalon, Frederic Barbarossa under his mountain in Thuringia.

P. T. TRAVERS, *About the Sleeping Beauty*

I like to think of Adoptees as being in the great tradition of sleepers. It is as if the act of adoption put us under a spell that numbed our consciousness. When we awaken it startles us to realize we might have slept our lives away, floating and uprooted.

The Adoptee is just beginning to raise questions that Travers explores in the Sleeping Beauty legend: "What is it in us that at a certain moment suddenly falls asleep? What lies hidden deep within us? And who will come at last to wake us, what aspects of ourselves?"

Put psychologically, Adoptees are asking how they managed to repress so much as children, to numb the natural curiosity within them, to accept society's mandate that they should not know something as primal as who gave birth to them. At what point did they give up and go along with the prevailing system, as if sensing intuitively that acquiescence meant emotional survival, and struggle meant disintegration? Even as they try to penetrate these mysteries,

71

they sometimes long to fall back into that former delicious sleep, so free of conflict and ambivalence. But it is too late. They know by now that the prince who placed the kiss on Sleeping Beauty's brow was but that aspect of herself which was ready to awaken. She had no choice but to arise and fulfill herself as an adult in the real world.

And neither do they.

The Adoptee awakens when he or she realizes that not to know would be to live without meaning. The curiosity has always been there, waiting to be released. Putting it in mythic terms, Travers tells us "things long unknowingly known have suddenly been remembered." Like streams, they had disappeared underground, become lost to us temporarily while we went about the process of living.

We could say that Adoptees have been searching consciously or unconsciously all of their lives. From the moment she is told she is adopted. From the moment he looks in the mirror and wonders whose eyes are looking back at him. From the moment she asks that first question: "Why did that other lady give me away?" From that moment he shouts in anger: "You're not my real mother!" From the moment she makes that first futile visit for information to the family doctor. From the moment he is informed by the hospital where he was born that everything he wants to know is on microfilm which he, being adopted, is not allowed to see.

And yet to awaken does not necessarily mean to begin the Search. There is still a lot of psychological work to be done before one is ready to pack and set out on that "mere" search for beginnings, which according to Erik Erikson harbors for us all some vision of an innocence lost or a hidden curse to be dealt with—and both with some sense of inescapable predestination.[1]

12

Who Searches?

In the past it was believed that only the psychologically disturbed, or those who were unhappy in their adoptive families, had the need to search. However, it is not that simple. Comparing those who search with those who do not, William Reynolds came to the conclusion that there are no conclusions—those who were happy in their adoptive homes might search because they felt confident in themselves, while those who were unhappy might be restrained from searching through angry guilt.[1] In the end he fell back on folk wisdom: some Adoptees just have more curiosity than others, and some were "luckier in the draw."[2]

The Sorosky team sees the Search as resulting from both a sociological and a biological need. "The need to have a sense of one's genealogy is probably a basic biological one, whereas the feeling of alienation created by adoption can also cause it," Sorosky told me.

Margaret Lawrence, an Adoptee with her own adoption research project, believes that the Search has nothing to do with the adoptive relationship or the need to find "real" parents. Rather, it is the need to be free to be oneself and to have the power to choose for oneself.[3]

However, most adoptive parents continue to be threatened by the phenomenon of Adoptees searching—fearful that they will somehow lose their children. In the same period that millions of her countrymen were rushing to genealogical libraries in response to Alex Haley's *Roots*, Eda LeShan, an adoptive mother, used her authority as a family therapist to compare the Adoptee's need to search with giving in to the impulse to lie or steal. "Maturity comes when we learn to control such impulses," declared LeShan, thereby suggesting that it is aberrant for the adopted to seek out their heritage.[4]

No wonder many Adoptees feel constrained about carrying out the Search—not only do they get the message that they are being untrue to their adoptive parents, but also that there is something immoral, even criminal, in the act.

There are other reasons, of course, why some people do not search. A few will admit that they are afraid of what they will find—afraid of rejection, afraid of disturbing the birth mother's life, afraid of their own lives changing, afraid of losing whatever identity they have, afraid they may be saddled with responsibility for an aging, indigent parent.

Some Adoptees are overwhelmed by disappointment after their first unsuccessful probe. However, getting information too quickly, before one is psychologically ready, can be an immobilizing rather than an energizing experience, as one woman found out:

> The problem is that I feel a good deal of anxiety associated with thinking over the whole childhood experience. In a dream my adopted parents and my natural parents became the same, and both were abandoning me. Knowing names has made me more curious than before, but because of the anxiety, I have put the whole thing aside for a while.

This woman may let the subject lie dormant for years before making another cautious attempt of one kind or another. Or she may become a permanent nonsearcher. Such primal anxiety is caused not only by breaking the taboo, but by the fear that if one ventures too deeply into this forbidden terrain, one might disappear into the abyss.

"Opening a dark and frightening tunnel which might have no end," is the way another woman put it. She wanted her birth mother to know of her existence, but even after locating the address, she was unable to take the final steps:

> Perhaps the day will come, maybe after my adoptive parents pass on, that I will again come to wonder "Who am I?" and whether my hangups are a result of being adopted, being an only child, or being me—or maybe a combination of everything. But for the moment, I am quite content to be the person I am today. The fact that I cannot put a face to the name is not nearly as important as it once was.

Such fears as those expressed by these nonsearchers have been felt by all Adoptees, even the most militant, at one time or another. There are moments when all of us have been tempted to leave those "hereditary ghosts" undefined—out there. When we have admitted to ourselves in the darkness of the night, "I'm not sure what I want from this."

The Militant Nonsearcher

I've found that nonsearchers often feel threatened by searchers. The clamor of militant Adoptees on radio and TV has the effect of loud music under the windows of those who are trying to sleep. It makes them react belligerently, like the woman who wrote this to me:

> I resent the melodrama attached to adoption and all of its aftereffects. It is passing from womb to home that is undeniably natural. Whether or not there is an exchange of hands is irrelevant. Spare me, then, the histrionics! I feel sorry for those who are beset by imaginary monsters; please, however, don't try to set them on those of us who are busy with the reality of living in the present.

It seems that militant nonsearchers have absorbed society's negative image of what they might find if they searched. One hears them say: "I don't want to rock the boat," or "Why should I open a can of worms?" They accept the position that it is an act of disloyalty to the adoptive parents. It becomes a moral issue, in which they see the searcher as an ingrate, just as the searcher sees them as an Uncle Tom. "Our adoptive parents accepted us for what we were with no questions asked," they might say, or "Meeting my natural mother would be an unnecessary trauma in my life as well as hers. I don't think there could be a more selfish quest than this."

Nonsearchers, for all their sense of righteousness and loyalty, have always seemed to me self-denigrating. There is the implication that they don't have a right to rock their own boat, to open their own can of worms. They seem to accept that they don't have a right to their own heritage. We see such internalized guilt in them that even if their adoptive parents should sanction a search, it would be hard for them to follow through. It is as if they have a will not to know.

Regardless of their personal biases, searchers and nonsearchers should not allow themselves to be put into adversary positions with each other, as sometimes happens when both are invited to debate on a TV panel or at an adoptive parent meeting. I made the mistake of accepting the latter only once.

Alfred, the nonsearcher, was a business executive and an adoptive father of a three-year-old daughter. I realized somewhere in the evening as we lashed out at each other that we were not unlike two gladiators putting on a spectacle in the coliseum before a bloodthirsty crowd. (In this case it was my blood they were after.) Wearing his hat as an adoptive father, which made him one of them, Alfred could placate the audience, make them feel that their child would never want to know, because he himself hadn't. "My adoptive parents were straightforward, told me everything," he said, "so why should I want to search? It was a simple enough story: two college kids got into trouble, and didn't want to interrupt their studies. I can understand."

Under Alfred's cool tone was the abandoned baby screaming: "They didn't want me then, I don't want them now." I've heard many nonsearchers declare that they wouldn't go out of their way to find their parents, but if they happened to hear they were across the street, they might glance over to see what they looked like. Alfred admitted, in response to a question, that if his birth mother contacted him, he would invite her up for a drink, just to see what she looked like.

"The child has the right to ask, but not to know," Alfred concluded. "He has the debt of life to the birth mother, but this is not paid back by invading her privacy, by seeking roots in a quasi-infantile way."

In such a situation, the searcher (who was me) is tempted to lash back (and I did) that anyone who has any curiosity about the origins of the universe he lives in—(the implication being that all superior people do)—would want to know his own origins; that Alfred has let those student birth parents remain stick figures on a frieze, forever poring over their schoolbooks; whereas in reality his young mother might have tried to keep him, and even now might be yearning to know what happened to him.

But the searcher should gain control of herself (which I finally did) and remember that the goal is not to make Alfred into a searcher, but to convince the audience that the records should be open for those who want to know. Alfred could do as he pleased, but he should have a choice. Of course, because Alfred is an adoptive father he may never wake up to this need, since he will never see his genetic mysteries reflected in his children.

Still, the fact that Adoptees like Alfred are not searching now does not mean that they will not be searching in the future. It is just that for the present they are raising their psychological defenses like barricades around their inner trepidations. And they are wise. Although one is never *totally* prepared, one should not tamper with the Search until one cannot do otherwise. I know a woman who had to wait seventeen years after seeing both her mother's and father's names on the adoption papers before she could say: "I am finally ready. I feel strong enough inside myself to do it without fearing I'll be destroyed in the process."

13

The Decision to Search

Black parental mysteries
groan and mingle in the night.
Something will be born of this.
MURIEL RUKEYSER, "Double Ode"

We see that although the desire to search has always been there, buried and seemingly lost except for the occasional thought, daydream, or outburst, the actual commitment to search is a special stage in itself. It is arrived at over a period of time, as the self gradually evolves from one level of consciousness to another, striving for authenticity and self-autonomy.

It is the moment of choosing yourself.

R. D. Laing once told me that in dealing with any difficult decision there comes a critical point when one either retreats or makes an aggressive charge into it. This is the moment of clarity of which one Adoptee said: "I think the decision to search and the acknowledgment of lost parents as every bit important psychologically as whatever turns up at the end of the search."

Of course, the timing of any internal decision is influenced by what has been happening in one's life. "There is nothing like shocks in the real world to jar loose repressions," the anthropologist Ernest Becker tells us.[1] The "shocks" that seem to trigger the need to search, according to the Sorosky team, can be anything from the death of an adoptive parent, divorce, the need for medical history, to the birth of a baby.[2]

78

Many of the Adoptees in my sample did not begin searching until their late twenties or early thirties, although I did hear from an octogenarian:

I am 81 years young. I would like to know who my mother and father were. I been adopted when I was four years. Well, I guess by now they're up there in God sky. I wonder if I had any brothers or sisters. Wouldn't that be wonderful to hear. I suppose they're all dead. I hope you can help me. If not, maybe we'll meet in heaven, or in the sky. Please let me know good or bad news.

The majority of searchers have proven to be women. This would seem logical when we remember that it is the girls who ply their adoptive mothers with questions while growing up, as if concerned even then with the problems around biological continuity. Women are closer to their feelings. They are the ones who face becoming mothers themselves, and who yearn for some knowledge of that woman who went before them into the rites of childbirth—an experience they cannot share with their adoptive mothers.

Men, as we have seen from their inability to recall their childhood feelings and fantasies, continue to suppress their conscious need to know more about themselves and are reluctant to approach the rage they feel toward the woman who gave them up.

Adam, who didn't search until he was turning thirty, feels that a man's reluctance to open himself to this subject goes back to those earlier days of repressing one's feelings. He remembers being told by his parents that little boys don't cry and, when he did, being ridiculed and humiliated and told to act like a man: "I think the decision to search requires a man to get in touch with feelings that are difficult, and that he is not used to being in touch with. The concerns of men are in the world of material things. They don't derive identity from their relationships. They're not as interested in defining and looking at biological and social ties."

Brian

Brian did not awaken to his feelings about being adopted until he was twenty-nine, but like most Adoptees, he had made stabs at getting information before that.

"As a child I asked few questions. My parents had told me I

was adopted at three months, but it never occurred to me to wonder where I was born, or the reasons I was given up. Any time I did ask anything, I sensed anxiety and discomfort. I don't think I even tried to imagine those other parents until I was at least sixteen. I realize now I was practicing the same denial my parents had in dealing with the adoption."

Brian's mother was an extroverted, smothering person who was the dominant one in raising him. His father was quiet, introverted, and withdrawn. When he was sixteen Brian became overwhelmed with the turbulence of adolescence, dropped out of school, and even attempted suicide with an overdose of aspirin. All that happened was that he woke the next day with a terrible headache and thoughts about who his birth parents were.

One afternoon shortly after that, when he was alone in the house, Brian did what many Adoptees have done: he went through his parents' drawers searching for clues to the mystery of his life, what William James calls "the worm at the core." It was then that he found his adoption paper with his birth mother's name on it.

"I was excited and fearful of what it might mean. I put the paper away and didn't pursue it further. I didn't want to go into it any deeper at sixteen. I was so involved in my own turmoil and troubles, I put the whole thing out of my mind. I felt I had to get away, so I enlisted in the Air Force. I told my parents I never wanted to see them again. I know now I wanted to hurt them. For a few years we were out of touch, but now that I feel better about myself, we have become friends again."

When he got out of the Air Force, Brian married precipitously —something many Adoptees do—divorced, started college, dropped out, reenrolled, and then finally got interested in studying psychology when he was twenty-four. As an undergraduate he was stimulated by his reading to let himself think once again about his origins. He wrote the adoption agency, asking for information on his own life as a means of developing his knowledge of the psychology of adopted people. He was granted an interview and learned that his mother had been twenty-three and single, his father married to someone else.

"Getting that information was exciting, intriguing, and I wanted to follow it up. But I didn't know how. So I dropped it and went on with my life."

Then at twenty-nine, Brian, now a graduate student, discovered an article by Arthur Sorosky on Adoptees searching. He wrote to him and was referred to an Adoptee group. He didn't go to a meeting, but the realization that it was possible to search helped him remember the name he had seen on that piece of paper when he was sixteen. He went to the library to look it up in an old directory.

"At first I was afraid to tell my adoptive parents I was starting to search," he said. "I thought my mother would be upset, shaken by it. I was amazed when she said it was fine with her, and she would give me the papers to help. I couldn't believe she was so unresistant. I gradually told her more and more as it developed, being careful to reassure her that I cared about her and father."

After Brian's mother gave him the paper he had glimpsed so long ago, it took him only two weeks to find his birth mother.

Jackie

Jackie, who replaced the dead baby, probably would not have searched if she hadn't gone into what she thought was an ordinary postpartum depression after the birth of her first baby.

"All during my pregnancy I had been terrified about whose genes I was carrying," she said. "I cried in the taxi on the way to the hospital and cried coming home. I'd look at the baby and cry. I had never thought of myself as having children. Never thought of myself as a mother."

The concept of motherhood is difficult for female Adoptees. Even the word *mother* is loaded. The woman who has never been born does not imagine giving birth. The woman who has never known her biological mother does not imagine becoming one. Her role model is the infertile mother. Her role is the eternal child.

Still, Jackie had thought about that *other* mother a lot. "Every birthday I used to wonder if my mother was thinking of me. And I wondered what my body would look like as I got older. I had no one to look at to see who I'd resemble. My cousin told me recently that when I was thirteen I told her that I wanted to search, and she had replied that I couldn't because records are burned every seven years. Strange, I don't remember that. But I do remember as a teenager going to the library and looking through microfilm copies of the birth lists in the newspaper. I thought I would mystically know if I saw my name. Then when I became a dancer, I would fantasize that my mother would recognize me from the audience and come backstage. But I did nothing about trying to find her."

When her depression didn't lift during a summer at the seashore, Jackie found herself receptive to a neighbor's description of an Adoptee search group she'd seen on TV. Without understanding what she was doing, she looked up the group in the fall and went to a meeting. She found herself sobbing as one Adoptee after another got up to tell about their searches and reunions. She knew that what had been troubling her would not be resolved until she too had searched.

Warren

Warren, who describes himself as a loner, did not begin to think seriously of searching until his adoptive mother, with whom he was very close, died. He was twenty-seven, without even a father to turn to. The man who was married to his mother when he was adopted left when he was three, and the man who adopted him after that stayed married to his mother for only four years. He had three fathers (counting his birth father), and none. And even though he had enjoyed being Mama's boy, much of her energy had gone into fighting alcoholism with the help of Alcoholics Anonymous.

Although Warren had fleeting thoughts about his birth mother while growing up, he stopped asking questions because his adoptive mother always became teary. It wasn't until he was a junior in college and needed a passport for travel that he saw his amended birth certificate with a doctor's name on it. "It made me wonder who my mother was. It was not a constant thought, but not buried either."

At that time he went to the reference room in the library and got out the telephone book for his place of birth. He wrote down the address of the attending physician and put the information away. "I thought, what should I do now? It took me a while to act on that. I was scared. Finally I wrote a long letter that began, 'According to my birth certificate you delivered me.' I had to be careful with the wording. If my mother came from a well-to-do family, I didn't want him to think I was after anything.

I told him I was in college studying to be a lawyer, though I was really studying music. I wanted to impress him. But he never answered.

"Then I wrote to the Legal Aid Society asking for advice. They sent their position paper on adoption records which discouraged me. Then a little later I saw a show on TV about Adoptee search groups. I wrote the station for information about how to contact them, but I got no answer. So I let the whole thing go for a few more years."

Within a year after his adoptive mother died, Warren's short-lived marriage broke up. Not having a mother to turn to, he began thinking of his birth mother again. "I found myself looking toward older women about the age she would be. I felt a connection with that generation. I was searching in other people for my mother."

Then he turned the symbolic search into an actual one. When he saw a listing for an Adoptee group in the phone book under *A*, he went to the next meeting. "I felt I belonged there. It was the first time I had gone into a group and felt the warmth of people like me. I knew I could relax. Mostly at a meeting I won't strike up a conversation, will listen or look around. But here I felt teary, even started to cry, had to wipe my eyes. It's nice to be with all these people, I thought. They told me how to go about my search."

Karla

Karla, whose mother supposedly gave birth to her before dying in the car crash, made her decision to search at twenty-eight. It happened at a friend's dinner party: "Two other people there turned out to be adopted, and we began talking about the circumstances. We each said our parents were killed in a car crash. Suddenly the ·absurdity of it hit us. We burst out laughing. It was then I knew I had to learn the truth of what happened."

Karla remembers vaguely wanting to check on the car crash story when she was in her teens. "I thought I would go out West, look up the newspaper clips, and contact the family doctor who was retired out there. But when I was passing through on a trip, I did nothing. I just gave up before I started. I guess I had to grow into it gradually."

All through her adolescence Karla never thought about whether her parents had been married. "I was a good student in high school, started dating at fourteen, and had good relationships with boys. On the surface, mother was excellent regarding sexuality. I believed what she discussed with me—that sex was beautiful and natural, although she stressed that it should be between two people who loved each other and were *married*. I did not realize this had any bearings on my origins. She sanctioned 'making out' in the living room as opposed to having to worry about me in parked cars. And gave me the confidence to stop any sexual experimenting if I was not comfortable.

"But on the negative and mixed-message side, she told me to come to her if I was going to need birth control devices, but that she would send me to a home for unwed mothers if I got pregnant. She warned me that men/boys will always leave a girl 'holding the bag,' and that 'sex was like a good sneeze for a man.' "

Now that Karla looks back on it, the crack in the car crash story really came when she was twenty-two. She had just graduated from college and was living at home with her mother, who had been suffering from various psychosomatic diseases ever since her husband died. One night shortly after she met Donald, who was to become her husband, Karla called her mother to say that she wouldn't be coming home and not to worry. Her mother became furious, but she stayed out anyway.

When Karla returned at 5:00 in the morning, she was stunned to find her mother waiting up. "She jumped on my back, pulled my hair, clawed my face. She was hysterical. 'Now you've become what you came from!' she shouted." It was the first time Karla realized she was illegitimate.

"I protected myself with my hands as she thrashed at me, but I did not hit back. The Vietnam war was on and I considered myself a pacifist. But she hurt my pride and I fled back to Donald's. I moved in and did not contact my mother again for two years."

Karla's mother wrote her a few letters during their estrangement, not to apologize for attacking her, but to accuse her of being responsible for her continuing bad health. "I felt guilty for quite some time, but my strings didn't respond anymore. I stayed away."

Karla and her mother had been reunited by the time of that

fateful evening when she met those two other Adoptees, and so she called her the next day to test her. She said she was going to write to California for newspaper clippings on the car crash that had killed her parents; since it was such a dramatic event, surely it must have gotten a lot of press coverage. Her mother was obviously nervous and got off the phone quickly, saying she couldn't discuss it with her then.

The next morning Karla's mother called and asked her to drop by. It was then that she leveled with her for the first time. There had been no car crash; she had found her through the family doctor.

"Her revelation of the truth to me was a beautiful experience. For a few hours—before the conversation disintegrated into anger and tears—I felt closer to her than ever before. It was truly shared fate."

14

Stages of the Search

Odysseus' erratic journey homeward after the sack of Troy
to his own kingdom in Ithaca consumed ten years.
There is a sense in which this sea-battered wanderer,
who at one point in concealment calls himself 'Nobody,'
represents the human journey toward eternity.
LOREN EISELEY, _The Unexpected Universe_

E very search has a life of its own.
Once the decision has been made there is a hazardous journey ahead—be it ten days or ten years. I have known Adoptees at various stages of the journey: at the threshold, when one is
just beginning; in the throes of obsession, when one can think of
nothing else; in the state of limbo, when all leads seem futile or
when the terror of what is on the other side of the veil is immobilizing. I have watched Adoptees tremble on the brink of
what we call _Reunion,_ but what could also be called _Redemption._

I have seen Adoptees go through all these stages as if some
law, as inexorable as the laws of physical science, were driving
them home to the blood connection. One's spirits alternately soar
and dive as one makes progress and then hits a seeming dead end,
as one feels positive about what one is doing and then is overwhelmed with guilt, as one believes that everything is possible
and then is overcome with frustration. Up and down on this
emotional roller coaster—elated/depressed, courageous/fearful,

86

mature/childlike, confident/hopeless. A drunken ride. Some jump off, but most try to hold on until it arrives at its predestined last stop, which was also its starting point.

We cannot call that station *home*, since we will see that it never had a place on the map. But we can call it *origins, reality, roots.*

Crossing the Threshold

Roots. Even the process of uncovering them is different for Adoptees than for the others. Mass market books on the subject advise anyone wanting to climb his family tree to write down everything he knows about himself, including his mother's and father's names, as well as mother's maiden name, and proceed from there.

Already the Adoptees are stalemated. They do not know their birth parents' names.

Alex Haley, who started the "roots" fever, recommends the "oldest means of historical record"—word-of-mouth interviewing of family members, or just plain overhearing what they have to say about each other in unguarded moments of revelation.

But there is no word of mouth for Adoptees. Lips are sealed in the adoptive family network as tightly as the records. And while it is true that all families have secrets that are guarded down through the generations—nymphomaniacal aunts, drunken uncles, bootlegging grandfathers—the secrets in the Adoptees' family are about them. Everyone else knows. These secrets are the gap in their lifeline.

How can they get through the conspiracy of silence?

If the Adoptee is lucky, his adoptive parents not only will have his mother's maiden name but will give it to him. Or it will be on her baptismal papers. Or he will discover it hidden away in the adoptive parents' drawers, as Brian did. Or some clerk will make the mistake of sending her the original birth certificate instead of the amended one.

Some Adoptees who do not want to confront their adoptive parents, for fear of hurting them, petition the courts for their original papers. According to most state statutes, the judge can break the seal if "good cause" is shown. Until now, "good cause" was left hanging loosely for the individual judge to define, depending on the condition of his gout that day, his own prejudices, or the largess of his spirit. There were some judges who found inheritance or property rights good enough reason, while others would accept psychiatric affidavits attesting to the petitioner's need. But a recent backlash around the Search phenomenon, which we'll discuss in the last chapter, has caused some states to place so many restrictions on "good cause" that Adoptees who could prove they had one would be worthy of Ripley's "Believe It or Not."

Petitioning the court, then, can be a costly procedure, both emotionally and financially, and does not guarantee success. A fifty-year-old Navy man, who was refused his records in Oklahoma in spite of the fact that he had three children with complicated medical problems, wrote me: "Neither the agency nor the court was willing to open their records. I am being treated like a fifty-year-old infant who lacks the good sense or sensitivity to handle his own affairs or those of others. They are saying I would bungle it like an idiot."

A few intrepid Adoptees hire detectives, who often are more adroit at escalating their fees than at tracing the missing parents.

Those who are fortunate enough to be in a city that has an Adoptee search group can learn the underground tricks of the trade—how to find one's original name if one has the date and place of birth, or the name of the doctor who was in attendance, or the lawyer who finalized the transaction. These organizations have acquired professional genealogical skills over the years and also supply much-needed emotional support.

But no matter what method one employs, the Search requires not only courage but cunning and persistence. It entails long, arduous sifting through old directories, hospital records, birth and death certificates, newspaper morgues, cemetery lists. Even the most law-abiding Adoptee, who is mortified by a traffic violation, soon finds himself sneaking about surreptitiously for information, often lying and impersonating others to achieve his goals.

The most difficult searches are those where the Adoptee was left as a foundling on some doorstep, placed privately by a mother using a fictitious name or by a black-marketeer who forged the documents. The Adoptee spends years in a fruitless quest for clues, and in the process becomes a chronic victim.

Those Adoptees placed by agencies, whose role, according to one disenchanted social worker, has always been "somewhere in between playing God and a complete hands-off policy," have a different kind of stress. They are put into the demeaning position of having to plead for their birthright. As the Sorosky team has pointed out: "When adopted adults, seeking background information, return to agencies, it is viewed as evidence of family failure and/or personal pathology. No one assumes they have a right to know. They are made to feel sick and abnormal for asking."[1]

In all but a few agencies throughout the country, some version of Mrs. Barker of the Bye Bye Adoption Service sits waiting for the Adoptee with her smug smile, her supercilious manner, her condescending tone, and her diabolically intimidating question, "But *why* do you want to know?" which, as one woman said, has the effect of "stopping all conscious wondering."[2]

The Adoptee puts out a wet, clammy hand, not sure whether to shake or salute with it. Mrs. Barker is still the official Scorekeeper of the Adoption Game, the Talleyrand of Taboos, the *sine qua non* of Confidentiality. One curl of her lip has the power to reduce the Adoptee to the helpless waif who was her original client.

When Brian went to see his Mrs. Barker, he took a list of written questions to make it easier for both of them: "She studied the list carefully," he said, "then took them one by one. She would go out of the room, look into the file, come back and answer that question. She did this over and over again until I suggested that she might want to bring the file into the room. She clearly had no intention of doing this. And I noticed she got more and more uncomfortable and ill at ease as she went down the list. She didn't answer the specific questions, only gave me descriptions. No names or addresses."

Warren took on his Mrs. Barker the way he took on much of the search—with relish. This was the project of his life. He enjoyed the drama of it, felt like a detective on a case. It was both personal and life-enhancing, since it involved him and allowed him to delay those other decisions he eventually had to face. He went back to the agency in the spirit of going back to the navel of the world.

With more hope than trepidation, then, he suggested the appointment with his Mrs. Barker. "I made a point of preparing how to behave with her before I went. I wrote it down on a piece of paper I carried in my pocket: 'Be sincere, but inquisitive; don't put pressure on her; make her seem important, right; let her start, nod a lot; make her feel my adoptive mother always wanted me to know, but didn't know enough to tell me; try different wordings for questions.'

"I was a half-hour early, she was a half-hour late. She had a legal pad with transcript from microfilm when she arrived. At the beginning of the interview she wanted to know what had happened to my life. It was maddening for the first forty-five minutes —having her make me talk about myself, interviewing me like I was up for a job. I kept waiting for her to get to the point where she'd give me something. Then at last she did. She looked at the pad, and the first thing she said was incorrect. 'You were born on May 18, 1950, at 9:30 A.M.'

"Now on the baptismal paper I had, it said May 16, so I told her and she put on her glasses and realized she had read it wrong. Then she told me my height and weight. I was nodding, like tell me more. That my mother was twenty-one, my father twenty-five. She said she had never met my mother, but another social worker who had taken care of her described her as being brunette with green eyes and about 5′4″. For a while I felt ecstatic. She was giving me the first facts I've ever had about myself. I felt I was receiving the foundations for my identity."

Warren himself has similar coloring and is not much taller. He has a handlebar mustache that seems to center his fragile body and even more fragile sensibility. Like many sensitive people, he is surprisingly tough—and this toughness enabled him to survive during the long period of his adoptive mother's bout with alcoholism, and it now gives him the tenacity to move into this painful journey.

"Just to be told her appearance is a sobering thing," he said. "I can almost see her outline. There is no face. At first I see her from the back. And after a while see her from the front. But no face. I see, of course, an idealistic stereotype—with no face."

Mrs. Barker said that his mother had completed two years of college. Home economics. Her parents were of Danish descent. "I pressed her on this. 'Was the name Danish?' I asked.

" 'Yes,' she admitted.

" 'Does it mean anything in Danish?' I persisted. She didn't know. 'Then how many syllables?' I had the feeling it was like 'twenty questions.' But I kept trying to make her feel good. I kept saying things like: 'I know I am fortunate you're talking to me at all. I know other social workers might not.' But I felt myself becoming angry. I didn't want to accuse her or let myself get too excited.

" 'This must be frustrating for you,' she said.

"I was thinking I could have picked up that piece of paper and read it, and then just put it back down on that desk and said, 'I'm sorry, Mrs. Barker, I had to do that.' Or I could have picked it up and run. But I couldn't do that either. She was such a sweet, little-old-librarian kind of lady. And she had me. She had the goods. I had to play the role she wanted. I noticed that when she got upset she would roll her chair a little back and away from me.

"She was trying in her way to be helpful. She said she wished my mother would call her tomorrow, for then she could arrange things. She also said that I wouldn't want to disturb my mother's life, would I?"

Obsession

At some point the Search becomes an obsession. A game to be played for its own sake. Although they may have entered the Search dispassionately, Adoptees now speak of wanting to solve the riddle of their lives, and they become obsessed with piecing together the puzzle, finding the missing parts. This riddle-solving, puzzle-making, becomes so attractive, so externalized, that they do not necessarily want this stage to end. It is a safe area, a zone of retreat from the reality that lies around the next bend. Ahead is the abyss. They are playing in the valley just above. They enjoy the lingering, the dawdling, the leisurely pace of posting things, going to the mailbox each day to see if there is a reply. They need this period to gather psychic strength for the moment they will penetrate the veil. They do not act hastily because unconsciously they know that to plunge forward too quickly might be to plunge into nothingness.

Warren became more and more fascinated as he got into the Search. "I have a thing about doing puzzles right. I like to know how it will fit first, not to have to erase it. I think of it as a piece of art. But it's like the last piece of the puzzle must be set in blood."

He likened his obsession now to his interest in antiques, which he was thinking of making into a career. "Handling old things makes me feel connected. Like a phrenologist's skull I saw in a show recently. I thought of the graveyard scene in Hamlet. It gave me some comfort to see that old skull. I wanted to touch it. But I didn't."

Still Warren knew that he was not in control of what was happening to him now—that he didn't necessarily know how things were going to fit. "I worry that if I keep thinking about this it can become an obsession. Am I taking it too far? The other night my roommate asked me if I didn't know how to talk about anything else. Are other things in my life falling behind? I don't know if it is a sane thing to do sometimes. Other times I think it is a useless waste of energy. 'This is crazy,' I tell myself. 'I have to forget it.' "

But it was exhilarating, too. "I never looked at people before I got those facts from the agency. I knew that we're all related from the Neolithic Age, but now that I know I have a mother and father somewhere, I've started really looking at everyone. On subways I stare at people. I could be classified as a weirdo. I wonder if they're looking at me for the same reason. I think, 'That woman could be my mother.' And now that I know she had a brother and sister I think that woman or man could be my aunt or uncle. I want to go up to people and ask them how old they are, to see if they fit into the right age range. You see, I was always a piece of pollen floating around before. Everyone else had trees with seeds on them. Now I had relatives, something I could never imagine in my floating on the wind experience. It's like something real, a fact. I'm not only looking for *her*, but there will be other people. And if she doesn't want me, they will be there."

Jackie found that looking for her mother now was as absorbing as being a new mother. The Adoptee group had convinced her that she must ask her adoptive parents the unaskable the next time they came to visit. She was astonished when her father said:

"We kept your papers for you, but never offered them because we didn't want to hurt your feelings. They're not destroyed. We'll even take you to the vault the next time you come down South."

Meanwhile they told her that the family name as they remembered it was something like Beck or Becker, they couldn't be sure. As soon as they left, she wrote to the records office, writing the name indistinctly, hoping it could be interpreted any which way. And shortly after, she was amazed to receive the long form of her birth certificate with her mother's name on it. Through some clerical error, her record had never been sealed. Within six months, during which she worked actively with the Adoptee group and researched every lead, she managed to find the phone number of her mother's brother. In the meantime everything had been subsumed to the Search, including her dancing career. Instead of making rounds, she went to the records office or Adoptee meetings. All of life as she had known it had stopped, waiting for the Search to be resolved.

As Karla got deeper and deeper into the Search, she was alternately wrenched with worry about possibly hurting her mother by bringing up new questions, and angry with herself that she was feeling so protective of her. "Still I was determined to get straight answers and documents, since at this point she was my only real source. My father had been dead for some years, and his brother was nice, but couldn't or wouldn't give any information except one tiny clue.

"During this time I read everything I could about adoption, and was creatively trying to deal with it in drawings and cartoons, before dealing directly with it in searching. I was really using this time to assimilate the new story, and, I guess, fantasizing, meditating, sublimating, procrastinating, while researching how to search. I ended up studying the question for six months. After that it took another four months to break through bureaucracies, to get my natural mother's date and place of birth, and the non-identifying social service report."

In the interim Karla finally got up the courage to contact the retired family doctor who had delivered her. She hoped for support from him, although she knew that his loyalty might be to her adoptive mother, who had arranged everything. Her fears were confirmed when he wrote her that although "any intelligent person with a similar nebulous background would want to know the answers," she should not let this become a pathological obsession:

> I have absolutely no recollection as to how your biological mother got into my care. I remember why. She was pregnant. I do not recall her name. Naturally I was curious to know her story. As I recall, she was living with brothers and sisters and stepmother somewhere in the Northwest. Following an altercation with her stepmother, in which the woman threw a butcher knife at her, she ran out of the house, never to return. By the time she reached my office, she was pregnant. She had a normal birth. . . . When she was on the delivery table and under the influence of "twilight sleep," I heard her muttering what I thought was a prayer. She was petitioning blessing for the "very nice people who had been so kind to her"—your parents.

The good doctor continued to warn Karla of the consequences of her obsessive actions:

> What if nature has finally smiled upon her, and that she has made a good life for herself with a fine husband and children who know absolutely nothing of her past. Now you show up. Would that make her, her family, or even you, any happier? On the other hand, suppose that she has sunk even lower on the social scale—that she has become a lifetime tramp, which I had no reason to think that she was at the time that I knew her. Possibly she might see you as a potential for blackmail benefits. . . . I do not deprecate her for this unsavory history. It has always been a pattern of life ever since man first stood on his hind legs, is now, and probably always will be.

Limbo

With such dire warnings it is no wonder that Karla spent a long time in Limbo Land—that state of being where one has some information and yet hesitates to contact the birth mother or anyone in the family who may have information as to her whereabouts.

Karla put it this way: "At first the time between asking for and receiving 'news' and acting on it was enormous, but gradually it has evolved to a matter of minutes. Also, the manic-depressive moods of the initial raised consciousness I experienced have eased off into a quiet, slow glow. It's actually very close now. I'm in Limbo Land, with enough concrete information to generate the leads to the current life of my natural mother. But I'm waiting for final clues to come back in the mail, preparing as best I can beforehand for whatever might occur, trying not to be absorbed every hour."

By then Karla actually had the telephone number of her maternal grandfather in a small Western town. All she had to do was dial it, and she could probably learn her mother's as well. But she could not pick up the phone. She said it was because she'd like to contact her mother directly, without going through anyone. She spent a lot of time imagining taking a trip there and setting up a painting easel in front of her grandfather's house. "Maybe he would be out on the porch and invite me in. And then I could ask him about his family, and learn where my mother was in a casual way." Such a trip, she told herself, would be easier than calling. But she made no plans for that journey. She was unable to act.

Many Adoptees fear that if they find their birth mother and father, they will no longer be a member of the adoptive family. One woman, whose adoptive parents are both dead, even fears telling her relatives she is searching. "This is my family and very important to me, and I don't want to hurt them or have them think I'm ungrateful, especially to my dead parents. Also I have difficulty understanding how our relationship will go on. Does my search and possible meeting of my natural parents make me not a part of my adoptive family?"

Warren wandered about Limbo Land for many months in a daze, seeking advice from everyone, but unable to do anything concrete. It seemed so simple to his nonadopted friends. All he had to do was to go back to the town of his birth, contact the doctor whose name was on his birth certificate, and check in the local vital statistics for the *first* names of babies born on his birthdate, since the agency had given him his own.

But he could make neither the phone call nor the trip.

"I've been having a good deal of ambivalence about knowing," he told me. "It's almost safer to have this dream. Maybe I don't want to know."

All his life he had been cautious, ambivalent, but this was worse than anything he had experienced. "I say, why do I have to see the roots? I think, you don't have to know how a plane works to fly in one. I know I'm connected to a past. Why dwell on it? I go back and forth like this. Wanting to know, not wanting to know. I'm wallowing in confusion. I have a way of procrastinating on things, numbing myself. I'm so confused, I don't know what day it is."

Another time he said, "I'm worried. I put myself in this position that finding my mother will change my life. I know it's an illusion. I say, 'When I find her, then I can start living.' I know this may not happen.

"Or I say, 'I know I had two parents. Two people who conceived me. What difference does it make if you know who they are?' I have cycles of depression and elation. Sometimes up and down within a minute. People tell me I must stop fantasizing about a relationship with my mother since I never had one. But I say the three weeks with her before she gave me up *was* a relationship—one that we can build on."

When Warren finally did decide to phone the doctor who delivered him, he plotted it like one might a business venture, or a murder. He would call him on the right day of the week—Sunday—at the right time, at night, when he had had a good weekend and would be rested. The time would be one minute to ten when the show he might be watching on TV was over and just the commercial was on. The secret was not to interrupt him or annoy him—to contact him at the optimal moment. But as it happened, at the moment when he did call—years of ambivalence dialed into the number—the doctor's wife answered. He wasn't home. So Warren had to go through the whole ritual the following Sunday night. The doctor proved to be cordial, but guarded. He offered no information but said Warren could come in to see him.

Still Warren could not bring himself to make that trip. There was a lot of depression now. "Will I freak out when I find the truth? I wonder. But it must be better to know than not to know. I guess I'm holding onto the hidden fantasy until the last minute

—savoring it. I know I should go, but there's something awesome about it. I like to keep it hidden—awhile. I like the fantasy of an ideal mother. I don't know—it's almost like I'm afraid of what I'll find. It's safer to have this dream. Maybe I don't want to know. If I was told my mother was in the next room I don't know what I'd do. I like to control things—don't like things done to me."

Adult Fantasies

Fantasy and fear make up the landscape of Limbo Land. But unlike the fantasies of the Adoptee's childhood, which we have seen as undefined and dreamlike, they now take on tantalizing form and substance. Parents now have personalities and identities in the real world. Adoptees conjure up wondrous possibilities, and not so wondrous ones. The yin and the yang, the eternal dualities, are still at play. Like people in a Robert Frost poem, Adoptees are still bewitched by the mysteries: "We dance around in a ring and suppose, / But the Secret sits in the middle and knows."

Warren said: "My fantasies take me everywhere. Like she may have died in childbirth. Or she's a prostitute. Or they were young, unmarried lovers forced to give up the child because of social pressure. Or I was lost and they're deliberately trying to find me. Or she's looking for me—watching for me. A paranoid thing, isn't it"—this is said with an uneasy laugh—"that she's watching me."

His fantasies did not include the father. "It doesn't matter if I find him. I'm not prepared for him. I suppose it's possible he could be with her. I hope not. I wouldn't know how to handle a father. I've nothing to model one on. I have a preference that she'll be all alone. Since I'm not connected, I feel she's not connected. I don't see her with people around her. I'd love it if she's looking for me and welcomes me with open arms."

Mark got to the point where he enjoyed willing his fantasies. "I'll have a fantasy, I tell myself. I consciously get into it—like meeting my mother. I see her very much like a woman I know who came from Austria. She'd have the same coloring and mannerisms. Every time I run into someone from Europe, I think maybe she'd be like that. I also imagine meeting my mother on an airplane on the way to L.A. I would happen to be sitting next to her. She has a German accent, and I ask her a few questions, and sure enough she turns out to be the one."

By now Mark had learned from the agency that his mother had come alone to America as a Jewish refugee child. The records described her as "attractive, intelligent, vivacious, charming," but included a notation that she had a problem letting people get close to her. She had moved from one assigned home to another.

"The social worker told me that her problems were probably the result of being separated from her parents. I felt like pointing out to her that I understood that problem. That's the trauma of being adopted too. It made me feel a kinship with my mother, the fantasy that she had the same kind of independence and bravado that I do, and a lot of the same feelings that are nurtured by the adopted."

Mark does not fantasize about the father. "I think the reason is that my mother is German-Jewish, and I can relate to that since my adoptive family is. But my birth father is Irish Protestant and that's alien to me. I have a hard time trying to develop my fantasies of what that's about."

Trudy had fantasies on many occasions about meeting her mother, but they were most intense during the Search. "She was different types of persons each time—some much better off than my adoptive parents, others much worse. Sometimes I would reject her, and other times she would reject me. I felt hurt most of the time while growing up, but then I started feeling anger and resentment that she gave me away. I felt that no reason was good enough to give up your child. My biggest fear was that she wouldn't want to see me. I was really afraid of being rejected again. In all of this, my desire was to find my mother. In fact, I did not think of my father at all."

Norman has been searching unsuccessfully for the past year. He has a recurring dream of a young woman, though he never sees her face. Sometimes he has the feeling he might marry her, and at other times that she might be his mother. He was in late adolescence when he realized that his birth mother was probably not married to that Naval officer his parents had told him about, that she might even be a whore. He wonders if it is related to his reluctance to marry, to take responsibility for a wife, and for his dividing women into the "good" and "bad" ones.

"I don't think too much about my father," he says, "although sometimes I imagine she has been raped by her stepfather. Or that she was a working girl knocked up by a black who lived in her boarding house. But I feel sorry for her, whoever she is, because it must have been traumatic."

Sometimes one gets so comfortable in Limbo Land one doesn't want to move on. Searching becomes a way of life, a reason for postponing other things. I've had men tell me they were not going to get a job until the Search was completed, and women say they were delaying marriage or having children. Sometimes their friends suspect that they are not doing everything they could, that they are resisting leads they might follow. Such Adoptees become known as "perpetual searchers." It seems that in spite of their protestations, they share with the nonsearcher a reluctance to pass through the veil.

We cannot overemphasize the terror that the Adoptees feel as they near that veil. Our mythology is filled with stories about those who were punished for daring to eat of the tree of knowledge, to seek out the unknown, to break a taboo. On this side of the veil one may be miserable, but at least one is still intact. One does not know what will happen if one tampers with the only reality one has—fragmented though it be. One fears complete annihilation, as if one were helpless before the dark forces of the universe. It is a time of nightmares—dreams about the death of loved ones—and oneself.

Penetrating the Veil

There comes a moment, after a few months, or a few years—perhaps when neither the Adoptees nor their friends can stand the indecision any longer—when they move out of limbo. It is as if the myth of the hero emerging triumphantly out of the dark woods takes over now. At last we see them mustering up the psychic energy to make contact between the past and the present, the living and the dead. One part of them is still terrified, but the other part drives determinedly on.

Now there is no turning back.

Having made the *big* decision, only the mundane ones remain —such as method of approach. How do you, the adult, contact the woman who gave you up as a baby? Should you write a letter? Telephone? Knock on the door? Use an intermediary to pave the way?

The letter takes longer, and now that you are ready for action it is difficult to wait. There is also the risk that someone else will open it, or that she will never answer. The phone call is more direct, but scarier. She might not be able to talk if someone else is in the room, or on an extension line. Going to the door is also precarious, since other family members could be at home. You want to make the initial contact as private as possible, for your sake as well as hers. You may or may not know a good intermediary.

Somehow, you manage to decide which method is the best one for you, and take action. As one woman put it: "It is like wakening the dead."

15

Varieties of Reunion Experience

"How are things going with your mother?"
"We're still getting to know each other. After all, could
you suddenly get to know any of twelve strangers you
might meet on the street? This is no different."
"Is she married?"
"Never married."
"You mean the only one is the illegitimate one?"
"What's legitimate?"
OVERHEARD AT AN ADOPTEE MEETING

We cannot speak of reunions as successful or unsuccessful. All of them, no matter whom one finds, are successful in that Adoptees are given a feeling of being grounded in the human condition, of becoming autonomous people in control of their own lives. But all reunions, no matter how positive, bring a tidal wave of emotions with them, and Adoptees ride these with varying degrees of skill. Jackie said: "You can't tell anyone it's going to be wonderful or terrible. It's going to be *everything*. And different for different people."

The types of reunion experiences are as varied as the types of people who search. No two are alike, and yet in a sense everyone

101

finds the same mother—a woman who has survived the trauma of giving up a baby. The way the mother perceives the Adoptee's return is directly related to how she handled that original ordeal.

For the most part, Adoptees find that their mothers are now married, with children a few years younger than themselves. A good many have kept the Adoptees' existence a secret from their present families; in other words, they are leading double lives.

In a few instances, Adoptees discover that their parents were married at the time of the relinquishment, or shortly afterward. Occasionally one finds the mother still unmarried.

If the mother has told her husband and children, she will be able to open her door, as well as her heart, to the Adoptee. But if it is still a secret, she may back off for a while until she gets the psychic strength to handle it. Even mothers who have remained unmarried or are presently divorced may feel some reluctance to reveal this part of their lives to others. A mother's ambivalence often causes Adoptees to pull back from their initial enthusiasm and may even plunge them into a deep depression.

However, whether the Adoptee is received warmly at first, or with ambivalence, there is a period of jockeying for a tenable position on both sides.

We can say that in most reunions there is an intense first meeting, often in a public place, which has the advantage of allowing both parties to meet anonymously, and without interruption. This is usually followed up by one or two brief meetings at the mother's home, if the distances are not too great, and if the mother has told the rest of her family. Often the relationship settles into little more than occasional phone calls and an exchange of holiday cards—although I know a divorced Adoptee who shares an apartment, as well as a talent for music, with her unmarried birth mother.

Some Adoptees are amazed to find how little they have in common with their birth parents, and others are equally amazed at the physical and emotional similarities. But the majority come to understand that time has moved on for their mothers and fathers as well as for themselves since that early separation.

We will look into the complexities of what happens after one has penetrated the veil, for as one Adoptee said: "Reunion is just the first step of a very long journey."

BRIAN—A Close Relationship

"It changed my life"

It is rare for an Adoptee to have as open a relationship with the mother as Brian did at first. It may be that because his mother's husband welcomed him as a surrogate son a close relationship with her was possible.

Brian was very nervous before he contacted his mother. His search had taken only two weeks, and he was moving with the initial momentum.

"I knew I had to learn the circumstances of my birth and relinquishment from the horse's mouth, so to speak. To know what kind of people I had come from, the social history of my parents, to have contact with birth relatives. I always wanted more of a family and hoped to find a large one which would supplement my adoptive one. And I was interested in having siblings. Knowing facts would not have been enough. I wanted to *meet* my family."

Still Brian's hand was trembling when he picked up the phone. "I feared she would not want to see me, but I told her right out I was her son. She said she couldn't talk then, she'd call back later. I was worried I'd never hear from her. But she phoned the next day. She said she had talked it over with her husband and he was agreeable to her seeing me. As a result she was relieved and positive about inviting me to visit her. Since I couldn't afford the plane ticket, she sent one.

"I was very apprehensive in the plane at the prospect of this first face-to-face meeting. We had exchanged pictures so I recognized her standing with her husband, Lou, just inside the airport as I walked toward them. She was smiling nervously. They told me later that I looked just terrified.

"As I walked up, Lou said, 'How are you, Brian?' He took my bag and shook my hand. And . . . let's see, did my mother and I embrace? I believe we did right there, yeah, I'm pretty sure we did. We hugged and kissed and said hello. It's hard to remember because it was very emotional for me. I was doing my best not to show it, but I was very upset and concerned about what she would think of me, what I would think of her, how we would get along, what we would do, you know. If in five minutes we decided we didn't like each other, what were we going to do for the next four days? And she told me later she was nervous about the same things, afraid I wouldn't be pleased with her, that I might reject her.

"Lou left us to ourselves, and we talked late that first night . . . about her experiences, being pregnant with me, where she lived and how she lived, and me talking about my childhood and reassuring her that I had been happy and well cared for and all that. And in the course of all this we really discovered that we liked each other, that we genuinely had good feelings for each other. Before we went up to bed, we embraced, and I felt very caring for her.

"We did a lot of staring at each other during those four days . . . the physical resemblance was absolutely striking. She is a wonderful person, what you would call a truly good person. So kind and warm and giving. The strain that she felt about how it would be was enough to make her lose her voice by the fourth day. She became hoarse, couldn't talk but in a whisper. And it was funny, it was laughable. But still she decided she would take me down to southern Oregon to meet the rest of the family. They were all waiting at the airport for us, and I felt like a kind of celebrity coming into this family, and everyone paying such a great deal of attention to me. They were all very polite and friendly, a little nervous about meeting me. We had dinner in a restaurant, and someone remarked it was like having grandpa alive again because I was the only man at the table. There I was, sitting at the head of the table being the father of this family in which there were no men. There was my grandmother, my aunt, and my three female cousins, and, of course, my mother. I was told there was a physical resemblance between my grandfather and myself. We were both large men, and I think that their identifying me with him sped my acceptance into the family. I liked everyone and keep up contact with them even now."

Brian has seen his mother a few times since then, once for a week in Mexico. "At first we had to maneuver to find out what roles to play together. She seemed to feel some responsibility to mother me, but I said right off that it was not the kind of relationship I wanted. I had my adoptive mother."

Brian's birth mother was very honest about why she had to give him up. "I approached her directly and she replied equally directly, enumerating the reasons why she had seen fit to do that. She seemed to have worked it through, given it a lot of thought, and to have absolved herself of any guilt. She presented it to me very matter-of-factly. But not in such a way that she could be said to be repressing feelings about it or defensively presenting it to me. She seemed to feel she had done the right thing. And that seems right to me, although I continue to have a feeling, 'Gee, wouldn't it have been nice if she'd kept me.'

"She didn't seem to have loved my father. They had a very brief affair. Apparently they had gotten drunk and had a sexual encounter in his automobile. They hadn't really gotten to know one another. She broke off with him after that, feeling that he was just not her type."

Brian has allowed Lou, who always wanted a son, to play the father role with him. They go fishing and riding together. But he has not been able to get close to his half-sister, who lives away from home. She obviously resents his upstaging her in the family. He hopes that with time this will change.

As for his birth father, Brian's mother was not reluctant—as many are—to give him the name. But when he called his father's relatives, he learned that his father had been killed in a plane crash a few years before. "There was some disbelief on the part of his family as to who I was. They were reluctant to believe I was his child because he had no children in his two marriages and was thought to be infertile. He had even adopted a son who strangely enough was given my same name, Brian. He was described as a flamboyant man who had made millions in the lumber business. I think his widow was afraid I might come fortune hunting and demand a share of her inheritance. But though I admit I thought about it, I would not try to push something like that. It would be a negative, emotionally unsatisfying experience. Not something I'd want to do."

Brian learned that he had his father's height and receding hairline; but otherwise they did not have too much in common. "I fault my father for being irresponsible, unwilling to acknowledge paternity or give financial support. But in some ways I feel positive toward him. I learned that he actually offered to adopt me, but my mother said absolutely not."

Brian is glad that he searched. He feels that it has been a catalyst in his life, galvanizing him into correcting unsatisfying ways of doing things, especially in his career. He has since decided on the direction he wants to take in psychology and is at present writing a dissertation on Adoptees and their searches.

"Before I searched I felt at loose ends in my career. I was not motivated. I feel better toward myself, pleased that I could effect the relationship I have and handle the whole situation successfully. I think I can say it changed my life. It has made me think in terms of family relationships in general. I consider myself a success now. My career is taking off; I am doing well. And I would advise others to search. It is a wonderful thing, an enriching experience. I respect the preference of those who choose not to, but I believe they are denying their feelings for their biological relatives, or are unwilling to recognize their fears and uncertainty about searching, or about adversely affecting the relationship with their adoptive parents."

As for the relationship with his own adoptive parents—"I feel closer to them now. The fact that I feel more trust and have a willingness to divulge different things and confide in them has brought us closer. It opened up our relationship, which was superficial before. I know now that I acquired some things from my adoptive family and inherited others from my birth family. Knowing this affects my personality, my make-up, my sense of who I am.

"Of course I've never told my adoptive parents *all* that's happened. Even though they are positive about things, they seem vulnerable from time to time. Mother saw the pictures of my birth mother's parents in my office when she stopped by at the university one day. She was hurt I didn't have pictures of her parents up. It is a sensitive issue, but by and large they have been positive. My adoptive father doesn't talk about it much, but then we don't talk about psychological things. He's not comfortable with his feelings. My adoptive mother took it best, and I discuss it mostly with her."

Brian feels there are no *real* parents now. "All four of my parents are my parents. But my adoptive parents are the people I relate to as parents in the most full and complete sense. Right now they're concerned about my having children. They want to be grandparents and I hope they will be."

When I last heard from him, Brian described moving away some from his birth mother. The intense need for her had subsided. "I need time and space now on my own to sort things out," he wrote. "But we're still in touch, and, of course, still very fond of each other."

KARLA—Mother in a Mental Institution

"My story is everyone's nightmare,
but it hasn't been a nightmare."

Although finding the mother institutionalized is the greatest fear Adoptees have, some, like Karla, find consolation in the warm acceptance of other family members.

While she was searching, Karla had only the most optimistic fantasies. "I imagine finding the kind of woman I will be twenty years from now," she told me. "A role model, I suppose, an intellectual like Doris Lessing who will reach out her arms to me. I need to hear my mother's voice. I want to find my father someday too, but emotionally I feel a stronger bond to my mother—the nine-month connection."

Then things began happening faster than she intended, taking them out of her control. A male Adoptee in the South, who had been helping her do research, made a series of phone calls on his own, including one to her grandfather's house. Speaking with the stepmother (to whom the retired doctor had referred in his letter), he learned that the old man had died two years before. The stepmother did not know where Karla's mother was, possibly in a hospital. She suggested he call one of the brothers, which he did, again without notifying Karla. He learned that the mother was in a mental institution, had been there on and off for the past twenty years. Only then did he call Karla with this information.

"I was shocked at first," Karla told me. "The fear of heredity was my first thought. But when I woke the next morning I felt a great sense of relief that the search was over. I didn't have to go out to the mailbox. Instead, I decided to call the hospital to find out about her condition."

Talking long distance to the social worker at the hospital gave her the story: her mother was extremely degenerated, psychologically and physically. Subject to violent outbursts, she was no longer communicating with anyone, just drinking coffee, smoking cigarettes, and pacing her room. Also, she was incontinent and had no teeth. Hardly the role model she had dreamed of, but Karla was now very decisive. She made plans to go out to see this woman who had given her life. "I think I can take it," she said. "Just knowing the truth gives me a fine, solid feeling. I no longer feel like Superman coming to earth on a rocket just as Krypton exploded. I know I'm of woman born."

It helped that Donald, whom she had been with for eight years, had been able to go with her. I talked with her just after she returned.

"I was relieved to find that the hospital was sunny with palm trees and flowering bushes everywhere. Inside it was clean with lots of activity, patients ranging from late teens through old age, most there for a short stay. My mother had been there for the past eighteen years because her husband, who was collecting her checks, would not allow her to be moved to smaller, more appropriate facilities. He was living with another woman and putting their two daughters out with relatives to raise.

"As we walked through the corridor I was, of course, looking everywhere to see my mother—sure that I would know her in some way. The caseworker knocked on the door to one of the wards. It opened, slowly, outwardly. My eyes, seeming to work independently, swept the room: windows, shades down; two desks, one on each wall; young fellow with beard sitting with desk lamp, papers; old woman across from him—this couldn't be my mother —very tiny, deep red-brown hair cut bowl-style—lower face collapsed, Gabby Hayes-style—spindly legs—blue wool dress—gray wool socks—a feeling of revulsion as I realized this was my mother.

" 'So that's her,' I thought. 'Goodness, she looks like a troll.' But soon the feeling passed. She stood up as the social worker called to her, somewhat mechanically and with a stiffness that suggested exercise was missing. I noticed her dress was wet on the seat and little droplets of urine were trickling to the floor. As she approached the door the odor hit my nose—warm and like no other—and we walked up the hall.

"My mother stopped at one point and turned to me. For the first time she lifted her head, and I stared into her face trying to reconstruct it prior to her toothlessness—her skin was lightly freckled, her eyes were clear, large, blue—her nose was not unlike mine—actually from her upper lip up she was just fine looking, not particularly elderly. The aged look came from her posture, stooped, her imploded mouth, and her institutional haircut. She was only fifty years old. She presented her full face and stared for what seemed a very long time into my eyes. It seemed that something was passing back and forth. She began walking. . . . I took her arm, it was all second nature. Her appearance and the faint but distinct odor triggered every ounce of discipline I could muster—but the long stare removed my repulsion.

"When we sat down, I explained I had come three thousand miles to see her. 'I'm really pleased to meet you,' I said. 'I've looked for you a long time. We knew each other once in a special way.' She listened, she looked, she asked for a cigarette by extending her hand and then two fingers held together. She squintingly eyeballed Donald. I explained he was my husband and that he was a very nice guy. I took out photos—first my adoptive father, did she recognize him? It was a long time ago, over thirty years—he worked in the shipyards during the war. Was he familiar? I knew she used to have a lunch concession which serviced yard workers. I showed her a picture of my adoptive mother. Eyes went down to two slits. Did she know her? She and her husband had adopted a baby. I showed her a picture of my mother holding me at two weeks. 'This is me when I was a baby. These are the people who raised me. See here they are with the child they raised.' It was hard for me to refer to my parents so dispassionately, but it seemed the only way to get through somehow.

"Then I said it directly, 'The special way we knew each other is that you are my mother. You gave birth to me.' She began to hunch in on herself.

"The caseworker turned to her: 'Are you angry at me for bringing your daughter to see you? For knowing your secret and not keeping it?'

"I continued, 'I've come all this way to see you, to tell you it is okay. You made a good decision.'

"She was by now physically withdrawn in on herself, and I found my head tilted almost perpendicular to my neck in order to keep eye contact. At that point I became aware of the body language and tried to get us out of it. 'I'd really like you to respond to me,' I said. 'It's very important. You did a good thing. My life has turned out fine. And I thank you for giving birth to me.'

"She pulled up her body at this. I told her I was going to visit her sister that evening. She is very fond of this sister, who has been visiting every two weeks for years, even though she no longer talks to her, either. She was listening, her eyes going.

"I gave her a large pad and asked her to write or draw something for me to remember her by. Anything. I put a felt-tip pen in her open hand. She grasped it and began to write—in script that dribbled off into a series of parallel lines that formed a curve, to which she added two branches, each line being made with great care, but monotonously repetitive. When she was done, she put the pen down. I gave her the summer duster I'd brought for her. She touched it. I explained that this was to remember me, so that when I was gone she would know it really happened. I said it was hard for me to believe I'd finally found her, and I was very glad about that.

"The social worker said, 'You can really be proud. You have a very beautiful daughter.'

"I said, 'I don't want to keep you from lunch,' for I had been told that she has always been totally food oriented. However, she sat rooted to her chair. She wouldn't get up. The social worker had to say, 'Come to lunch now.' She finally began to stir. And again with physical stiffness she uprighted herself. She was a bit unsteady, got her balance and toddled out numbly. As we passed the dining room, a little later, I could see her sitting at a table, sitting up very straight, hands folded, waiting."

Karla concluded, "I'm feeling very good about that visit. Overwhelmed, emotional, satisfied. It's hard to assess what she understood. Was it *me* or me as a nice person whose visit she was comfortable with? The social worker felt her lack of negative response was positive, though I think it's probably that she knew me on several levels. Mostly I needed to see her. I would have liked a verbal response, but the visit was enough. She is a victim-type person. I was rushed with empathy, but did not feel that she was me or I her. I tried to imagine how I would be if I were in her shoes. At one point I told her what beautiful eyes she had, and what a gorgeous color her hair was, and how when it was longer it must have been spectacular. She allowed me to touch and stroke her hand, but she did not return the gesture."

Although it was too late for her to be reunited with her mother in a meaningful way, Karla did get a sense of belonging from her aunt, who greeted her warmly and welcomed her into the family. She had not known about Karla, but had heard rumors about a baby who had been given up. Now she was thrilled to have Karla back with them. "She said I resemble the family—my face and my body were indeed proof; yes, I looked like her sisters and many of my cousins. I had Sally Jane's mouth, someone else's coloring, the freckles, and so on. I loved it. Silly as it is, it meant a lot."

Karla has not attempted to meet her two half-sisters because her aunt warned her against their father—who may possibly be her father. She wants to absorb what she has learned so far without pursuing this further. In fact, she is luxuriating in her invitation to the family's yearly reunion of fishing and relaxing together in a state park. "I can't even imagine what such an experience will be like. I do feel a small tingle like the call of the wild, an intense curiosity."

For now, she is working through her feelings about coming from a family so different in religious and cultural background. Karla's mother grew up in a farm family which, being Baptist, allowed no smoking, drinking, or dancing, while she was brought up in the Jewish faith in a large city. "It fascinates me, this peek into the life that might have been. It's really fine to know. To have seen. To have some answers. And I don't feel very different. Just stronger and better, like someone sprinkled Accent all over my psyche. I feel delicious. Not soaring, but very much grounded. From all I've heard I see my mother realistically. She was too sensitive. She lost her own mother when she was four. Things never went right for her after that. I am glad that I know—it helps me understand."

A few months after our last talk, Karla sent me an invitation to her wedding with Donald.

WARREN—Mother Is Ambivalent
"She's torn between me and her family."

Often a mother may be genuinely happy to be reunited with the Adoptee but too filled with guilt toward her husband and other children to encourage a deep tie.

Warren didn't know what to expect when he found himself on a train to the city where he had been born. The clerk at the town hall let him go into the vital-statistics file when he explained he was looking for a lost cousin. There he discovered that only three babies had been born on his birthday, and one had his first name. Then he went to see the doctor whom he had so much trouble phoning, and learned from him that the other boy born that day was the doctor's own son. The doctor had even offered to adopt Warren to raise with him. However, Warren's mother had already made arrangements with an agency in another state.

"It gave me a strange feeling to think that this doctor's children could have been my brothers and sisters," Warren told me, "and that he could have been my father." Before he left town, Warren even visited the boarding house where his mother had stayed before having him. The woman there remembered her as a sweet, young girl, all alone while her husband was overseas.

Now that he had his mother's maiden name and hometown from the birth certificate, it was easy for Warren to look up his grandfather's phone number. But he found he didn't have the courage to dial it. An Adoptee friend had to do it for him, pretending to be a distant cousin researching the family tree. She was able to find out that his mother was married, had three children, and was living in Peoria, Illinois. She even got the phone number.

Once again, Warren found it difficult to act. He swung back and forth between writing and calling. "If you write, you can say all the things you want to," he told himself, but he was finally persuaded to call by the friend who had been helping him. "You're putting yourself through a lot of misery," she said. "Why write a letter? You'll only have to make more decisions, like what kind of stationery to use, what to say. A phone call is over quickly."

And so Warren planned the call to his mother as carefully as he had planned that earlier one to the doctor. This one he would make at ten o'clock in the morning when her husband would probably be at work, her kids at school. If her husband happened to answer, he would pretend it was the wrong number. "In some ways, it was not as difficult as calling the doctor," he said. "That was like breaking through the barrier. This was scary, but not so much as the time approached. I thought, I *want* to make this call."

As it happened, a young child, home sick from school, answered. "I thought of hanging up, but I heard myself saying, 'Is your mother there?'

" 'Yes,' she said, and went to get her. I heard a voice say 'Hello.'

" 'Is this Marilyn Alyward?'

" 'Yes.'

" 'This is your *son.*' I put the ball into motion. It was out of me now.

" 'It is?'

" 'Yes.' I could hear her working through it.

" 'How old are you?' she asked.

" 'Twenty-six.' She was sniffing and gasping. 'Are you all right?' I said.

" 'Yes,' she replied.

" 'I've been looking for you a long time,' I said.

" 'Thank God. I always prayed this would happen. You sound beautiful.'

"In the course of the conversation, it came out that she had become very religious in the past few years. 'Do you know Jesus Christ?' she asked. 'Do you believe in God?'

"I said yes. That made her happy. It wasn't such a lie since I have taken courses in religion and philosophy.

"She said her children didn't know about me. Her husband did because he married her shortly after my birth, but they hadn't talked about me since. In fact, her husband had been a friend of my father. She had broken the engagement with my father when she learned she was pregnant. Still she had thought about me for years. She said she always wanted to find me and was afraid I wouldn't want to look. Then she asked how I found her. I told her. She said she always feared I had been killed in Vietnam, or become a hippie or a drug addict. I kept saying, 'I'm alive.' I think my happiness was as amazing to her as hers was to me. She wanted to see me. I said I'd like to meet everyone and have them know who I am. She said that in her newfound religion she could justify telling them.

"I think we could have talked for hours, but she said to call back at two o'clock because she had to take her daughter to the doctor. Then we talked for an hour till the other kids were due back from school. She laughed a lot. She said things like, 'Oh wow!' 'Weird.' It must be her children's language. That made me feel good.

" 'Do you want to know about your father?' she asked me. 'I won't tell you his name now. I don't want you to contact him.'

"I said, 'You don't have to talk about it. Just tell me, is he alive?'

" 'Yes, and married.'

"After that second call I sent pictures. I wanted to get on a plane, but she asked for time to tell the family. I'm so grateful for this little bit of pleasure, I don't mind not seeing her right away. I like to dole out happiness. I feel high."

A few weeks later, after she had told her family about him, Warren flew down to Peoria. His mother was waiting alone for him at her house. "It was incredible to see this person who looked like me, and to touch her," he said. "It was like a mirror. I couldn't believe it was happening. Her eyes and nose and the upper half of the face are identical to mine. We both have green eyes flecked with blue. I didn't blink, couldn't keep my eyes off her. We talked and talked but I don't know what we said. She kept saying, 'I'm so happy you found me.'

"When her kids came home from school, they got introduced, but didn't hang around. The oldest boy said, 'Well, how are you doing? Want to buy a car?' Things like that. It will take a while to know them as people. I didn't stay to meet her husband. I felt overloaded. I had to get out, couldn't handle it all."

Warren has been talking to his mother a few times a week on the phone since then. "I'm running up twenty-dollar phone bills. It's so unreal. I'm glad she's there now. I've got somebody. I see her as a friend, not like a mother/son relationship. We don't have to go through that. She says I'm her secret confidant, her outlet for things she can't share with her family. They're so familiar, they just take her for granted, while for me every little thing has meaning. I sent her flowers on Mother's Day. She said she'd like to take me back to her hometown someday. I'd like to go alone with her, not have to share her with the others."

The last time I saw Warren he was down from his high. His mother seemed to be withdrawing again. When she and her friend made a two-day trip to his vicinity with her religious group, she insisted she could not get away to meet him. "I have a feeling she doesn't know how to handle it with the family. They may feel jealous. Right now it's still like a clandestine relationship in the closet. She hasn't invited me back down."

In the meantime, Warren has his father's name and phone number, which he has been sitting on for three weeks. "I don't have the same intensity about finding him," he said, "but I can't decide if I should write or call. What do you think?"

TONY—Mother Tries to Deny Relationship at First

"She had her phone number changed and
unlisted to avoid me."

It is not uncommon for a woman to deny that she is the right person when first contacted. Taken by surprise, she needs time to
work through her emotions before she is able to reopen this painful and often secret part of her life.

On one level, Tony could understand this. He had seen his
mother's name on his adoption papers when he was sixteen, but
it had taken him fifteen years to get the "guts" to search for her.
Still, on another level, it hurt.

Tony's childhood had been like something out of Dickens—
the worst Adoptee story I heard. The adoptive father, to whom he
was deeply attached, died when he was nine. His mother then became an alcoholic, under the influence of a tailor with whom she
began living. This man was a sadist and obviously jealous of Tony
and his brother, also adopted. As a punishment for not behaving
satisfactorily, he packed up all the boys' possessions, many of them
presents from their adoptive father, and sent them off to the
Salvation Army. There were continual beatings, and many nights
the two boys went to bed without supper. There were even a few
years when the tailor wouldn't have them in the house, and the
mother had to put them out to board. Yet when this man died,
Tony took his mother into his home with his wife and children.
He was grateful that she took a grandmotherly interest in his
three children. "I guess I loved her, but she didn't deserve it,"
he is able to say now.

After her death, Tony still did not think of looking for his
birth parents. Completely self-made, he had a good job, owned a
few houses, and was putting himself through college at night. "I
was too hung up with other things in my life, but my wife started
saying 'You've got three children, you've got to find out what
your heredity is all about.' My adoptive brother was urging me, too,
though he won't search himself. He's been in trouble with the
law and is not very proud of himself. It's like the rich man/poor
man syndrome. I've been successful, and he hasn't. He's gay and
leads a kind of hippie life, in and out of jail.

"I was going to hire a detective, but my wife found this
adoptee group, and they advised us to do the easy things first. Call

the name you have, they said. Call on anyone in that town with the same name and see if you can get information. You might be talking to your mother, but it doesn't matter. At least you're not going to have to go crazy looking at records.

"So I called the first number in the phone book with that last name, and it turned out to be my mother's former sister-in-law. I got the whole story from her. My mother already had a child when she got pregnant with me. Her husband was away in the service. She was convinced that if she got rid of me, everything would be all right with her marriage. So she did, but still they got divorced. Now she's remarried and has a few kids."

This woman gave Tony his mother's phone number.

"I had my wife call for me. We used a different last name which I'm sorry for now because I think it made my mother suspicious of me for a while. My wife got her on the phone and said, 'Are you alone? Can you talk? I have something personal to tell you.' She wasn't alone, but she said, 'Like what?' My wife said, 'I have someone who would like to speak with you.'

"Then I got on the phone. I was very nervous at first but afterwards I got mad. Because she started to deny me. I started to interrogate her like Perry Mason. Finally there were just these incredible long pauses where she could have hung up but didn't."

Tony played the tape he had made of the call, commenting as it went along. It is an interesting example of how the birth mother's first instinct is to pretend she is not the person being sought:

"Hello. My name is ——— (and I gave her a false name)."

"Yes?"

"I have recently been doing some checking on records and I have . . ."

"Yes?"

"I know this is an odd call. If you are my mother, I'm not calling to screw up your life or anything. I just have to find out who my natural mother is. It seems very right to me. I have three children and I'm concerned about my heredity. It's very important to me."

"Umhm."

"Am I on the wrong track? I mean . . ."

"I believe you are."

"Is that true?"

"Yes."

"You have never had a child?"

"No" (*shaky voice*).

"You haven't?"

"No."

"You didn't?"

"Where are you calling from?"

"My home."

"Where's that?"

("I gave her a fictitious town in New Hampshire.) I've done some extensive checking and you are the only one that meets that description."

"Umhm."

"Your name was ———?"

"No."

"You were Mrs. ———?"

"No."

"You weren't married to ———?"

"No. You're a little confused."

"You are ———?"

"No."

"I do have this fouled up then?"

"Yeah."

"What was your maiden name?"

"I think that's personal."

"I don't understand. All the records I have point to you. Did you ever live on Broad Street?"

"No."

"You have two children?"

"No."

"This is very confusing to me."

"Yes, it is."

"Then you don't know anything about this?"

"No."

"Gee, I'm really at a dead end now."

"Yes, you are."

"You're not interested in seeing this person I'm talking about?"

"What person?"

"Me. I mean, you really aren't my mother?"

"No (*laughs*). Not really that I know of."

"I must have an awful . . . Your husband's name is ————?"

"No."

"What's his name?"

"You have the wrong number, I think."

"You lived on Pound Road once."

"No."

"My wife just asked you if your name was ————."

"No, it isn't."

(Long pause.) "It isn't? I think it is. It's obvious you don't want to tell me anything now."

"No. I have nothing to say."

"Can I call you some other time—when your husband's not home?"

"Yes."

(*Relief.*) "That'd be great. When can I do that?"

"Any time in a couple of weeks."

("I didn't understand that she was moving then and she'd be out of there in a couple of weeks.")

"Within a couple of weeks?"

"A couple of weeks."

"He won't be home? But he's home now and you can't talk to me?"

("I told her I'd call soon and hung up.")

Second call: Two weeks later. Mother admits identity.

"I'd like to talk to you. I'm sorry the way I called."

"I'll tell you what's happening. We're moving. We sold our big beautiful house. (She's trying to impress me.) Going to a small apartment. (She sounded relaxed.) And I discussed this with my husband."

"You discussed what—my call?"

"He said it would be all right. He'd like to see you."

"He'd like to see me?"

"If you want to see me."

"Do you admit you're my mother?"

"Yes."

("I groaned with relief. She laughed.")

"I'm so happy."

"I told one of my daughters."

"I'd love to see you."

"We're not settled."

"Can I see you before you move?"

"We're moving today."

"How can I find you? (*No answer.*) This is wonderful. I have so many questions. Do you know who my father is?"

"I don't. Well, I mean I do, but I don't know his name."

"It's important for me, for my heredity and everything."

"If I find him, I'll let you know."

"You have three grandchildren."

"No, I have only one."

"I mean *I* have three children."

("She didn't comment on her grandchildren. I was like an old friend—not mother/son.")

"I tried to call a couple of days later but discovered that when she moved she had a different unlisted phone number. She changed it because she was trying to avoid me. Even though she accepted me on the phone, she must have thought, Still I can avoid him. Maybe I won't have to see him. So for six weeks there was silence. Then I wrote her at the old address and had it forwarded. In the meantime I was in touch with Mrs. R., her former sister-in-law, who had given me the information. She took me on a tour of the town, showed me where I was born, where I would have grown up. She also showed me where my mother had moved. There I was outside my mother's house. I could hardly fight off the urge to walk up to the door, but, you know, this was a Sunday afternoon, the whole family was home, cars all over the place. I knew that would be disastrous. So I fought the urge, and I came back.

"Mrs. R. went to see my mother for me, which I found out later made her angry because she didn't speak to the family anymore. But she gave Mrs. R. my sister's phone number for me to contact. She had told all of her children and her husband about me, but she still wasn't willing to meet me. So I called my sister and we discussed ways to get my mother to come around. My sister said, 'I don't think she's ever going to meet you because she's nervous. She wouldn't mind seeing you in a public place where you couldn't see her.' But I wouldn't agree to that. I wanted to meet her face-to-face, and I wanted her to be brave enough to do it. Finally I said to my sister: 'Look, I know where she lives. Call her and tell her I'm going there tomorrow.' My sister called back to say my mother had said 'No, I'm not prepared' at first. Then she said she'd call me in the morning.

"I was so happy. I took the day off work, but she didn't call. So I phoned my sister and said 'Look, she didn't call and tell me *not* to come, so I'm going there.' When my sister called her again, she agreed to see me.

"Well, I was really nervous and anxious. I was speeding all the way there. I realized I was not as objectively cold about all this as I thought I was. I was really getting emotional about it. I finally got to the house. I was late. The main door was open, and I started to walk up the walk. My mother came to the doorway and that's when I saw her for the first time. We stared at each other. We didn't kiss or anything at first. As I stared at her she said, 'Are you disappointed?' I said no. In fact, I was impressed. I thought she was going to be older. I thought she was going to be a witch. I didn't know. I had this horrible feeling about what she was going to look like. On the phone she was not well-spoken. I thought she was going to be an incredible dumbbell. And I met this woman and she was very nice. She told me everything, just like I had heard it from Mrs. R., except she put the blame on her first husband. Anyway, we hit it off very well, you know. I didn't feel love right away. We did kiss eventually, like I would kiss an aunt I was just meeting for the first time. I expected just to stay there for a little while because I didn't think she wanted me to meet her husband right away. But she did. She invited me to dinner and I met her husband and children. It was a great thing. I left about ten o'clock that night. I had been there for ten hours.

"On the way home I cried. Forty-five minutes of crying. And I don't do that very often. That kind of thing never happened to me. I am cold and objective about most things. There's been a big change in me because of all this. I was crying for a lot of reasons. Because she looked so beautiful when she accepted me. I was crying because I didn't have her for my whole life, and I felt that I should have. Because I thought of different times in my life which were so terrible that I wished she was around, and I could have gone to her. At a later time I had the feeling I was cheated, but not then.

"We've met twice since that day. Once when I took my wife and children to her house. And when she came to visit us.

"She showed me pictures of the house where I was born, even the bed I was born in. The fact that she was looking through those pictures—I felt, oh man, she's not emotional about it. But I learned she's not a real emotional person—to her other children either. I have to keep holding myself back—my wife holds me back, too. I'd like to call her every couple of days. I want to bring her close to me. I haven't gotten close enough to know whether I want the relationship or not. It's not like I finally found my mommy, or that I'm looking for a grandmother for my kids. I want to know more and more. The closer our relationship, the more information I'm going to get. I do think that after a while I could learn to love her—you know, as a mother. I don't think it would ever bother me, the fact that she gave me up. Because I understand the circumstances. I can really be objective about that and sympathize with the feeling she had at that time. I know it was a hard thing for her to meet me because she didn't know what I wanted. She and her husband had had difficulty in the past, and she didn't want her life all messed up with me coming back. She didn't know how he'd react to it. That's what she said.

"But recently I've had the feeling the relationship is not going so well. She doesn't seem particularly interested if I come down or not. And my wife is closer to Mrs. R. She's totally different from my mother, very emotional, very loving, very interested. My wife compares her to my mother. I tell her Mrs. R. wouldn't be Mrs. R. if she went through what my mother went through. I said my mother's probably got some scars.

"Sometimes I think my wife is sorry I searched after all. She didn't know I'd get so carried away, so obsessed."

Four months passed before I spoke with Tony again. By that time the relationship with his mother was over. Upset that he had sent Christmas cards to her sisters, she had accused him of tormenting her.

"I'm not really your mother," she told him. "Your mother's in the grave. I'm going to have a nervous breakdown if you don't stop abusing me."

"You're putting me up for adoption twice," Tony said. "I came back and you were nice, but now you're sending me away again."

"You're not the product of a love relationship, but of rape," she said. "I could never love you because you remind me of that bad time. What do you want from me? If I give you $10,000, would you leave me again?"

"That hurt most of all. I said I never wanted anything from her. After all, I came to her in pretty good shape. I wanted nothing more than to be acknowledged. I don't like being put aside."

Tony still is not sorry he searched. "I would do it over again," he said. "I know now that the family I came from is healthy. There's no cancer or heart trouble. It puts my mind to rest for my children and my children's children."

ALICE and FAY—Mother a Suicide

"It's too late now, she
wears the ground as a coat."
ALICE, AN ADOPTEE

The novelist Peter Handke called the book about his mother's suicide *The Sorrow beyond Tears*. It best describes the emotion felt by Adoptees who find their mothers dead of self-inflicted wounds. Like Handke, they continue the search for this woman out of personal need and as outside investigators. Some, like Alice, are turned away by their mother's relatives, who are reluctant to revive the pain of the past. As a result, she has never been able to resolve the reality of her mother's death or life. "I have such a sense of emptiness and loss," Alice wrote me. "I must ask, Why do I dream of her? I have images of what I believe she would have looked like. Strange, even when I'm awake, I see her, and go deep into thought about how things might have been. I blame my mother's death on society for condemning the unwed mother."

Alice continued to send me notes and poems as she tried unsuccessfully to persuade her mother's family to see her. "I have been told 'You must put the past behind you and live in the future,'" she said in her last letter, "but how can I live in the future when I have no past? How do I go about finding this peace of mind I want and need?"

Fay was more fortunate in securing such peace because she was received by her mother's brother, slept under the roof of her grandfather's house, where her mother had been raised, and visited the grave.

Like so many searchers I have met, Fay was the Good Adoptee. Although she smarted under the rigid regime of her elderly Southern Baptist father, who occasionally called her "a child of sin" and allowed no smoking, drinking, or dancing, she tried to comply as best she could without offending him or her more permissive mother, whom she adored. She married another Adoptee whom she met in boarding school, and picked up the cue from him that it was disloyal to their adoptive parents to even speculate about their origins.

Fay would probably never have thought of searching if she hadn't taken a part-time job as a companion for the children of a divorced man in her community. Her employer, Ira Denberg, had been through marriage counseling that stressed analyzing one's past behavior with parents and siblings in order to understand one's present behavior patterns. Like a convert to a new religion, he prodded Fay when she refused to talk about her adoption.

"Wasn't I curious to know where I came from? he kept asking. It made me mad. I said it was impossible to know anything more than I did. I had my mother's name on the adoption papers my parents had given me when I was sixteen.

" 'You cannot know the future until you know the past,' he kept saying. 'You wouldn't react so strongly if it wasn't bothering you. Make a game of it. Let's get a phone book for Kansas City.'

"Now I guess I really was curious, because when my son was born a few years before I couldn't help thinking how little we knew about his heritage, neither of us knowing our own. And so I let Ira do the research, and he came up with a name that matched my mother's. I wrote her a letter, vaguely pretending to be a friend, but requesting that she call me. Her son phoned soon after that.

" 'I think my mother, Barbara, is your mother,' I told him. He was stunned. His mother was a very religious person. 'I don't want to confront her until I'm certain,' I added quickly. 'I'd be happy to accept you,' he said.

"But as it turned out, when I wrote away for my birth certificate, I discovered that my mother had put her former married name, not her maiden name, on the adoption paper. I had the wrong woman. It was very embarrassing, but I had to write her son that I wasn't his sister. It took a few more months of searching before Ira managed to locate a woman with my mother's last name in her hometown in the West. I called saying I was a friend trying to locate Barbara. She said Barbara had died twenty years before. She didn't know how, but suggested I call Barbara's brother, which I did. His wife answered. She said Barbara had had two children, and a baby who died.

" 'I think I'm that baby,' I said.

" 'Oh, my goodness,' she gasped. And we both laughed.

"And then I said, 'What did she die from?'

" 'She shot herself.'

"I started bawling.

" 'Are you all right?'

" 'Yes, I am . . .'

"But I couldn't stop crying. The disappointment was overwhelming. My greatest mistake in all those months of searching was that I never seriously considered the possibility that she might no longer be alive. I kept crying through those next few days. I cried for my mother who had found living unbearable by the age of twenty-seven, and I cried for myself, as I was twice-cheated of knowing her.

"Fortunately, my mother's sister-in-law was a wonderful, sensitive person who never threw anything away. She sent me old letters and pictures of my mother and compiled a ten-page biography of her life, everything from medical records to her taste in music. She also invited me to visit her and my uncle."

Fay learned that Barbara had not only been married and divorced, but had two other daughters before she gave birth to her. Her own mother had died of pneumonia at the age of twenty-seven, the exact year that she took her life. By a strange coincidence, Fay was twenty-seven when she stood at her mother's grave. "I felt so empty. I realized that I didn't just want facts when I began the search. I wanted to talk to her, to have real communication."

The picture that Fay got of Barbara was of a shy, withdrawn girl growing up without a mother. She didn't talk about her problems, according to her brother. She never swore, smoked, or drank, and didn't laugh often; she liked opera, always had a job or two, especially waitressing, which she did even after her children were born. There was a period of a few years, after her divorce, when she .put her children out to board and was a waitress in another town. It was during that period that Fay was born. Her brother remembered rumors that she had had a child who died then. No one knew who the father was.

Four years after that, Barbara, who was still a waitress, put a bullet through her brain as she lay alone in her rooming house. The only letter she left was to the couple who were boarding her two girls. She instructed them how to get some money owed her by a man at work and apologized that she couldn't leave anything more. She asked them to raise her daughters. What was clear about the letter was that it had a sense of authority in it, as if the act of dying enabled her to put matters into place more effectively than she had been able to do while living.

At the time she first began her search, Fay had been afraid to tell her husband what she was doing. When she finally confessed, he admitted that he had always wanted to know too, but was reluctant to say so. Now he began his own search. She was also nervous about telling her adoptive parents, but finally did when she came back from visiting her mother's grave. Her devout Baptist father was even more shocked that her mother had committed suicide than he was that she was an unwed mother. However, his love for Fay now overcame his moral judgments—he offered to make the 150-mile trip back to the agency to learn what he could about her birth father. "If your parents were living I'd drive to the end of the earth," he told her.

When Fay's parents met the agency director, an old woman in a wheelchair, she informed them that Fay was the last child she had placed. She still had her files intact and managed to uncover the name of Fay's father, as well as a note from her mother written a few weeks after she had relinquished her. It read:

DEAR MADAME,
I left my daughter for adoption. I now find it possible to keep her. If you have not already released her, please let me know.

Fay had been placed just three days before. There was no further word from her mother in the records. But Fay's aunt was to recall that Barbara had visited them during that time and had lain for eight months in their guest room like someone who was already dead. They guessed it was grief over the "dead" baby. Then she had gotten up one day and returned to her waitress job in that town.

Ira helped Fay trace her father now. It turned out that he, too, was dead, having died of a heart attack in his early fifties. Ira managed to see the widow while on a business trip out West, and learned she had been a bedridden invalid for two years in the period Fay was born. She knew nothing about the affair, but was kind enough to give Ira pictures. She said her husband was the finest man she ever knew.

"I was mad when I learned he was dead," Fay said, "that I couldn't know him either. For a while it was hard to hear other people talk about their reunion stories. But now when I talk about my natural mother, I often forget that I did not know her before her death. There was a reunion between us, perhaps not in the way I expected when I began looking for her, but a good one just the same. I still see the grassy slope of the mountain where she is buried. All the stones in this cemetery must be flat against the earth to preserve the natural beauty of the view. There are no houses anywhere in sight. One looks out only on the snow-capped peaks of the Black Hills.

"But my life is not built around this," she added. "It's been a year. I don't dwell on it. I can accept her sordid life, and her suicide, and still like her. If I met her today I would realize she was a weak person, but feel affection for her. Ira was right. It is better for me to know the truth as I do. If your life was good, you can take it. I had my adoptive parents' love and now I have my husband's and child's."

MARTHA—Mother Refuses to See Her

"She asked if my adoptive parents knew
what I was doing."

One of the most devastating experiences for the Adoptee is when the mother—because of shame, guilt, or pride—refuses to meet with the child she once gave up. She has so effectively sealed the wall around that original loss that she cannot respond when the child returns—as if all of her defenses would crumble in the process.

Martha had thought of her mother all her life. She had looked for her on buses, fantasized what she might be like. She had never felt close to her adoptive mother, who was prone to explosive anger during frequent bouts of drinking. "You're as bad as where you came from!" she would scream at such times, or "If it wasn't for me, where would you be?"

"I used to think I'd rather be somewhere else," Martha told me. "I guess I used adoption as a cop-out, because I kept telling myself they weren't my *real* family."

In spite of their wealth and high social standing, her adoptive parents had had their lumps. Her younger adoptive brother had died of leukemia when she was seven. It was after that that her father had an extramarital affair and her mother began drinking. The boy they adopted as a replacement was a problem from the beginning, has had a few nervous breakdowns, and, when last heard of, was on heroin. Martha herself rebelled by running off to live with someone of a different religious faith, and was told not to come near the house as long as they were together.

"My father had groomed me to be somebody," she said, "and there I was kicking him in the teeth instead of paying dues."

When she was twenty-two, Martha went back to the adoption agency to get the hour of her birth so that she could make an astrological chart. Her ardor was dampened when the social worker, misunderstanding her ·purpose, informed her: "They didn't want you then, they wouldn't want you now."

She did no more thinking on the subject until she was married and was about to have her first child. "I was so happy when I was pregnant. I wanted to tell my birth mother how I felt for her, that she had done the right thing."

After the child was born, Martha decided that since she had her mother's name on her adoption papers, she would search for her. But, like Fay, she spent the first year tracking the wrong woman. When she finally did find the right one, she discovered that she had recently moved to another part of the country.

It was with great hope that she made that first call. It went like this:

"I'm looking for ———"
   "Why?"
   "I was born March 10, 1941."
   "Do you know we're talking on a country party line?"

"I'm sorry."

"I hope you understand, I can't talk now. Give me your address and I'll write you."

"I was so happy when I hung up," Martha said. "That is, until I got the letter. It referred to me as Mrs. ———, and went, 'This matter has been private between two young people and attorneys. It is a secret and should remain one. I beg you not to pursue this further. My life is all set. Do you want to destroy it?'"

"I wrote her that I only wanted information about myself, nothing else. When I didn't get a reply, I called her a few months later. This time she said she had nothing to say. She asked me if my adoptive parents knew what I was doing, and demanded their address. I said I wouldn't give it to her, that I was thirty-four, not a child anymore. Then she hung up.

"That got me angry, her hanging up on me. I'm a battler. So I called her daughter, who is my half-sister. She sounded nice on the phone. She didn't know anything about me. We talked for an hour and a half. I didn't learn too much about my mother except that she is stubborn.

"My sister must have told my mother she heard from me, because I got a letter from her lawyer the next week. He accused me of harassment and invasion of privacy. He said he represented both my mother and her husband.

"I had my lawyer call him to say that I just wanted information. But her lawyer demanded a declaration from me that I wouldn't bother his client again. He offered a bribe. Can you imagine, offering me money to go away?

"After this exchange I went into a decline. I was so depressed I could hardly function. I thought of suicide. But a few months later, I phoned my sister on her birthday. She was very nervous and wouldn't talk."

Somehow, the birth mother's lawyer managed to trace Martha's adoptive parents and notified them of what she was doing. He accused her of extortion, and even hinted that the recent break-in of her mother's home might be connected to her activity. Martha's adoptive parents were appalled and told her they wanted to see her immediately. "It was like I was a child again," she remembers. "My father saying, 'Come into the den, I want to talk to you.'"

Still, Martha's adoptive parents were more conciliatory than she would have expected. If anything, they started making overtures to her. Her mother brought out the family silver and heir-looms as a kind of offering. They said they would take her child for part of the summer, so that she could travel. In return, Martha promised them that she would not make any more contact with her birth mother. She wrote a note to the lawyer to that effect.

She was still depressed, but determined to rise above it this time. We talked about how the refusal of the birth mother to recognize you is a devastating blow. It is as if only she can confirm or deny your existence—her rejection consigns you to the realm of the dead.

"I can deal with it now," Martha insisted. "I know I have to give birth to myself."

However, over the next year she began putting on weight, and when we met again, I hardly recognized her.

JACKIE—No Shock of Recognition
"I didn't like her at first."

An Adoptee may be disappointed to find that she shares no physical resemblances or similar interests with the mother she has dreamed of all her life. She may not even like her at first. It takes time to give up the fantasies and accept the actual person. Jackie was to learn that you need more than one meeting to fully understand the story of the past—and the person who is telling it.

Jackie had located her mother by first calling the brother, who was listed in the phone book. She pretended to be a friend of his sister's from out of town, and was overwhelmed when he gave her the number. But it took her six months before she could get the courage to dial it.

"I told her my name and birthdate and said, 'I've been searching for you.' 'Yes, you called my brother,' she snapped. 'What took you so long to call?'

"I thought she meant until this time in my life, but later I realized she meant after calling her brother. It was a dumb comment when I thought about it. After that her next words were 'I had nothing to do with it.' I was stunned, disappointed. Then she said, 'Do you love to shop?'

"I found myself getting angry at her for not being what I wanted her to be. She didn't even remember my birthday. She said things like 'I almost died giving birth to you' and 'I had to leave school to go to work afterwards,' as if I was the reminder of a bad experience. At another point she said, 'What do you have to complain about? You're lucky. My past is coming back to haunt me.'

"Then she told me that she was married for the second time, and had an adopted daughter since she couldn't have more children. She'd told her daughter that her parents were killed in a car crash because she doesn't want her to search.

"We agreed to send each other pictures and arrange for a time when we could meet. I sent her a picture right away and was appalled when she sent one with her adoptive daughter taken a few years before. I thought that was pretty insensitive."

A month later Jackie flew up to her hometown to meet her mother at noon in a restaurant.

"I sat there for twenty minutes waiting. I noticed an older woman waiting too, but she didn't look anything like what I imagined my mother would be. I went to the ladies room and came back, but still she was the only one there. Then she turned to me and said, 'Are you Jackie?' I was shocked. It was her. She hadn't recognized me either.

"As soon as we were seated at the table, she said, 'I suppose you want to know what happened?' I nodded yes. Then she went into a long, involved story about how she married young, but her brother didn't think her husband was good enough for her, and forced her to get an annulment. When she discovered she was pregnant, it was too late, and she had to give up the child. It sounded implausible to me then. I was sure she was lying. I thought, Yeah, tell me another one.

"I noticed she seemed defensive, almost angry at me a good deal of the time. When I told her I had had my nose altered, she was insulted. 'What's wrong with that nose?' she asked, and I realized it had been just like hers. Then I found myself resenting it when she asked about my child. I thought I had a right to pry into her life, and get explanations, but she had no right to mine. I think we were both relieved when the lunch was over."

For some months after the meeting, Jackie could not get herself to write a note to Helen, as she called her. "I wanted to say I was glad I met her, but I didn't know how honest I could be. I knew I was annoyed that she wasn't going to tell her adopted daughter about me, and that she hadn't leveled with me about what happened. I felt guilty about feeling this way. I wished I didn't have to deal with it. I even found myself wishing I could forget the search, forget it ever happened, although I knew I didn't mean it. I was happy I'd done it, but I knew I didn't like the results. I wanted to go back to my old fantasies."

DEAN—The Foundling

> LADY BRACKNELL: Now to minor matters. Are your
> parents living?
> JACK: I have lost both my parents.
> LADY B: To lose one parent, Mr. Worthing, may be
> regarded as a misfortune; to lose both looks
> like carelessness. Who was your father?...
> JACK: I am afraid I really don't know. The fact is,
> Lady Bracknell, I said I had lost my parents.
> It would be nearer the truth to say that my parents
> seem to have lost me.... I don't actually know who
> I am by birth. I was...well, I was found...
> LADY B: Found!
> OSCAR WILDE, *The Importance of Being Earnest*

Writers from ancient times have been fascinated with the role of the foundling. The mystery of the lost child lends itself to endless possibilities. In Wilde's play, Ernest, who was abandoned in a handbag in Victoria Station, for reasons which Lady Bracknell surmises were to "conceal a social indiscretion," learns that he is really Lady Bracknell's nephew. It seems the absent-minded nursemaid left *him* instead of her manuscript in the cloakroom at the station. Before all this is unraveled, Lady Bracknell advises Ernest to "try to acquire some relations as soon as possible, and to make a definite effort to produce at any rate one parent, of either sex, before the season is quite over."

In what we call "real life," the endings are not so humorous or fortunate. The foundling, of all the searchers, has the fewest leads—if any—and usually can uncover no clues. Having not even a hint as to nationality, religion, or the circumstances of his parents, the foundling is the most susceptible to fantasy and despair.

I knew Dean for several years before I learned he was adopted.

I thought of him as a talented actor who always had a beautiful woman in love with him. Just about the time she became serious, he would phase out the relationship.

It was from one of his former women friends that I learned the secret of his adoption. "You too?" he asked when I confessed that not only did I know about him, I shared the condition. And then we talked, really talked, for the first time.

So much of his adoption experience was like mine—overly protective Jewish parents, mother slightly hysterical, father sweet but conservative, playing life "close to the vest." But while I must have taken sustenance from knowing that one Jewish clan had passed me on to another through a Jewish agency, Dean knew only that he had been found on the steps of an orphanage about eight hours after birth. His parents said that they knew nothing about his past, and he both believed and didn't believe this while he was growing up.

"I tried to think about it as little as possible," he says now. "Adoption was like a fact of life, neither positive nor negative— it just existed like a scar on the lip. The story was so closed— abandoned. There was nowhere to go for information, not much to ask."

Dean remembers being morbidly shy in his early years, but his parents always told him he was a rebellious baby, screaming if his demands weren't met. He was extremely bright in elementary school, even skipping a grade, but just before puberty, from the age of twelve, he began losing interest in his subjects, copping out. "Everything went downhill after that. From a brilliant child, I went to a nonperformer."

The rules of the household were laid down primarily by Dean's mother. "When I was fifteen, if I came home late, mother would be in the living room crying, while my father slept unconcerned. She would say that I was worrying them both to an early grave. I had a feeling she thought of me as a sexual being. Once she found condoms in my drawer and asked, 'What are you doing with this?' When I replied, 'What can you imagine?' she said my behavior was disgusting. She made some comment about *bad blood* then, too. I remember wondering if it was communicable.

"There was resistance from both parents if I asked anything about my adoption. I used to say I didn't care who they were as long as I could know."

When he was expelled from school for having a bottle of liquor in his car, Dean's mother took him to a psychiatrist. "He asked about my sex life with my mother sitting right there. I thought he was a moron. My adoption was not mentioned. But I remember thinking that my friends were just as outrageous in their behavior and didn't get into awful trouble with their parents."

Dean left home at seventeen to attend the local college, but after a half year, he dropped out. For the next few years he was in and out of schools.

One memory stays with him. "When I was nineteen I was in a coffee shop and a woman came up to me. 'Where's your father?' she asked. I just sat there thunderstruck. 'Isn't your father a faith healer?' When I still couldn't answer, she got nervous and left. I didn't ask her anything, but I would now."

Dean's parents were not pleased when he became involved in theater. "My father looked on actors as bums. He maintained that the important things in the cosmos were security, respectability, and fitting in. I was imbued with a different nature. I was a loner, getting satisfaction from listening to music and reading Shakespeare. I couldn't help wondering where I came from. Acting was the only thing that could engage both my body and mind. I thought, 'I don't belong in this family, something's wrong. I'm not fitting into the scheme.' I never broke with them completely, but the communication never improved."

It did not occur to Dean to pursue his origins until an actress friend remarked casually that he looked like his adoptive father. "I thought, Could he be my real father? Maybe he had me by another woman. I decided to check it out. My mother got very upset when I began asking questions. She said I didn't love her, that I was ungrateful. I accused her of lying to me. I figured they wouldn't pick a kid they knew *nothing* about. My father told me I could call the children's home if I wanted to.

"In the end I wrote. I received a letter back that it was true, I was a foundling. I had been left there unwashed, with my umbilical cord still untied. They sent me a Xerox copy of the note that had been pinned on my blanket. 'Please take care of this laddie. He was not wanted in the house to which he was born. He is some part Jewish.'

"When I read the letter, I thought, 'I was born. There was a time they were together, married or not. Whatever reason, they couldn't keep the baby.' But I had a curious feeling of sadness, poignancy, of being somewhat alone."

Dean and I talked about what the note could mean. The word "laddie" sounded as if it was written by someone Scottish. We conjured up a nursemaid, much like that of Shakespeare's Juliet, who secretly delivered the baby and then carried it away to protect her young mistress.

But do such nursemaids know how to type?

"Still, no matter how mysterious, the letter was something solid, real," Dean said. "For that moment I did have a feeling of reality. Now when I ask myself who I am, I say 'Everybody is everything. Nothing is foreign to the life of the imagination.'

"I know the place that adoption occupies in my mind is awesome. It's a part of me. Something that's always there that other people don't have. But there is nothing more for me to find out. All I can do is translate the experience into my work, create other worlds. Sometimes when I'm acting, I think, 'There's no me here. I'm just playing the part of the Other.' "

Recently he's tried meditation, hoping it would give him some insight. "I thought if I concentrated, I might have access spiritually to my parents. If my father really was a faith healer, maybe I have inherited some of his ESP. I even went to a psychic and told her I was adopted. She said, 'Your father is dead, and if you want to see your mother's face, look in the mirror.'

"Sometimes I think I may be descended from Edmund Kean, a famous actor. He had been an orphan too. Or Jack London. I look like his father, who was an itinerant astrologer. Since his mother was a faith healer, maybe there is a relationship there."

When I last saw Dean he was fretting over turning forty, drinking heavily, and breaking up with yet another woman. It was as if being unable to attach himself to his past, he was unable to attach himself to anyone, rejecting each woman before she had a chance to reject him.

"Something in myself, in my life and career, keeps me away from the things I think I want," he said. "I can't blame my adoptive parents. They did what they could. They were playing out their roles. But my script has no ending."

After Dean's father died, his mother raged at him in her grief: "You're not married, you have no children, no real life. You're hopeless!" But he cherishes the memory of that adoptive father, so different in temperament, loyally attending his performances. On his deathbed he had looked up at him and said with resignation, not untinged with admiration: "You are a free spirit, aren't you?"

HARRY, JOAN, LUCY—The Myth of the Missing Parent

"Be, damn it, be."

In the past it was not unusual for one branch of a family to adopt the illegitimate offspring of another and make a pact of secrecy around this. When Adoptees learn the truth, they feel humiliated and enraged by the deception.

Unlike the true foundling, who must eventually come to terms with not being able to know the past, the Adoptee who suspects that the missing parent is really masquerading as an aunt or uncle gets double messages that may become unbearable at some stage of life. Dr. E. Mansell Pattison calls this kind of situation "family mystification."[1]

Harry

Harry, one of Mansell's cases, had been told he was found on the doorstep of his two maiden aunts while they were living together. When he was five, the gentle aunt, Millie, married, leaving the stern spinster aunt to raise him. At the age of forty, unable to fight the depression that overcame him upon marrying his deceased's wife's best friend, he turned to alcohol, and then therapy. He began to realize that he was associating the personalities of the two wives with the two aunts, and that he had to solve his feelings around all the relationships.

Mansell recorded the last session they had together, just before Harry was to confront his aunts about whether one of them was his mother:

> Where, oh where is my mother? If my mother is dead, then let her be dead. But maybe she is alive . . . but just to know that I came from somewhere, that I belong to somebody . . . that I'm not just a nothing. Mother, mother, mother, where

are you? Dead? All right. Give me your grave. Let me put flowers on it. But be, damn it, be! You know, sometimes I think Millie is my mother. I don't want anything from her. I just want to know. I have to have a mother! God, O God, have mercy on me.

When the two sisters once again denied knowing anything, Harry committed suicide. Only after his death did they finally reveal to his wife what could not be told while he was alive. Millie was indeed his mother. They had made a pact to protect her reputation, as well as that of the father, by never telling anyone. And they had been true to that pact. The secret had taken on a life of its own, superseding the lives of anyone involved in it.

Joan

Joan was also a victim of family deceptions that were played behind her back for the convenience of the adults involved.

When she was eight, Joan's adoptive mother admitted that her real mother was her Aunt Mary, her adoptive father's sister. However, Joan was sworn to secrecy, and did not tell her birth mother she knew the truth until she was seventeen. By that time her mother was married with three children and could not muster the courage to admit to her double life.

Joan did not feel close to her adoptive mother, who was domineering and abusive, nor to her rather weak adoptive father, who died of alcoholism when she was nineteen.

"But the biggest problem in my life was being connected to two families and yet not really being a part of either one," she said. When she had tried to press her birth mother to tell her two sisters, her mother had countered: "But I am *not* your mother."

"It was an impossible situation," Joan said. "Growing up with two mothers, and two families, was a form of hell on earth. To make it worse, my two mothers hated each other, although they tried to hide it. When I watched the two of them together, I wanted to scream with rage. I felt like a pawn, used and manipulated for their own ends."

The other members of Joan's family—the aunts, uncles, cousins—also played the game, pretending that Joan's mother was not her mother. "It was like living in an Alice-in-Wonderland world or some futuristic society where nothing is as it seems. After a while I came to feel that this attitude was a denial of my very existence."

When she realized that her birth mother had no intention of admitting their relationship, Joan took her younger sister aside and told her. "She was quite surprised, and said that she always thought she would hear something like this one day, only that it would be she who was adopted." She said it explained a lot of things about her mother, but she felt she would have to digest it for a while before discussing it further. That time never came, and the sister seems to be avoiding her.

Joan's birth mother has also been avoiding her. "I know now that I let my family cram a situation down my throat without any thought as to what was best for me or what I wanted. I can say with authority that when a person suppresses their feelings and thoughts for thirty years, an enormous slush fund is built up, a slush fund of tremendous anger."

Lucy

Lucy, on the other hand, never suspected anything when the poor Jewish family into which she had been adopted was visited once a year by a wealthy friend she called Aunt Nettie. She remembers feeling awkward and badly dressed when she was sent alone by train to visit Aunt Nettie in her large house in a nearby city on holidays—especially when they sat at the long dining table surrounded by Nettie's husband and her two grown daughters, Martha and Jacqueline. Martha, a housewife, was always friendly, but Jacqueline, a successful career woman, seemed to go out of her way to ignore her. None of them gave her presents, not even a book, or took her to plays or concerts during those tense visits. She was just here, another place at the table until it was time to be sent back on the train home.

It wasn't until she was a married woman with teenage children that Lucy looked up an Adoptee group she had read about in the newspaper. It had never occurred to her to search. She had no clues, but one member of the group suggested she call Aunt Nettie, whom she still saw occasionally, and ask her what she knew. Lucy was amazed when Nettie began gasping and stuttering on the other end of the line and finally turned the phone over to Martha, who happened to be there. Martha offered to meet Lucy for lunch that week. She then revealed that Nettie was her grandmother, and Jacqueline, who had died the year before, her mother. Her father had been just a casual acquaintance who had died a long time ago.

Lucy fled the restaurant and did not contact Nettie again for years. She felt enraged that they had all duped her, but did not tell her adoptive mother what she had learned.

By the time Lucy was ready to probe into the reasons *why*, Nettie was in a nursing home. Lucy began visiting her and gradually overcame the old woman's crafty lapses into forgetfulness, which were a way of avoiding the subject. She learned that when Jacqueline refused to keep her, Nettie had taken her with a nurse into her own home, hoping her daughter would change her mind. By the end of Lucy's first year, Jacqueline remained adamant, and Nettie was exhausted. Remembering the childless wife of a truck driver from a nearby mining town who had been in the hospital for an operation at the time of Lucy's birth, Nettie devised an adoption plan. She would give this woman the baby in return for visiting rights. She, herself, promised she would not reveal her true identity or try to influence Lucy's development.

Lucy has begun to forgive the old woman, even to appreciate the early struggle she put up to keep her, and then not lose track of her. Her visits to the nursing home are now out of genuine concern for Aunt Nettie, once the mystery figure in her life.

16

*The Journey
after Reunion*

how to go on
from the moment that
changed our life,

the moment of revelation

proceeding from the crisis,
from the dream,
and not from the moment
of sleep before it?
MURIEL RUKEYSER, "Searching/Not Searching"

The hero, according to Ernest Becker, was the person who
could go into the spirit world, the world of the dead, and
return alive. The Adoptee returns from his phantom world
only to discover that the journey is not over—only one stage of it
has passed. There are others still ahead.

There is the shock of that initial encounter with the mother
when one feels so deeply affected one can hardly remember what
was said.

There are the subsequent meetings in which one begins to
see the birth mother as a real person rather than a blown-up
illusion.

There is the period of adjusting to who she is, and deciding
what one thinks of her.

There is the moment when the Adoptee must deal honestly

with his or her expectations. Was he only looking for his origins, or was he unconsciously hoping for a relationship? Was she the rational adult researching the past, or the deprived baby trying to return to the womb?

In that period of soul-searching there are all the human entanglements to be solved. As a birth mother who was reunited with her son wrote me: "Can anyone *not* involved hope to sort out two incredibly complex family orbits that have collided, shear some sort of constructive individual path through the tangle of circumstances and emotions?"

It is important to stress here again that, until now, both mother and child have been frozen in time. Just as the Adoptee expected to find that young, vibrant fantasy mother who existed at the moment of separation, so does the mother respond to the *lost baby* there on the other end of the telephone line. The return of the lost one seems possible to both. It is only as the days pass that reality sets in for the mother—it is not the baby who will appear at the door but some unknown adult whom she must not only cope with but explain to her other children, her husband, and the neighbors. It is then that she experiences the panic which may make her hesitate or withdraw completely.

So, too, the Adoptee, faced with a mortal, vulnerable woman who is shrunken in size from that all-powerful fantasy goddess, must accommodate to the reality that the answer does not lie with her.

Robert Jay Lifton believes that the myth is broken for both Adoptee and birth mother when they find each other. There is a partial compulsion to retreat back to myth. To de-realize the actuality of it.

Who Owes What to Whom?

As yet, relationships after reunion have no precedents in our society—each is an uncharted course.

What do you do if the birth mother wants more of a relationship than you do? Wants to play grandmother to your children as well as mother to you?

Even as I write these words an Adoptee drops by with this problem. "I wish I had been more cautious after contacting my mother," she says. "If I had it to do over again, I would not have rushed in so quickly. I would have told her not to share this with her family for a while—not until we got to know each other better. She doesn't understand she is making demands I can't meet—like calling her 'Mother.' "

The tension is mounting. She cannot tell her adoptive parents, for fear of hurting them, and cannot tell her two young sons for fear they'll blurt it out to their grandparents. One of them is always asking when she's going to find her mother. Meanwhile, her birth mother keeps appearing at the house disguised as a friend. And her husband is getting tired of all the intrigue.

"I'm trying to consider everyone," she concludes, "but I'm getting confused. I wonder if I'm being fair to my husband and my children."

There are other equally complicated scenarios. One Adoptee was stunned to find a sick and incapacitated mother who had lost interest in life. "What is our responsibility to our mothers?" she asks me. "For example, do we owe them financial assistance? I learned she never had any interest in me. I don't want to go near her, but I'm haunted by negative fantasies about her."

Conversely, there are situations where the Adoptee wants more of a relationship than the mother is willing to give. What do you do if she is reluctant to introduce you to her family or incorporate you into her life?

I think of the birth mother who once took me aside at a gathering to admit that she would only want to see the son she gave up if he were successful. "I wouldn't want some down-and-out derelict knocking on my door," she said. "Someone I'd have to take care of. My life is too active. My husband doesn't know a thing. I wouldn't want that kind of responsibility now."

Adoptees are learning that with rights come responsibilities, as they struggle to find their own way. Certainly we can say that the birth mother owes the Adoptee, whether a success or failure, at least one meeting to hear her story. Certainly the Adoptee owes the mother the courtesy of respecting her privacy, and not disappearing the moment the story is told.

I remember the mother who complained: "My daughter used me like an encyclopedia, for facts, and then took off."

However, beyond the initial human considerations, both parties must try to be sensitive to the needs of the other. This is difficult, especially in the case of Adoptees, who may feel that the mother, as the one who abandoned them, owes more than she is offering—though they may not be clear themselves as to what it is they really want from her.

Tony was in this situation.

Well, it's almost like two animals that are wary of each other, you know. I hadn't thought "She owed you, so you don't owe her anything"—because you can say, well, a business deal was made, a property transferred. That's us, you know. And then they don't owe us anything any more. That's all. It's in the courts, it's legal. And then if that piece of property comes back and says, "Well, here I am," what obligations are in the relationship? I don't know. Certainly you don't owe her anything, that's for sure.

But as he thought about it more, Tony decided that maybe she did owe him something after all:

Well, I never did anything bad to her. But she's done something bad to me. Or what she didn't do was bad. If you look at it from that point of view, she was the only one who could possibly owe anything in the relationship. You know, she did give me away. So she owes me. I felt she owed me the chance to meet her. But whether she really owes me more than that— I guess sometimes you lose track of what you went in for.

Paradoxically, when the birth mother is dead, or immobilized in an institution, one is spared many of these questions. The parameters are defined. One is not plagued by all the untidy emotions that wreak their own havoc as the new relationship is worked out. One begins to suspect that perhaps our business is best conducted with the dead, or those who have checked out from life.

Karla found that, far from being desolated when she discovered her mother in a mental institution, she was somehow freed to marry the man she had been living with for eight years. And Fay felt enormous relief at being able to visit her mother's grave. There was the sense of completion which those who must come to terms with functioning parents are not granted until much later.

Everyone finds different solutions to these problems, but the degree of fantasy or illusion one brought to the reunion (and everyone brings some) will influence the degree of accommodation as time passes.

The Letdown

I made a note of something John Le Carré once wrote—I no longer remember where—that seemed to me to apply to Adoptees at the end of their search: "Coming home from very lonely places, all of us go a little mad: whether from great personal success, or just an all-night drive, we are the sole survivors of a world no one else has ever seen."

It is important for everyone to be aware of the possibility of some kind of reaction so that he or she is not taken by surprise. Those of us who write glowingly about the Search as a means of finding self-autonomy have the obligation to give warning of the dangers inherent in the process of self-discovery. For while the Search promises to make us free, it also stirs up previously repressed material that has lain dormant until now. I am reminded of Ernest Becker criticizing psychotherapists for promising their patients unadulterated joy:

> I have never seen or heard them communicate the dangers of total liberation that they claim to offer; say to put up a small sign next to the one advertising joy, carrying some inscription like "Danger: real probability of the awakening of terror and dread, from which there is no turning back."[1]

The searchers I have been in touch with are only too ready to warn their fellow Adoptees of "the demon of confusion and helplessness that is inflicted on you," as a woman in her late twenties put it. "No matter how high you may think the price, it is still higher," she said. A seventeen-year-old, who found her mother on her own, advised other teenagers not to search unless they were ready for shocks. "Make sure you can handle it. Don't stay in a dream world."

How does one know when one is ready? Or just how debilitating the "shocks" can be? In other words, how does one know one's own emotional threshold?

For some Adoptees the letdown after reunion with the mother is greater than for others. I've talked with both men and women who have walked away seemingly unscathed by the experience, and others who spoke of reactions that left them temporarily "immobilized," "catatonic," "fearful," "filled with rage."

One woman believed that the severe mononucleosis which sent her to the hospital at the age of thirty-five (where she retreated like a passive infant) was a direct result of her mother's refusal to acknowledge her.

What is so frightening about these violent reactions is that they descend upon one suddenly, like a sneak attack.

I remember being so overwhelmed with anxiety on a trip abroad shortly after meeting my mother that I had to hibernate in my room, as if only in a dormant state would I be safe from the furies that threatened to devour me. The woman I had found was like a defeated star, no more fire or passion banked in her. I couldn't accept that my mother could be anything but strong. Was this what was devastating me? Or her refusal to introduce me to her husband and son? Or was it my guilt that I had broken society's taboo against looking for the woman who had given birth to me?

Gradually over time my depression lifted, even receded in my memory, until years later, when talking with Adoptees who were experiencing similar attacks, I could say, "So that's what that was." They all seemed to be going through that same period of depression once the euphoria of the reunion wore off. They, too, were unprepared for it. Jackie said, "I thought when I found my mother everything would fall into place. But I still don't know who I am. I am falling apart, rather than getting put together."

There seems to be a period where one has to disintegrate, become immobilized, as if connecting with those early primal anxieties that all people experience. One relives the fears of the infant struggling with basic trust and mistrust—a battle that most Adoptees lost with the *actual* loss of the mother. Erikson tells us that these fears of alienation are a mixture of anxiety and rage which persist into all later phases of life. As one struggles to become a person, that early panic is recapitulated: one feels abandoned by what has become familiar and fears "being left a victim to crushing forces; the terror of the evil eye and the dread of being alone in a universe without a supreme counterplayer, without charity."[2]

Many Adoptees described agonizing feelings of worthlessness

at this time. One woman spoke of the pain as being located in the solar plexus area:

The pain was like a sob, yet much lower. There may be a term for this but I am unaware of it. I began talking to my husband about it, then I just started saying whatever would fit the soblike pain in my abdomen, and then it became like screaming. The words were like "I am nothing. There is nothing to me." Even while doing this, a part of me kept saying, no, that isn't true, but the other part kept on with its nothingness.

Fay found that she was feeling acute anxiety during the Search, even before learning that her mother had committed suicide:

I was sick to my stomach a lot, had headaches. I even had the fear I was going to die. Once in a supermarket I had an overwhelming feeling of terror. I couldn't remember what I was buying. And in the car on the way home, I was sure the brakes wouldn't hold. I had to pull over to the side for a while, stop the car.

Jackie also felt overwhelmed by death imagery:

When I was searching, I had dreams I was uncovering death. Now I dream of running downstairs pursued by people in masks, like the Arabs wore when they were attacking the Israeli compound at the Olympics. I feel I'm being chased by death.

During this initial stage of depression, Jackie, like many others, found a free-floating anger merging with her anxiety. She remembers screaming at taxi drivers, being impatient with her young son, intolerant of her husband. She seemed to hate everything and everyone, but most of all, herself.

At times when I come across a moving reunion picture in the paper—mother and daughter clutching each other with seemingly unambivalent joy—I want to believe that nothing will ever change for them. I latch onto anyone who looks as if he or she might be immune to what the rest of us have been through.

That's why I tried to keep in touch with Erica (the lesbian poet) who had stood up in the audience to tell her story when I was on the Phil Donahue TV show in Chicago. "I'm on an upper," she declared breathlessly. "I've just come back from meeting my mother this weekend. It was the greatest thing that ever happened to me. We share the same artistic interests—we are soul mates!"

Erica had been searching for years. In her first letter she sent me one of the poems she had written during that period:

I looked for you
spinning the wheel of my horoscope
I lied for you in court chambers
I performed for your benefit in catholic charities.

But you were always with me,
every time I loved and left
each time I put my life in suitcases
as I watch the coupling of friends
and know I can not follow
envying the simple faith of the world's majority
with the clairvoyance of daughters
I wrote you five years ago
knowing even then
I was writing myself.

However, a few months after meeting this mother, Erica informed me that she was struggling out of a deep depression. She had precipitously quit her job and left her lover—the woman she had been living with the past year.

The disillusionment set in after Erica's mother had flown out to visit her for a week. Erica realized that this bohemian artist mother of her fantasy was on drugs the moment she stepped off the plane, and she was unprepared for the revelations she was to hear: her mother had given still another girl up for adoption, had aborted a baby by an Arab lover in North Africa, but kept the two boys she had with the man who was to become her husband.

The bohemian style which Erica had romanticized until now was not as tidy and manageable as the disciplined life she had led with her staid adoptive parents. There were no boundaries, no supports here. She felt threatened in spite of herself, felt that she would be swept away in this torrent of emotions emanating from her mother.

This, too, she expressed in a poem:

No wonder you wear watches
synchronize every clock
panic when someone seems unconcerned.

We are all fleshed out pivots of your time

I am here
but only because discreet phone numbers
were not yet published in underground papers

My sister you sold to Miami Jews
for red shoes and a purse to match

The boys you kept
hoping it would be easier
not to raise your own incarnation

and the nameless one
decomposing somewhere in North Africa

the final ticking under your heart
before your racing timepiece
was disconnected.

Freud aside, all our fathers
do not matter
A woman bleeds through her mother

I love you for trying to stop the flow.

"When she left I was in a rather devastated state," Erica wrote. "I had drawn closer to her, and yet battled with a feeling of anger at the carelessness of her life—primarily in regard to her off-spring."

I have come to accept that depression, with its handmaidens of anger and rage, may be a natural aftermath of the reunion process, the "slush fund" of emotions which can be contained no longer. It seems to be a transitional stage between reunion and integration, between lost and found. As T. S. Eliot says: "We all of us have to adapt ourselves/To the wish that is granted. That can be a painful process."[3]

Oedipus, My Brother

Perhaps it is force of habit in repressing their feelings, but men seem to be prone to less severe depressions after reunion than women. A number of men, like Tony, insisted that because they had entered the search in a detached way, they were not really emotionally involved. When his mother seemed disinclined to invite him over, Tony shrugged and said, "My life is so complicated beyond her, I don't have time to dwell on it. I see she is not strong enough to deal with it. I've decided I don't really like her anyway. I was never comfortable with her."

But a few months later he was saying, "I'm not going to give her the benefit of my going away. I won't let her stop me from sending her Christmas cards or turning up at family funerals. She'll know I'm around till the day she dies."

Adam told me that he felt no severe reaction because he didn't have a fantasy of finding a goddess at the airport. "And I was right, a goddess did not meet me at the plane, just a simple, ordinary woman." Adam seems to have successfully rationalized the outcome—for the time being anyway.

However, many women who also had thought they had little involvement and no great expectations found themselves profoundly depressed, letting their true feelings wash over them to the point of drowning.

Is it that men are just as depressed but have a need to cover over their feelings? And that their rage is of such an order that to release it, as David Berkowitz, the "Son of Sam," did, would have the same disastrous effects?

I think of the phone call my husband received one night from an acquaintance asking for advice. His friend's son—the one she had given up for adoption twenty years before—had recently knocked on her door. She had admitted her identity, and since he had traveled a long way, invited him to stay with her for a while. The night of the call the son had supposedly "raped" his mother. The acquaintance wanted to know how to find psychiatric help for him, and for her. And what it all meant.

Perhaps the meaning is in the Oedipus myth, not as Freud interpreted it, but as an Adoptee might. Perhaps Oedipus recognized Laius as his father in those flickering moments before he killed him in the chariot. Perhaps he had a flash of recognition as he merged with Jocasta on the marital bed. Perhaps he knew what he was doing—he was getting revenge.

In the Heart or in the Head?

It would be satisfying to locate that exact place where rage comes from—to be able to draw an anatomical diagram of the Adoptee, and say the anger is centered here—in the right hemisphere of the brain, in the left ventricle of the heart, or squarely in the gut.

But perhaps it is easier to find the answer in metaphor. In his *Uses of Enchantment,* Bruno Bettelheim tells us that when the genie in the bottle was asked why he was threatening to kill the man who had just released him from hundreds of years of imprisonment, the genie explained that for a while he thought he would reward his liberator. But as he waited and waited over the centuries his anger and frustration built up. By the time his rescue came, he was in a state of murderous rage.

So, too, the Adoptee thinks he will be overjoyed, but the anger, submerged all his life, eventually overtakes him. Jackie was amazed that something as simple as finding her parents' names in the phone book could set it off. There, on that printed page, was proof that they had been going on with their everyday lives, while she had been trapped like the genie in a world of fantasy and pain. "It was as if there was no meaning to anything," she said. "I was just an accident, not a person. My being here was nothing more than a great mistake."

Over and over we try to trace the source of this mysterious depression so intermixed with rage, a sickness unto death that seems not to be part of the ordinary human condition—that seems so undeserved. We try to capture it with words, to domesticate its wild course. To believe that it must be something more than disappointment over what we have found. One woman said:

> People don't realize, regardless of what they say, what it's like to think and dream for twenty-three years about a person you've never known, and then suddenly discover she's not at all what you dreamed of. Pop! The illusion is gone, and cold unrelenting reality swarms over like a flock of vultures that preys on your dreams.

It keeps coming back to that Ideal Mother. The mother who should have been. For although we have been mothered, usually by devoted *psychological* parents, we cannot be sure it was legitimate, because it was not by the mother who conceived us. We are not even sure we know what true mothering is, for we have not experienced the mothering that natural children take for granted. Like the changeling, we received the alien mothering that the child who never was should have had, just as we missed the biological mothering we should have had.

Because we are adopted, one part of us will always perceive our mothering as inauthentic—for in a literal sense it was. It is hard for us to understand that even those who are raised by their own mothers have a sense of frustration, a feeling that they too have missed something. Something that existed back in the Platonic Ideal of an era long lost to all of us.

In her book *Of Woman Born*, Adrienne Rich reminds us that many people have been mothered in ways they cannot yet perceive:

> ... if a mother had deserted us, by dying, or putting us up for adoption, or because life had driven her into alcohol or drugs, chronic depression or madness, if she had been forced to leave us with indifferent, uncaring strangers in order to earn our food money, because institutional motherhood makes no provisions for the wage-earning mother; if she had tried to be a "good mother" according to the demands of the institution and had thereby turned into an anxious, worrying, puritanical keeper of our virginity; or if she had simply left us because she needed to live without a child—whatever our rational forgiveness, whatever the individual mother's love and strength, the child in us, the small female who grew up in a male-controlled world, still feels, at moments, wildly unmothered.

I would add here that under such circumstances the male, too, feeels "wildly unmothered." Freud told us that a man who has been cherished by his mother will not fail, but he did not say what happens to the man who has been abandoned by the mother. (According to one male Adoptee, he will not trust another woman until he is lowered into the ground.)

For all Adoptees there is the paradox of having not one mother, but two—and often feeling one has none. After reunion there is the task of separating out one's feelings for the birth mother from those for the adoptive mother. There are times when the two merge into each other, as Jackie pointed out:

> I find myself tangled up in the myth of motherhood. I made a myth of what the reality of a mother is from the ideal mother I had fantasized. But she turned out to be not like either my adoptive mother or my fantasy. I felt angry at her for not being what I wanted her to be. And I realized that much of

the anger I had directed at my adoptive mother had come from the rage I felt for having been deserted by her.

In sorting these mothers out, one has to accept that the adoptive one cannot be everything, and the birth one cannot fill the void. Erik Erikson believes that Adoptees panic during this period because they have destroyed both the exclusive bond with the adoptive parent and the ideal fantasy of the biological parent.[4]

It is like being between the two worlds of Matthew Arnold, the one dead, the other powerless to be born.

Forgiveness

The psychiatrist Norman Paul told me that reunion is healthy if for no other reason than that it gives the Adoptee a chance to forgive the parent, and the parent a chance to overcome his or her guilt at relinquishing the child.

Yet I have found that it takes time, this working through to the point of forgiveness. Jackie, who went into therapy, says: "I can't forgive until I can sort out who I am angry at for what. Half of the anger is absurd, but I have to reorganize myself intellectually. I know rationally that I wouldn't have wanted to be raised by her—I might not have gone to college, or even survived in such a household—but part of me would like to have grown up with blood relatives. So I still feel some anger at my mother for messing up her life in such a way that she couldn't keep me."

Erica also went back into therapy for a while. "Now I'm evolving very positive growing, and in touch with results following that initial catatonic state. I feel I have permission for being my entire self. Heady, scary, challenging and strengthening. I take a great joy in my mother as a human being. She's no longer the terrible mythical figure that she was before I met her, and after. I see her, I can place her in context, it fits much better. Considering the climate of the times, I probably would have done a similar thing. I came to understand, after taking a trip with her back to her hometown, that giving up the girls and keeping the boys had something to do with her sense of worthlessness from her own mother."

17

Father–
The Mini-Search

And which of us shall find his father, know his face...
THOMAS WOLFE

To say that man has a mother is not to
deny that he has a father.
AFRICAN PROVERB

I met my father and he denied it.
Said he was in the navy at the time.

So what else is new?
AMERICAN ADOPTEES

Tracking down father is the last stage of the Search, but one does not usually embark on it until one has absorbed the reunion with the mother. Having expended so much energy on this first quest, the Adoptee does not have the psychic energy to pursue the father too quickly. Once again, time is a factor. It varies for everyone, but Adoptees seem to have a slower internal clock than others. Their friends often marvel that they can let months, even years, pass between one stage of a Search and another. Adam said that even his adoptive father was wondering why five years after finding his mother he had done nothing about tracing his birth father. It took me ten years before I could ask my mother who my father was. Yet I know of others who were ready for the hunt after a few months.

152

I call the quest for the father the Mini-Search.

One is ready to take on father when one realizes that to be whole one needs the *whole* family tree. Also, if one has been disappointed in Mom, one may have more luck with Dad. He may still live up to the fantasies. But it's a big risk too. If he denies responsibility, it can be a bitter disappointment—a confirmation that one is really cut off from one's origins.

It is the last chance.

The name of the birth father is seldom on the birth certificate, or even in the agency record. Only one person knows, the birth mother, and often she will not tell the Adoptee. Either she is bitter about the past, or does not want to reexperience the pain of his rejection. She behaves as if her uttering the name of the man who was the cause of everything—the loss of her reputation, the loss of the baby, the subsequent depression—might resurrect him on the spot.

In his autobiography, *Because I Was Flesh*, Edward Dahlberg describes his mother's recalcitrance when he asks his father's name:

> She sat immovable. No grave was more silent than she, and no matter what words and sounds I made, she did not move. I stared at her helplessly, for she was a terrible headstone, without an epitaph, from which no secret could be wrung.

A mother's reticence about the birth father often depends upon the degree of resentment she harbors toward him. It is rare for her to still be in touch with him, but Jackie learned that her mother and her mother's husband had been playing poker with her father and his wife every Saturday night for the past twenty years. When her mother invited her to lunch with him at her apartment, Jackie flew up for the occasion. It proved to be a much more rewarding luncheon than that first one when she and her mother had not even recognized each other:

> I was nervous as we waited for him. I was sitting on the couch when he sauntered in and sat down. I really liked the way he looked. He's slim and wiry, with pixie features. The kind of person I'm always attracted to. I said, "I'm Jackie." He and my mother started talking about me—Who does she look like? "She's got my chin," Helen said. "My eyes," he said. "Isn't she cute!" Helen added. "Hey, yeah, if she was a stranger, she'd be the kind I'd go for."
>
> That made me laugh. He was actually shy, but he had a

gentle, appealing way of talking. At lunch I toasted them, and thanked them for bringing me into the world. I felt seven years old. I felt they liked me. It was strange to meet your parents at thirty-five and find they approve of you. But more important, I learned that my mother had been telling the truth after all: not only had they been married, they had actually had a baby who died. Her parents forced her to annul the marriage after that, since they had never approved. But she continued to see him over the years. By the time she knew she was pregnant with me, he was already married to someone else.

I realized that theirs was a love story. "If we had lived in a different time, we'd still be married," Helen said. And he nodded in agreement. I got a different picture of her when he was there. She seemed soft now, and I realized that the toughness I had recoiled from before had been a defense for her pain. She had somehow confused the date of my birth with that of the first baby. When you think of it, giving me up was like having to bury two children. My coming back must have been both a joyous and a difficult thing. I was like the avenging angel, reminding her of what she'd done, and raising the possibilities of what might have been. I feel better about *her,* having met him. She was witty and ironic a good deal of the time, as if he still turned her on, made her feel alive. They even joked about their former marriage. "A shotgun wedding," my mother said merrily. "And a shotgun annulment," he added.

Jackie cannot visit her father's home, because he doesn't want his third wife to know about her. Nor can she visit Helen, whose adopted daughter has still not been told about her existence. But none of this bothers Jackie now. "I know the full story, and I feel better," she says. "It was unrealistic of me to expect Helen to tell me everything at that first meeting. You don't spill out such things to a total stranger. Everyone has to get over the shock of that initial encounter. Then you get to know each other as people."

A father's acceptance of the Adoptee often depends upon his past relationship with the mother. If they had once loved each other, even been married, as in Jackie's case, the father will probably respond warmly to the reunion. A woman whose father had hoped to marry her mother was overwhelmed by his eagerness to welcome her into his family of five sons. In fact, she worried he was only remembering her mother, and not seeing the real "me":

> He apologized for any anguish I had suffered due to the adoption. I can see that he wants to make up for any of that. I am amazed at his perception of the situation. If it is possible to have inherited parts of someone's personality, I think I have some proof. We have so many similarities that I am astounded. It is marvelous.

However, if the father hardly knew the mother, and was badgered by her family into making some kind of financial settlement, as Tony was to learn happened in his case, the reunion may not be a very warm one.

Tony found himself filled with ambivalance when he set out on the Mini-Search. For although it would seem that men might be more eager than women to find the father, it often proves to be quite the opposite. Perhaps it is male pride. For if it is true that every father wants to pass his life onto his children, particularly the son, then the male Adoptee must be painfully aware that his father opted out on this. Furthermore, he has been chosen to continue the adoptive family line.

Tony hesitated even after he had located his father's address in the neighboring town:

> I'm afraid of rejection from him more than my mother. I didn't expect to be rejected by her because I came from her womb and, you know, how can you reject something like that. But with my father ... I think I see it from his position—a one night stand, maybe. Or maybe he did love her, maybe they courted for a while. But maybe she was just running around. I mean, I don't know. This guy probably has no feelings about it at all. I was just another one of those things he left behind. He may have three or four other children. So I really fear rejection from him on the one hand, and on the other, I have no love feelings for him. I really think of him as the biological parent. He was just like the part of the experiment that was necessary for it to happen. She's the one that had to have me, had to arrange for everything. He didn't have to go through any part of that, so in a way, I don't think he's as guilty. I know that's terrible, but you see, he didn't make the *decision*. She made it. But yet I'm afraid of him. If he rejects me, I'll be angry—but I won't be emotionally hurt.

Tony's father neither rejected nor accepted him. On the phone he admitted he was the man involved in the affair, and agreed to meet Tony at his garage:

> We drove around for about forty-five minutes. I never did get to see him standing up. Right away he began shedding doubt: "I don't want to say it, but your mother was running around." Still he seemed friendly when he realized I didn't want anything, almost emotional. He answered questions, but didn't offer any information. I gave him my phone number, but he hasn't called these few months. I've really been down on this whole thing. That was the last straw, to have him not call back. Both my mother and father seem to feel the issue was settled thirty years before. I'm not a person. I don't exist. I wasn't angry before for them giving me up—my anger is for *now*.

The Macho Father

Margaret Mead reminded me that human fatherhood is a social invention, while motherhood is a palpable fact. She was referring to the fact that paternity has convenient loopholes—while it can be proven who the father is *not*, it cannot be proven who he is.

Not a few men take advantage of nature's ambiguities by denying their paternity. My father was one genre of this macho species —what we used to call a bounder, a cad, a heel. He had been turned on quickly during a date with my mother—he twenty-one, she sixteen—but turned off even more quickly when informed by her aunt that she was pregnant. He refused to marry her, even with the promise that it would be annulled immediately after.

If one wanted to be generous, one could say that men like my father are victims of their biology, too—in that they cannot control their prodigal sperm, sent forth in a moment of vacuous ardor—in that nature has not endowed them with enough imagination to project nine months hence when that impulsive union will emerge metamorphosed into a real live baby girl or boy, perhaps an exact replica of themselves.

I see my macho father and his type in the chimpanzee male who, having had his sport, is off to other parts of the forest.

I see my macho father in the irresponsible soldiers who spawned and are still spawning millions of babies in Japan, Korea, Thailand, Okinawa, Germany, wherever our troops are stationed throughout the world—babies they will leave and have left without names, without support, without caring, and without their families or governments holding them accountable.

And yet—I have sympathy for my father, too. He is dead, so I will never know how he would have received me. Those who were close to him say that his guilt may have accounted for the rage he carried within him all his life, and for his devotion to other people's children. In spite of myself, the part of me that yearned to see my father's face grieves for the macho father I will never know.

It should not be surprising that some macho fathers who denied both paternity and responsibility at the time of birth will still deny it when contacted by the Adoptee years later. A call to him could prove like the one Donna and her husband, Conrad, made after sleuthing around his hometown for his present whereabouts:

CONRAD: I am calling because I believe you are my wife's father.

FATHER: I expected your call. I received three calls from my friends back home yesterday.

CONRAD: I'm sorry if I have caused you any embarrassment.

FATHER: Don't worry. I couldn't get their attention while I lived there. I am delighted if they are standing around on street corners discussing me now.

CONRAD: In any case, I hope it doesn't shock you after all these years to find that you have a daughter.

FATHER: I've never been shocked by anything in my life. I've had paternity suits against me in Korea and Europe. What's the story?

CONRAD: My wife was born in Lima, Ohio, on February fourth. . . . I guess you know the year.

FATHER: Why should I know the year? I didn't know anything about this until yesterday.

CONRAD: Do you want to talk to her?

FATHER: Maybe I'll call her tomorrow. Oh, well, if she's there, put her on.

DONNA: Hello.

FATHER: Well . . . I guess you have found a father.

DONNA: I guess I have.

FATHER: You sound relieved.

DONNA: I am. Do you remember my mother?

FATHER: My lawyer wouldn't want me to answer that.

DONNA: Tell me something about yourself.

FATHER: I was in the Army. I was a speechwriter for General Van Fleet in Korea. I got the Purple Heart when the poker table collapsed on me. Anything else you want to know?

The Father Who Cares

There are, of course, situations where the relationships were so brief, the father did not even know about the pregnancy.

In his short story "The Child," Arturo Vivante writes about a man who has just made the discovery:

> He couldn't get over it. A daughter, fifteen months, whose existence he had never heard of or suspected. And he thought he was telepathic. No, it had never entered his mind, never occurred to him. The pregnancy, the delivery, all had happened without his being even remotely aware of it. . . . The diaper was moist on his forearm, and soon she was so heavy his arm began to ache, but he didn't mind. She sat heavily now, comfortably, sensing his strength. He wondered if she had ever seen such hairy arms or such black hair. Probably not, not so close at any rate. She looked at him, kept looking at him. And he, he felt one with her, part of the same substance.

Erica had not expected that her father would fall into this category:

> After the years it took me to find my mother, it seems ironic that only a few hours were required to find him. But best of all, his response. He couldn't be more thrilled, even though, or perhaps because, he never knew I existed before. He lives in Boise, has five children, and was in the Navy for twenty years. He's called me almost every day. He's very warm and open about the whole thing, even called my mother, which flipped her back to the summer of '46.

Research studies are beginning to show that the birth father is a much maligned figure. Far from being a "swinger," or the older man who seduced the young girl, he was usually the same age and social level—sometimes he was the boy next door.[1] His dependency on his own family often made it difficult for him to accept responsibility. He may have been advised by his parents to deny paternity rather than risk a large financial settlement. Or it might have been the girl who refused marriage, even when the boy was willing, because she was not ready to settle down. In that case, she might have been the one who insisted on adoption as the solution for the baby to have a family life, while she had her freedom.

There are some instances where the "putative" father, as he is called, has actually gone to court to gain custody of a baby born out of wedlock. Because one such father, Peter Stanley, took his case all the way to the Supreme Court to gain custody of his children after his common-law wife died, an unwed father, like other fathers, is now entitled to a hearing on his fitness before his children can be taken away from him.[2]

However, some fathers have tried to take the law into their own hands. On February 12, 1977, a man with a sawed-off shotgun made the headlines when he barged into a home for unwed mothers in Cincinnati, Ohio, and demanded the whereabouts of the son he and his wife had given up twenty-three years before. He was finally tricked into letting his pregnant hostages go fifteen hours later when a police officer, impersonating the son, spoke to him outside the barricaded door. One could not help feeling relieved for this man's hostages, but the lie about the lost son seemed but one more callous deception in the adoption system.

The Missing Father

A birth father's disappearance does not always indicate his indifference. There are some who have suffered psychic wounds from the experience, just as the woman did.

When Jean learned that her father had left town before she was born, and had never been heard of since, she spent a year-and-a-half blanketing the country with tracers, while researching his origins "all the way back to the Norman Conquest." One of her letters, to a motor vehicle department in the South, finally paid off with his present address.

Her father acknowledged her written request to visit by return mail, but just before she was to leave, his wife called to warn her not to be disturbed by his appearance. He had been an alcoholic for thirty-four years, that is, from the time of her birth.

In the airport when I saw him and shook hands, I felt shock waves rolling over me. Although he was only 54, he looked more like 70. His face was lined and leathery. He had white hair, but since he didn't like that, he shaved it, making him seem bald. But when I looked into his eyes, there I was. I was looking in my mirror. His eyes were all that I could establish connection with, since the years of drinking had obviously ravaged him. Still, over the next few days he reached back through the alcohol-fogged years and dredged things up for me out of the past. He said that he had not thought about these things in many, many years. I felt like I was waking up Rip Van Winkle. Later I heard from his wife that he is now writing his relatives for the first time in over thirty years and is talking about visiting some of them. I apparently had some effect on him.

Fathers, too, it seems, can find catharsis when the past is laid to rest.

The Ambivalent Father

Some men, like some birth mothers, may deny at first, admit later, but behave ambivalently, as if they would like to forget it ever happened.

When Susan contacted her father by phone in the Midwest, his first words were "I am not your father." Still he agreed to meet with her when he came East on a business trip the next month. He was charming then, a dapper man in an expensive business suit, leather briefcase, and all. He handed her the letter he had not mailed, which admitted knowing about her. He promised to tell his wife and two sons when he returned home, and to send her a present.

As it turned out, he did none of these. She wrote him. No answer. She called him at his office, and always he promised things which he never delivered. And always she kept coming back for more rejections, as if she believed that he would begin behaving as a *real* father should. The last excuse he gave her for not telling his family was that his sister had just died after a long illness, and he was making preparations for the funeral.

When I met Susan she had just bought a ticket for that small town. She was going to go "incognito" to the funeral. Did I think it was a good idea? I didn't. I worried that she would be spotted as the "outsider" there, and if her identity were revealed, it would be as the "bastard." There was the danger her father might never forgive her for exposing him on such an occasion. I suggested that the funeral was her aunt's moment of tribute, and she should wait for another, hopefully more felicitous, occasion, to meet the family.

For the next twenty-four hours Susan agonized over this decision. "They are my relatives, too," she argued, more with herself than with me. "I want to see them, share this with them."

It was as if her father's mercurial charm had captivated Susan, as it once had her mother. Her adoptive experience as an only child had been a difficult one, mainly because of that mother's recurring mental breakdowns. Her birth mother, divorced, a loner, had showed little initiative in establishing a relationship. Susan needed to believe that her father might still supply what was missing.

At the last minute she did not fly out to the funeral, but spoke of going out "unannounced" another time. During this period she left her job, spoke vaguely of future plans, but remained immobilized, as if deferring life itself.

> I can't come to terms with it. I keep feeling I am an orphan. I feel sadness first, and then rage. When rage takes over, I get migraine headaches. All I want to do is eat, sleep, and read children's books. I know I've got to grow up, handle my own life, even if it means going through this. But last night I felt I was going to die. I felt it was the end of all things. I felt I was going crazy. My mind was slipping from me. I can't help believing that the natural mother and father are the most important people in your life. A tie that cannot be broken— that's what life is all about—life and death.

Perhaps hoping to break the impasse with her father, Susan picked up the phone one night and called his oldest son, whose number she found through information. He refused to believe that she was his sister, and hung up on her.

That too was devastating.

"I'm still not sorry I did it," she told me later. "I have a right to meet my half-brothers. They are blood relatives, aren't they?"

18

Siblings

They locked into each other
like brother & sister,
long-lost relations,
orphans divided by time.
ERICA JONG, "The Puzzle"

O ne of the unexpected bonuses of the Search is the acquisition
of brothers and sisters, especially when the relationship with
the parents has proven disappointing. It is possible that
Susan's brother would have responded to her call had she been
acknowledged by the father. When the Adoptee is introduced
by a parent, siblings usually welcome having a new member of
the family. Being closer in age, they often have much in common.
The relationship can be simpler, too, uncomplicated by past
history.

Here is a letter from an Adoptee's nineteen-year-old half-sister,
received shortly after she had contacted their mother:

I just found out about you a few weeks ago. And Mama told
me the story of you, and how she would have given anything
to have kept you. Mama told me when she was fifteen she fell
in love with a man older than her, got pregnant, wanted to
marry the man, but my grandmother and grandfather wouldn't
see it. They made her give you up. She told me while she was
pregnant if someone came to the house they would make her
hide under beds, in closets, etc. Mama said that grandma and
grandpa got the man on statutory rape. And he was driven
from the county. I believe everything my mother told me because I knew my grandparents and what they were like. My
grandmother was a stubborn woman, everything went her way

or no way at all. She never showed anybody any love. And she didn't care about anyone's feelings but her own. Mama's had a hard life. I think you are her dream come true. I want you to know you will be welcome in Mama's home until the day she dies. She told me that in the last thirty-seven years you've been in most of her dreams and always in her heart. Please write.
Your found sister

Occasionally the sibling resents the Adoptee as an intruder, a competitor for the mother's affections. Brian learned that his sister was angry at her mother for not having confided in her, and at him for upstaging her in the family circle. Another woman was shunned by her half-sister, who complained to the mother: "Why does she need you? She has a husband and four children while I have no one but you."

It is usually a great relief to the birth mother when her children welcome the Adoptee. It is an acceptance of her, too, as well as a forgiveness. However, when the siblings show their jealousy, the mother often becomes torn in her allegiances, and may feel more comfortable excluding the Adoptee from her everyday life.

Adoptees who find that the birth parents were married to each other at the time of the relinquishment or shortly afterward are usually upset. They cannot help but resent that they were the one given up while the other children were kept. Why me? they ask themselves. On the other hand, the mother's children may envy the Adoptee for being better educated and having gotten a better start in life.

Sometimes the birth mother refuses to tell her other children about the Adoptee. It is somehow embarrassing to have to admit this sexual role to them, as well as reveal the fact that she has surrendered a child.

What is the Adoptee who has been yearning for brothers and sisters to do? Many, like Susan, insist they have a right to know their siblings, whether the mother approves or not. Everything in them resists being pushed back to the other side of the veil— treated as if they are once again the invader they were in her womb. Their insistence on being admitted into the family circle is a cry of "I exist! I exist!"

Does the Adoptee have a moral right to defy the birth mother's wishes?

This is a question to which there may be no moral answer. We can say that the birth parents owe us our story, but not necessarily entrance into the life they have made for themselves—just as they do not have a right to intrude against our wishes into our adoptive family relationships. But the right to meet one's siblings may depend upon each individual circumstance.

In my case, my unmarried half-brother still lives with my mother, and to interject myself into his life would be to disturb hers. And so I have not. However, I do not know what I would do were he living down the block from me, or if I felt that because of similar professions, we had a lot in common.

Ideally, we might hope that the birth mother could be persuaded over time that it would enrich her children's lives for them to know each other. But once she digs into her position, this seldom happens.

I know one woman who has managed to become a friend of her half-sister's without revealing their relationship. "It would serve no purpose to tell her now," she says. "It might cause conflict between them. But I will tell her when our mother dies."

Many Adoptees speak of looking up their siblings after the mother's death. But considering that often not too many years separate them from the birth parents, everyone may be a geriatric basket case by the time these sibling meetings take place.

A Touch of Incest

> Of such, one may almost say, that the world is
> not theirs, nor the world's laws.
> JANE AUSTEN, *Emma*

The fear of incest is something that many Adoptees have experienced while growing up. Like Freud's *exceptions,* they feel outside the mainstream of society—as if they were throwaways for whom it didn't matter. Some of them fear they will unknowingly commit incest with a brother or sister. A few reported engaging in sexual relations with adopted siblings in early adolescence, using the justification that they were not really related.

I've heard Adoptees wonder if they would be physically attracted to their mothers or fathers when they found them. Both men and women expressed the wish to see the naked bodies of those original parents, almost in the spirit of scientific investigation. But something else is also at play in this voyeuristic desire. Shades of Oedipus (the most magnificent of all exceptions) hang over us. Not having worked through incestuous feelings that blood-related people deal with in their everyday contacts, Adoptees worry that they will be overwhelmed by the mere physical presence of someone who shares their genes.

None of the Adoptees I've interviewed reported physical attraction to the adoptive parents, although a few women were aware of the father's seductive manner toward them.

But siblings of either sex often seem drawn to each other physically, like magnets. One sees them holding hands, embracing, or hugging each other frequently. Usually there is an innocence about it—like children clutching each other, so as not to become lost again. Yet sometimes the intensity of the attraction can be so strong that they can be overwhelmed by it.

Jackie was astounded at the attraction she felt toward her father's son when she looked him up, even though she had heard through mutual friends that he was gay. It was not only her imagination that an electricity seemed to be passing between them. Her husband, present at that meeting, admitted later that he felt jealous of the mutuality and enjoyment they were finding in one another.

"I felt irresistibly, magnetically drawn," Jackie told me. "My body reaction was to move toward him. I wanted eye contact. I liked what I saw. Because he was like me. We made ribald jokes like 'We'll go to Florida and tell our father we're going to get married!' At the time I felt exhilarated, like we're going to get revenge on our birth parents."

Jackie will never know what that meeting meant to her brother. It must have frightened him in some way he found impossible to deal with. Although he promised to come for Thanksgiving dinner, he never showed up. And when she rang his number a few days later, a voice she recognized as his snapped "wrong number." She was positive he knew who it was. For a while her passion turned to fury toward this brother who was deserting her by withdrawing, just as his father had once done with her mother.

Trudy reported feeling the same attraction to her half-brother, Leonard, four years older than she. Both of them are unmarried and confess to never before having been able to find anyone they felt totally satisfied with—intellectually, emotionally, sexually. Leonard had experimented with some bisexuality, but was living alone when they met.

"I felt attracted to him as a man," Trudy said. "He was articulate, assertive, everything I admired. He told me that he felt more like a lover than a brother, and asked me if I had ever thought about incest. We talked about it a lot, how it operates in families when kids are growing up, but that we hadn't grown up together. And we discussed the danger of trying a physical relationship, that it could damage what we had together now."

Nevertheless, Trudy agreed to meet with Leonard in the South on their spring vacation.

"This time I noticed he seemed to be avoiding me," she said. "We didn't discuss incest openly, though there was some innuendo in our speech. For instance, Leonard said things like 'With our luck, if we made love, you'd get pregnant.'

"I knew he'd been thinking a lot about it, and that he didn't touch me because of the social taboo. But my feelings were somewhat different. Socially, I don't give a damn. The reason I am resisting making love to Leonard is because I think that I would fall in love with him completely, and it would be too frustrating knowing we couldn't have children. I guess it just couldn't be a healthy relationship."

Still she added, "Incest is very romantic. Like making love to yourself. You know, flesh of my flesh."

Greg, now in his mid-thirties, has known his full sister for one year. Right after he was born his father divorced their mother, and in desperation she put him up for adoption, while keeping her two-year-old daughter. "If we had met under other circumstances, we would have been lovers," he told me. "I am deeply in love with her. The only thing that prevents our having relations is the fact that it would be incest. Intellectually, emotionally, it's like we're stamped out of the same cookie cutter. The same taste in dressing, cooking, the same pictures on the wall. She starts a sentence, I finish it. We live in different parts of the country, but I'm in touch with her all the time through telepathy. I called her this morning and said, 'You're not feeling well, are you?' She wasn't."

What are we to make of this attraction? Can we say that it is the attraction toward the *double,* each seeing the sibling as some extension of the self? I think of Narcissus falling in love with his reflection in the stream. And of Lord Byron's passion for his half-sister Augusta.

Can we say that, having been cast out of the natural flow of generativity, Adoptees as outsiders feel less bound by the taboos that inhibit others? That having broken the taboo of searching, the fear of other taboos no longer intimidates them?

Or is it that the romanticism Adoptees feel toward the blood tie is eroticized when they meet the sibling of the opposite sex? Perhaps it is that need for physical bonding, a yearning to merge, to belong completely, in a way that one learns is not possible with either birth parent.

19

The Unsuspecting Spouse

Sometimes I feel sorry for the men and women who unwittingly marry Adoptees. How can they know that locked within this winsome partner is the waif who can never completely trust, and perhaps not even love—the *searcher* who may one day wake up to his or her need. Even the Adoptee does not know, until it is too late.

I was fortunate in that my husband had empathy for my need to know my origins and shared every stage of the Search with me. However, I have heard of husbands and wives who feel threatened by their mate's sudden self-absorption, their disappearing alone into a territory where they cannot follow. The phantom parent can even assume the dimensions of a rival since he or she is draining off so much of the Adoptee's emotions.

Some marriage partners identify with their in-laws and believe the Adoptee is being ungrateful to them. Others, not close to their own families, may try to belittle the quest. A few get tired of the subject upstaging them for so long and take lovers as a way of reasserting their own needs.

Adoptees who get support from their spouses find that their marriages are strengthened. It is liberating to be able to express their dreams and fears without guilt. The spouse becomes a protector, who goes into battle for the Adoptee, righting past wrongs. As one husband said, "How can I not be involved? I'm in the fall-out area."

In his book *Jody,* Jerry Hulse describes searching for the mother of his wife as she lay desperately ill in the hospital—her life depending on the medical information he would find. During this difficult time, Hulse thinks of his original attraction to Jody: "She was different from other girls I'd known. She was quiet and withdrawn with an innocence that was rare even in the winter of '41. I promised myself that someday I would marry her."

Adoptees often have an innocence and fragility that non-adopted people are attracted to, without understanding the source. Jerry did note that Jody's folks thought she was the kind of girl who needed a lot of protection, who needed parents, not boyfriends—or a husband. The irony was perfect—yes, Jody needed parents—more than anyone could have guessed.

> Later, after we were married, I would hear her beside me at night, sobbing softly, and I knew what it was. The old nightmare. Everyone had run away and left her alone again. Occasionally she'd dream a happy dream in which her mother held her in her arms and she felt warm and loved and wanted. But when she waked it was always the same, a vague melancholy, a longing.

Husbands and wives may rise to heroic dimensions in trying to ease the pain of their spouse's suffering. We have already seen what happened when Conrad contacted Donna's macho father, but that was nothing compared to the ordeal he went through trying to devise a strategy to get her mother to acknowledge her. After their letters went unanswered, Conrad thought he and Donna might try to confront her outside her husband's medical office, where they had reason to believe she worked part-time. The problem was to learn her schedule.

Conrad did this part of the sleuthing alone, to spare Donna the tension:

> The two vigils at his office yielded only the sight of *him,* getting out of his car. Now I thought I would wait for my wife's mother to leave her home. I saw his car and two others parked in front of their house. I followed a man who drove off in one

of the cars, saw in passing that he was young, and returned to the house. Soon the husband came out, made a U-turn in his car. I waited a while, did the same. My wife's mother was standing in the door: taller and of bigger frame than I had thought, and quite gray. After my U-turn, I passed the house again. She was gazing at me, I looked squarely at her for a brief moment; I thought, "she knows." Rare opportunity. I needed only to press a bell, she's there, probably no one else in the house, why not go up to her. But I felt it would be wrong. I only wanted to see her—it was Donna's turn to face her.

My mission accomplished, I meant to drive home. On the highway, I saw the husband's now-familiar car in front of me. I had not looked at him. I passed him several times, had the best look yet at him. He had come without a jacket, a fact I had instantly registered, but ignored. He never looked left or right. He took a turnoff. I thought he knew a shortcut, so I turned too. We were now on country roads. Before I knew it, he drove into the state police station, parked and went in. A sign said "DEAD END." I knew what was up, so I turned around and stepped on the gas. Not fast enough. I was stopped by a trooper. "The attorney thinks you were following him. Do you know him?" "No." "You want to explain to me?" "No." "Then I have to take you to the station." On the steps I saw him. "Good morning," I said. We went inside and sat on benches in the hall.

I began like this: "I believe my wife is the daughter of your wife." He said: "That does not make a difference to me, or to my wife." He did not seem to know of such a daughter, but he showed no excitement. I, however, with the police stoppage, had butterflies in the stomach. He did not even dispute, or examine. The only slight reaction he showed was when I mentioned his wife's name: that seemed to clinch it for him. He said quietly: "I shall not permit an upset to my wife nor her children." He reiterated this, stressing the *permit*, and I said I would not permit that either. He took down my name, address, telephone number, name of Donna's father. He also said: "For any further talk, you call me, and nobody else."

He said he would live with this, and let me know in a few weeks. He offered to show me the way back to New Jersey, and I followed him.

A few days later Donna called him to say she was sorry

if she had caused him any trouble. Apparently he had been ready to call me, for he read her a statement—to stop her fantasies and hallucinations. He had spoken with his wife. To desist from further contacts. Donna was so upset. As for myself, I was totally exhausted when I heard. I knew the time had come to look into the future and not to manipulate the past anymore. We couldn't go on like this. It was self-preservation. Well, at least we had to stop for now.

As we have seen, it is often the wife who awakens the husband to his need to know the heritage of their children. She is amazed that he has so little curiosity on the subject, and finds herself stirring him up whenever she gets the chance. She may do the necessary research while he is at work, and even attend Adoptee search meetings for him.

However, some women, like Tony's wife, may begin to regret the quest once their husbands become obsessed with it. They had not suspected the depths of emotions that would be released, and the endless preoccupation with it—that it would cause their husbands to relive the repressed childhood pain and fury. At times it seems they have been dropped for another woman—a woman they resent for failing their husbands twice, as babies and now—a woman whose mystery is too deep to compete with, and whose influence they will have to wait out, but for how long?

20

Aftermath: The Restless Pulse

After ten years of terror in searching the way home to
Ithaca, Odysseus found that it did not calm the
restless Pulse within him.
LOREN EISELEY

Just as it is hard to pinpoint that moment when a search actually begins, so it is hard to know when it ends. Is it over after
one finds one's mother or father? After one is united with
siblings? After one has met grandparents, more distant relatives?
Is it ever over? Or is it as Robert Lowell once said of life: "In the
end there is no end, the thread frays rather than being cut."

Many Adoptees find that the Search has become a way of life,
a compulsion, a habit that can't be broken, as if the repressed ener-
gies, once unleashed, cannot be reharnessed. They behave like
runners who have overshot the goal: the momentum cannot be
turned off.

Anticipating this, Tony had told me, "I'm concerned that
when I find my father, it's the end. The search has been an exciting thing for me. I don't want it to be over."

Some Adoptees busy themselves by searching for relatives of
relatives. Brian spoke of possibly searching for other illegitimate
children his father *might* have had. Many throw themselves into
the searches of others as a way of reliving the excitement of their
own quest. Searching has become a metaphor for a life of explora-

172

tion. It may be desperate and compulsive, but it is a time when one feels totally alive, liberated from the mundane concerns of everyday existence.

None of the Adoptees I interviewed were sorry they had searched, no matter how difficult their journey. Erica might have been speaking for them all when she said: "It has been the most liberating experience of my life." And Ernest Becker's words are applicable here: "If there is tragic limitation in life there is also possibility. What we call maturity is the ability to see the two in some kind of balance into which we can fit creatively."[1]

We might say the tragic limitation is that Adoptees have become mortal. One who was never born need never die—but once they have traced their birth, even held the certificate, Adoptees know they must die like everyone else. They are cast down from mythic heights; they are no longer magical.

But the possibilities are there, too. One realizes that, as in fairy tales, one has to give up something for the privilege of becoming human. Just as the little mermaid had to experience pain and accept dying in order to become a mortal whom the prince might love, the Adoptee has to take on mortality when he or she finds the birth parent.

For all the suffering, Adoptees find that it is a relief to be part of the human condition. Those who, until now, felt bypassed and abandoned, can now allow themselves, in Erikson's terms, to be *chosen* and *confirmed*. They can dare to give love, and to receive it in turn. Having actively mastered what they had passively suffered, they are resurrected as their own person. They can know their strengths are of their own making, rather than deriving from that phantom mother and father.

We can say that maturity comes when we can accept the complexities and ambiguities of our situation and make them work for us, rather than against us—and go on.

It comes when we can enjoy the positive side of being adopted —not being entrapped by roots as others are. When we realize that our sense of not belonging has given us the freedom to move easily from one world to another, rather than being "nailed down to a life without escape," as a nonadopted friend expressed it. We have the satisfaction of knowing that we have mastered our fate on both the immediate and ultimate levels. The immediate— what Lionel Tiger calls the Little Optimism (you'll make the bus), and the ultimate—the Big Optimism (you'll get to heaven).[2] Now the Adoptee knows he'll make the bus and get to heaven, too.

It comes when we can see our quest as but another of the many searches for meaning that all people must take: it is the search of the artist for images; of the scientist for the possible; of the philosopher for meaning; of the astronomer for infinity. Its lack of conclusiveness is its universality. It is the painter Raphael Soyer writing in his journal at the age of seventy-six, "I'm still trying to understand . . . to what purpose is the journey." It is Blanche DuBois's last line in *A Streetcar Named Desire*: "Whoever you are—I have always depended on the kindness of strangers." It is Edward Lear converting tragedy to so-called nonsense:

> Calico Pie,
>   The little Birds fly
> Down to the calico tree,
>   Their wings were blue,
>   And they sang "Tilly-loo!"
>   Till away they flew, —
>   And they never came back to me!
>   They never came back!
>   They never came back!
>   They never came back to me!

It is knowing how to laugh at yourself:

ADOPTEE: I finally feel at peace.

HUSBAND: You just lost your status as an orphan.

ME: Why don't we know who we are after we find them?

HUSBAND: Even the nonadopted don't know who they are. You Adoptees ask for the moon.

Part Three

ROOTS and WINGS

There are only two lasting bequests we can give our children—one is roots, the other wings.
POPULAR SAYING

Adoptees need both sets of parents if they are to have roots and wings.
A BIRTH MOTHER

21

Taking Wing

Adoptees who have taken the journey through Search and Reunion know that what is lost can be found, but never fully recovered. It comes back to us in new forms, but never in the shape of what might have been. And though we feel complete in knowing our story, in being grounded, we cannot say that the integrating process is ever concluded. It may take the lifetime left to absorb. Additional insights will catch us at unexpected moments, like light throwing new patterns on a familiar water view. Flashes of the old depression will repossess us when we least expect it. The childhood weeping, of which Proust speaks, remains with us "like those convent bells which are so well masked by the town noises during the day that one thinks they have stopped, but begin to sound again in the silence of the evening."

Not until death claims all the characters, and not even then, will the impact of our drama be over. It will live on in our sons and daughters because it influences their heritage. The children I leave behind are the offspring of a woman who bequeathed them not one, but two family trees, neither of which she could fully claim as her own.

But she left them *roots*, without which they could not have wings.

22

Telling the Adoptive Parents

S ome Adoptees feel that they cannot truly have wings until they tell their adoptive parents about their reunion experience and receive their sanction. But this is sometimes more difficult than the decision to search. Where the message has always been: "We are your only parents," how do you confess that you have found those others?

Obviously such news could be devastating, or the adoptive parents would not have turned off the communication channels years before. Their terror of such a confrontation is akin to the Adoptee's terror. The irony is that just as the adoptive parents once had to steel themselves to tell the child he was adopted, the child now has to steel himself to tell the adoptive parents what he has done.

Adoptees differ on how best to do this.

"Adoptive parents should be led gently to the disclosure that their child has decided to search," one woman advised. Another said, "I eased into the discussion on the broad topic of adoption over a period of a few months. I think they were prepared for it. They knew I was loyal. And though they didn't quite understand, they knew I had to do it."

Many Adoptees put off telling the adoptive parents for some indeterminate future time. Some never tell, fearing that their parents could not possibly understand. I was one of these. It seems a kindness to keep silent. But others may not tell out of deep resentment about the secrecy of their parents while they were growing up. They do not want to lose the autonomy they have so painfully worked for by sharing this with them now.

Those who can confide this secret usually find that it is a great relief to their parents to realize that their children are still around, that they haven't deserted the ship. The parents are also surprised to see how relaxed the Adoptee is. "If I had known how happy it would make him, I would have insisted that he search years before," said one mother who had been through a difficult adolescence with her son.

The Adoptee is also relieved. Brian does not believe he could have handled the guilt if he had not told his parents. "One should delay the Search if necessary to give the adoptive parents time to come to terms with their feelings," he said. "In the long run, it's easier for everyone. It takes a lot to get through to the realization that there is life after the Search—that the parents won't lose the child, and the child won't lose the adoptive relationship."

Jackie's parents had reacted with predictable panic when she informed them she was searching. Her mother made remarks like "She may want to reclaim you," even though Jackie was in her mid-thirties. But after Jackie called to tell them that she had met her mother, it was her turn to feel panic: "My adoptive mother was so different on her next visit with me. Instead of being critical and competing with me for my son's attention, she was almost formal—as if she respected me. She said nice things, like how well I looked. Even my husband noticed her change."

Jackie found that instead of enjoying the shift, she feared the direction it was taking. However stormy the former relationship, at least it was familiar. Now it was almost as if her critical mother had withdrawn from her, and a kindly stranger had taken her place—as if her mother had a new kind of secret to hold over her. What was she really thinking? Had she forgiven her for searching? Did she still look upon her as her daughter? This overly possessive mother, now defused, lacked the passion of any kind of caring, even the negative kind, and Jackie felt rejected. "I think maybe it's better not to tell the adoptive parents," she told me at that time. "It's like telling your husband you have a lover. You can't expect them to accept it. Something has to change."

And yet, in the long run, things do not really change that much. Nor do people. Adoptees are discovering that after an initial outburst of anger or hysteria, adoptive parents often revert back to that same denial mechanism that has been operating all along. Many never refer to the incident again. If they don't talk about it, they can believe it never happened.

On her next visit, Jackie's mother did not mention anything about what they had been through, and was her old critical self. Jackie was so relieved, she didn't even mind.

Karla, on the other hand, is bothered that her mother never refers to the fact that she has found her birth mother. She feels her mother's silence as a flaw in the relationship. "By not talking about the Search, she is denying a part of me—like she is disenfranchising me. As if she's saying she doesn't think my search had value. It's a carryover from adolescence, keeping a part of yourself to yourself. I cannot accept that it's back in the closet."

Many Adoptees feel closer to their adoptive parents after reunion. One woman found her adoptive mother was the only one she could turn to in the midst of her turmoil:

> For years I couldn't decide whether to search or not because I wanted to wait until my adoptive parents died. But now I'm glad I've done it. It's a tremendous relief knowing that my adoptive mother is still around. That she's always there. If I had waited for her to die, then I wouldn't have had her now when I need her.

Much of the tension that has been in the adoptive relationship falls away if the Adoptee can share the experience with the parents. One woman, who never felt close to them while growing up because she was aware of their physical differences, could now see both her mother and father in a positive light.

> I was able to accept them for themselves, and I could accept myself as being different. It was okay for it to be that way. I realized how glad I was to have had them as parents. They gave me music lessons from the age of six and the discipline to practice. I learned that it is because of them, and not an inheritance from my birth parents, that my life is entirely involved with music.

Another woman felt that this improvement in the adoptive relationship was worth the whole effort of the search.

> Once my parents broke down and gave me the information, they were on my team, and I kept them abreast of all the events leading to my reunion with my natural family. They were thrilled with the results. They are closer to me than ever—in fact, my father is warm and approving of me now, where he was always cold and sarcastic before. This was the biggest unexpected reward I got from the search.

No matter how they receive the news of the search, most adoptive parents do not want to meet the birth parents. Even the adoptive father who wrote his son, "We shared you when you got married, we can share you again," could not do the sharing in person. Adoptees understand this reluctance on their parents' part, but a few, like John, are disappointed. "A reunion isn't a reunion until *everyone* meets," he told me. He has a close relationship with his birth mother, who has no other children, but feels guilty when he is with her. "I feel split this way," he said. "I'd feel better if my adoptive parents knew her."

Those adoptive parents who also have biological children seem less threatened by the Search, and sometimes agree to visit the birth parents.

Trudy, whose parents had three children after adopting her, feels she would have searched much earlier if she had known how secure her parents would be.

> I was willing to sacrifice finding my biological mother rather than risk hurting my parents. That's where therapy really helped. I learned I was treating myself like a child. I had always discussed problems with my mother, so why not this problem? And my mother was delighted with the idea of my search. She called the agency to get background information for me, and even petitioned the court. Together with Dad she went to dinner at my birth mother's house. It went very well. "Thank you for doing a wonderful job," my birth mother said. "It was our pleasure," replied my adoptive mother. And then she told her what I was like as a child, fussy eater and all that. And my birth mother said, "My second son was, too." They kept on like that all evening.

By sharing her search, Trudy's parents were also able to share her struggle to integrate the birth mother into her life. For although the found parents prove not to be *strangers*, as they've often been called, neither are they parents in the nurturing sense of that word. As yet the relationship has no name and, like a vestigial organ, no function. The birth mother or father is more than a friend, less than a parent. As Trudy put it:

> I feel they're not my family, but *special*. I did feel guilty about seeing my bio mother at first. I felt if I saw one, I had to see the other. My adoptive mother said it was natural I would seek my birth mother out, since I didn't know her well. But I don't visit her so much now that I'm beginning to know her as a person. I had wanted someone educated, doing interesting work, and I had to admit she disappointed me; that I must accept her for what she is. My adoptive mother is independent and assertive, while she's passive and dependent on her husband for everything.

We see that the birth mother often has little more in common with the Adoptee than that shared moment of birth and separation, and that adoptive parents who can take the journey back to that moment and connect with their child's reconnection will reenforce their own parental relationship. For Adoptees cannot truly claim their adoptive mothers and fathers until they have claimed themselves and the people from whom they spring.

23

The Chosen Parents

If we are to understand why it has been so hard for adoptive parents to accept their children's need to know, we must go back in time, back to those people making up the chosen-baby stories, and see the difficulty they had in admitting they were not the *real* or *blood* parents.

For they, too, were "chosen," by the same social workers, doctors, and lawyers who decided the baby's fate. Contrary to their stories about that "cast of thousands," they took the solitary baby chosen for them by those go-betweens. They had no more choice in matching than the baby. In fact, they had spent years of frustration trying to conceive their own, years measured by monthly cycles and temperature charts.

In his tragicomedy *Ashes,* David Rudkin records the tribulations of one such English couple:

> (*In darkness, loud* ALARM CLOCK *on speakers. Screen fully drawn. Sounds of walking, shifting,* CUT ALARM.)
> ANNE (*Yawning, unseen beyond screen*): God, what an hour. Why so early?
> COLIN (*Yawning, unseen there*): Specimen, love.
> ANNE: Mm?
> COLIN: Specimen. We have to provide a characteristic sample of our mixture. Fresh.
> ANNE (*Miserable, tired*): Oh, fuck—
> COLIN: Something like that.

ANNE: I'll have to have a pee. (*Anne heard stumbling away off beyond screen.*) Put 'fire on, love.

COLIN (*Grumbles, moving*): Mouth like a bloody parrot cage ... (*Slow* DIM GLOW *as of electric barfire beyond screen: form of* COLIN *before it.* LOUD ON SPEAKERS: *urine trickling into water; rip, scuff of tissue paper; chain pulled.*) Romantic.

The couple manage to conceive, only to lose the baby in a miscarriage. Now they are bona fide candidates for a trip to the adoption agency where they, like all prospective parents, are put through grueling interviews in which they must reveal financial, psychological, and sexual intimacies. In the play, Anne and Colin encounter the English equivalent of our Mrs. Barker.

SOCIAL SERVICES OFFICER (*Gentle, absolute, enshrining a hardness: He must prepare his hearers for the worst.*): We, in the Authority, realize you come to us as a last resort. We accept that. You have discovered for yourselves, there is no "host of unwanted children" awaiting adoption: This application you have lodged with us is thus virtually your last chance for parenthood of any kind. If then, as I speak, you are furtively assessing these other couples' chances against us as against your own, that is only understandable. For you know this is not a rivalry so much between you; and yet you know also—if not, you are not ready for adoption—to adopt means, not to find a child you think suits you, but for us the County to find a home we think right for the child. Thus in the nature of things we can never say yes to you all. . . . You must be prepared, for prolonged and deep investigation: medical, professional, financial, marital. You will flinch from this inquisition; at times feel laid out on our slab just once too often. Appreciate our reasons. Nor is it pleasant for us, submitting a man's or woman's deepest motives to dissection.

That there are always ways to beat any game—even this one— we learn in Rael Jean Isaac's *Adopting a Child Today*, which gives prospective parents twenty-eight suggestions on how to outwit the social worker—a tip sheet worthy of a satirical novel, if not a musical comedy. To mention just a few of the ways to avoid "The Major Sources of Danger": use the pronoun "we" instead of "I," for it means you are a team; say you get on well with parents and relatives, but not so well that you arouse her suspicions; speak of a happy childhood, but not too happy; an active social life, but not too active; be reconciled to your infertility, but regret it a little; admit to intercourse twice a week, a wholesome amount, but not excessive; do not indicate too much preference for a boy or girl, nor any desperate need for a child. And this above all—be "relaxed, self-searching, and unguarded."[1]

Those couples who went through the ordeal and were fortunate enough to pass bore the social-work stamp of approval— "super parents." The adoption papers were their diploma.

But something in these couples must have suspected that they were not so "super," that in some way they were still defective. They had to take the child they were offered, rather than choose one, and they had to accept the limited family background they were given, rather than all the facts they might have wanted. Adoptive applicants were never supplied with information that might be considered too damaging for them to know. Those who were too curious were in danger of being considered "anxious, narcissistic and unconsciously sadistic," good candidates for psychiatric treatment rather than parenthood.[2]

John Brown feels there is something even more vital that these couples were not given by the agencies—a realistic assessment of the true nature of the adoptive relationship:

> A fraud is perpetrated on adopting parents when they're led to believe that they're going to have the relatedness of birth with this child because there's no way they can get that no matter how much they love him, or how well they take care of him. They anticipate a relationship they would have to a child born to them and this anticipation can never be fulfilled, so there's always going to be some disappointment or bitterness.[3]

Once the adoption papers were signed, the social worker's responsibility disappeared along with her autonomy. Just as she could not police what the parents were telling the child, or how many times a week they were actually sleeping together, she could not control the attitudes of their neighbors. She may have declared them super parents, but she could not make their various communities look on them as being exactly like everyone else, let alone superior. Two levels were always at play simultaneously: on one, adoptive parents were seen as perfect, golden people who had rescued an unwanted child from the gutter; on the other, they were viewed as unfortunate people who were not able to bear a child of their own. Perhaps as a reaction to the latter, adopters often tell their children: "Other parents had to take what they got, but we were able to choose you."

In his classic book *Shared Fate,* sociologist David Kirk, himself an adoptive father, speaks of the reluctance of adopters to admit their marginality in a society where kinship is measured by blood relationship. He defines them as falling into two groups: those who "reject the difference," by trying to maintain the myth that the child is really theirs and that they are no different from biological parents; and those who, by showing empathy for the child's special situation, "acknowledge the difference." His own conviction is that there is more communication and trust in a family where the difference is admitted.[4]

Kirk was ahead of his time. Only now is it being recognized by other professionals that there are inherent stresses in an adoptive family that other families do not have. No matter how close or antagonistic blood relatives are, they are secure in their biological tie. The very certainty of their relatedness gives them a sense of belonging that they take as much for granted as the air they breathe. But deep in the psyche of both Adoptees and adoptive parents is the knowledge that "they're not mine."

Many psychiatrists believe that, as a group, adoptive parents bear the scar of infertility and its psychological aftermaths. Enid, who has two young adopted children, was one of the few women who was able to discuss this openly:

> It never occurred to me that I would be an adoptive parent. I imagined that I would get married and have two girls and one boy—the boy in the middle. Then I had to go through the infertility thing. It is done so coldly. And we had to come to the decision to adopt. It was hard since we both came from Irish Catholic families who had plenty of kids. The social worker kept saying, "You'll get over it. You'll accept your infertility." She said the pain would break like a boil, and be over. All the while I felt I was playing a game, this getting instant motherhood. When the call came into my office that a child was available, the operator congratulated me. I went out immediately and picked up the baby, but I felt like I was playing dolls. I was happy but I had terrible dreams. I would

go to the store and when I came home, she would be gone. "What am I going to tell my husband," I would think. "That I left her?"

I love my two children very much, but I have an inner fantasy I would never admit to other adoptive parents. They'd think I was disloyal. I would like to see the face and body of the biological child I couldn't have. We have gorgeous people in our family, and bright people with brilliant minds. I'm sure it would have been a wonderful child.

By being honest with herself, Enid has been able to work through her very natural disappointment about not having been able to raise her own children. Not facing this ambivalence can prevent a woman from feeling secure in the mothering role, making her overanxious and overprotective as she compensates for fears of inadequacy. Adoptive parents who can be frank about their uncertainties have a better chance of overcoming the problems. For although blood relationships may not be perfect, they do not have to be explained.

24

Telling the Child

Telling the child that he or she is adopted is often an ordeal for the adoptive parents: having been advised by the professionals "to make the child your own," they must somehow inform him he isn't. Most do not want to admit this, even to themselves. It's known as the *double bind*.

Enid remembers her daughter at the age of seven looking at a pregnant relative and saying: "Did I grow in your tummy?" "It was painful having to say no, having to admit that no babies could grow in my womb. It didn't seem to bother her. But it bothered me."

Adoptive parents have always placed great emphasis on *when* to tell, as if there were a magic moment, as in fairy tales, when one could safely reveal such loaded information with no consequences. How nice the adoption tale would be if, right after the Wicked Fairy approached the crib with the disgruntled curse, "Someday you will learn you are adopted," the Good Fairy could always be counted on to step forward with, "But it will never trouble you!"

Until now, the word the social workers passed on was that it would never bother the children if they were told *early*. They would simply digest the news along with their orange juice and pablum. As one parent who took this advice seriously told me: "We introduced the word adoption at the age of one, along with Mommy, Daddy, cat, and dog." And another: "In our house everything was adopted—we had an adopted turtle, an adopted rabbit, and an adopted dog."

This "tell early" school flourished after World War II, apparently inspired by psychiatrist Robert Knight, who said that it would relieve the parents of "continuous dread" that the child might hear it from a third party, with "the resultant loss of faith in their word." He also assured everyone that the child would "very likely think little of it and forget about it."[1]

However, in recent years professionals have been differing about the wisdom of telling early. There is now a "tell later" school that believes the Adoptee does not have the ego strength to master this information until he is over six. Analysts like Herbert Weider say that when a child asks about conception at the age of four or five, he is asking about a piece of general information, and not necessarily about his own origin. He believes that children who are told carry a burden of knowing, which may turn them off knowing other things as well and cause them to expend a great deal of energy in fantasy. Underachievement in school and learning difficulties could be the result.[2]

At a conference I attended with Weider at Hofstra University in the spring of 1977, adoptive parents felt deceived on hearing this "tell later" view. There were moments when their anger at the "experts" resembled that of a lynch mob. One parent shouted, "Now the advice is changed, I feel everything we've put into the child is down the drain." A father, reflecting the underlying despair of the group, said, "Most of us feel we're floundering. Can't we develop a philosophy to follow through on?" A few parents argued that the adopted child was being undervalued, that he could cope with more than the "tell later" doctors were giving him credit for.

Trying to calm the group, Jules Glenn, who chaired the panel with Weider, conceded: "No one knows the exact age that is best—there is danger either way. There are no rules. You can only figure out the problems as they come up when you raise a kid." Trying to clarify the opinion he shares with Weider, he went on: "If you tell a child at a half-year, he won't understand. It may ease the parents' mind, but it won't influence the child. At a year and a half, or two, the child won't get the message you're trying to give; in fact, there's the danger that he may misunderstand. He may get the message he was not *taken in,* but *sent away.* At four he may have the cognitive ability to understand, but still find it hard to get the message right."

A woman interrupted here: "But at six he's just starting school.

Won't telling then interfere with his learning?" She was raising a point that the adoptive parents could identify with—that any stage has its problems, no matter how long one delayed.

One of the few women who could relate to what Weider and Glenn were saying took the floor then. "I'm grateful to this panel," she announced. "No one has said before that maybe the problems we're having are because the child is adopted. I'm glad to be hearing about the vulnerability of the adoptive parent. When my son was three, our social worker told us we couldn't have another child unless we told the first one. We told because we had to. Then our child had fears about being kidnapped. He was not ready for this information. It made him fearful. As he got older, he was reluctant to make relationships out of the home. He is still isolated."

There were assents as she spoke, as if those parents wanted to believe it might have been different had they done it differently. This need to see the age at which they told as the source of their child's problem is shared by many adoptive parents.

I remember a woman in New Mexico telling me how sorry she was that she told her son so early. "Everyone said 'make it natural, you're our darling adopted baby.' But it wasn't natural to me telling Alex at the age of three. I didn't think he could handle it. He was bright and asked a lot of questions, but I noticed a change in his personality afterwards. He just wasn't the happy boy he had been. I felt he had bad feelings about the fact that he was adopted. I could tell by the questions he asked, like 'Why did my *mother* . . .' I'd interrupt him and say 'I'm your mother,' so he'd change it to 'Why did the lady who birthed me give me away?'

"It was tense the first few times he did this. He was so young. My husband and I just looked at each other. At five he asked, 'Where's the lady who had me?' Then another year would go by, and out of the clear blue sky, when we weren't talking about adoption, he would just suddenly work something in. How come we couldn't have children? We never lied. I told him that our twins had died at birth. Or he'd say, 'Where does she live?' and I'd answer 'I don't know,' because I didn't.

"I can't say definitely it's because we told him, but after that he began sucking his thumb, and he's immature for his age now, does poorly in school."

When this woman and her husband adopted a girl privately, they were determined not to make the same mistake.

"We agreed not to tell her until later—much later," she said. "But we arranged to have Alex there the afternoon she was brought home from the hospital by the lawyer and his secretary. We thought it would be terrific to have our son share his sister's arrival with us."

This second child, Judy, whom they didn't tell, seemed to confirm their suspicion about early telling. She was an easy, cheerful child, according to her mother. However, when she was seven, she blurted out one night at dinner: "Did you have me in your tummy?" Her mother, taken by surprise, admitted she hadn't, and Alex came to the rescue by saying he hadn't come out that way either.

"I was pleased with how well things had gone," the mother said, "but shortly afterwards Alex confessed to me that all those years he had been suffering over the fear that he would be given up. When I asked him why, he replied, 'Well, Judy's mother and father gave her up that afternoon.' We realized he thought the lawyer and his secretary were her real parents. I explained who they were, and it seemed to make him feel better. But I don't know."

Nor does this mother really know what her daughter had been feeling all this time. If Judy suspected that Alex was in on a family secret she was not part of, she could have had a sense of being excluded. And all those years that Alex was keeping the family secret about Judy, he was being forced to hold in his own questions and fears, which he had been able to express openly when he was the only child.

It is because of situations like Alex and Judy—where one evasion leads but to another pitfall, when communication is turned off—that we can see the dangers inherent in the "tell later" system.

Marshall Schecter, one of the earliest advocates of telling later, is always careful to qualify that each family constellation is different. "Some parents come to me and say, 'I have four older kids and there's no way for the three-year-old not to know.' They're right, they obviously have no choice. But otherwise, I see it as a question of *timing* and by *whom*. I would prefer children being told by parents at a time when the communication system is open and good feelings abound. This is usually between seven and ten. But we have to admit that even then the adoption factor is a constant, a time bomb that may show its effects earlier on some, later on others."

Some psychiatrists, like Thomas Harris of *I'm OK—You're OK* fame, would try to avoid that time bomb altogether by lying to the very young child:

> I honestly believe that it would be better for the child to be told "yes, you grew in mommy's tummy" even with the implications of dishonesty, than to go into great detail about growing in some other mommy's tummy. If the little person is made to feel he truly belongs, he will have a strong enough Adult a little later in life to comprehend why his parents may have lied to him: out of love for him, to avoid burdening him with confusing and troubling truth.[3]

What Harris does not understand is that he will not be around to signal when the truth switch should be pulled. It usually gets jammed for life.

Karla feels very strongly about this. "Asking the child to forgive the parents' lies later is like asking him to be another version of Christ," she said. "I think my parents' falsifications account for the real pits of depression I had while growing up. I was told one thing, but I was feeling something else. I never questioned their story, but now I wonder what was going on unconsciously in me. I was too smart in too many other places to have accepted it so blandly."

Alas, it seems there is no magic age for telling, and no consensus among therapists as to the best time. There are the few professionals who believe the child should *never* be told; those who would lie until they felt the child was old enough to know; those who would tell from the beginning; those who would delay telling until the child asked; and those who would tell the child by age five if he or she had not asked.

I tend to agree with this latter position. Parents should obviously tell when they themselves feel most comfortable about it, but if the child has not brought up anything about how babies are born by the age of five or six, they might broach the subject along with how babies are adopted. By initiating the discussion, the parents are demonstrating that, although being adopted may be different, it is also natural in this society, and not something to be ashamed of.

What is important is that there not be a dogmatic attitude about the age the child is told. One should belong to neither the "tell early" or the "tell later" school, but should decide what is best for the needs of one's own family. Robert Jay Lifton feels that the whole subject of telling should be defused. "Telling does not have to be flaunted or pressed upon the child. In fact, parents should take the pressure off the issue of *when,* so as not to falsify by not telling, or find themselves confessing to a toddler out of guilt or ostensibly expert opinion. By being more relaxed about telling, the parent will be able to tell in the most natural way possible according to the child's curiosity and need."[4]

Knowing Too Little

Some adoptive parents feel they do not have sufficient information to give their child. Many who were afraid to ask the social worker for more than was offered, for fear of losing the baby, are now genuinely distressed that they cannot give their children satisfying answers to their questions.

One woman who prided herself in giving "nice answers" still remembers her feeling of inadequacy when her daughter Anna was five:

We had a little girl staying with us for a few days while her mother was away. The child must have been feeling anxious because soon she was leading Anna into a situation with me that I had no control over. I was painting in the back room when Anna came running in. "Mommy, did I have a bracelet when I was born?"

I said, "Yes, all babies do, I think."

She ran back to her friend, and then came back to me. "What was the name on the bracelet?"

I said as calmly as I could: "They put Baby Girl on it, and then the last name of your mother."

Anna ran back to her friend and then again came racing to me. "What was that name?"

I said as carefully as I could, "I don't know what it was."

Then the little girl, she must have been about six, joined us. "Why didn't her mother keep her?" she asked me. I got down from the ladder and said: "We don't know. For the same reason she couldn't bring up a baby."

"I know why she didn't keep her," the child said to me. "Because she didn't want her."

"Not everyone can keep their child," I said lamely. And meanwhile I was thinking this is a terrible story, that a mother can't keep her child. So I said, "She wanted the baby to have a home, to do the best she could for the child." But I was thinking it's not very satisfying for a mother to say this about another mother. I couldn't turn it into something wonderful. I was in anguish. I felt I had to round it out and make it a good story. So I brought them into the living room with me and had them sit down, like for a story. "Would you like to hear about the day we got Anna?" I asked them.

They both nodded yes.

I went back and got the little dress she had worn, and the announcements we had sent out. And I told the story like a fairy tale—how we wanted a baby, and we were waiting and waiting, and then we heard about a baby in Chicago. And we went there, and we found Anna.

Anna was beaming, as she always did, when I told the story. It was, after all, a nice story, as I intended it to be. But from the point of view of the child, I was thinking, this should be a story with two sides. I felt inadequate. I wasn't able to solve everything. It was not satisfying to say I don't know some things. Like about her birth mother. And I really do know just a little about her.

The social worker felt it was best for us not to know, that it would avoid her building fantasies. Without the facts, the child won't fantasize, she told us.

Such were the fantasies social workers projected onto adoptive parents just a few years ago.

I was amazed at the number of adoptive parents who seemed relieved to know as little as possible. One woman said, "I deliberately learned *nothing*, so I won't be lying to my daughter when I say I don't know the answers to her questions."

I was to discover from my questionnaires and interviews with adoptive parents how prevalent this *know as little as possible* attitude is. The adoptive parents' reluctance to know and the adoptive agencies' reluctance to tell come together here in perfect collusion.

Here are some of the statements from parents on their attitudes about knowing:

The agency told us everything they felt we would benefit from knowing. Nothing definite about backgrounds, no serious illnesses. To be frank, I didn't want to know.

We know very little—that her parents weren't married—that her mother went to college. But I would never want to tell her those things because it would make the mother more real, and I guess I would never want to do that.

We were afraid to ask. We just wanted to please the agency so they'd give us the baby, and not do anything that would make them take it away. I guess it's too late now.

I had the fear that I would find out too much. I wanted it to be an anonymous thing. I wanted to know enough to be assured the baby would be relatively healthy. Just knowing she had Jewish parents was enough for me.

In answer to a later question—what they hoped for their children—these same parents were unanimous in replying that they wanted them to lead happy lives, be successful in their work and secure in themselves. They did not understand that the lack of knowledge of their heritage might be the very stumbling block to their children's becoming those mature, trusting, well-adjusted adults in the future; that if their past was an "anonymous thing," their children could well become anonymous people.

Parents who have adopted from overseas often feel less threatened by their children's questions, since they cannot emotionally or physically pass as the *real* parents. Many of them have expressed a desire to get more information but don't know how to go about it.

No one can say for certain that, even if they were to take a trip to those countries, they would be able to trace their children's origins. It's difficult, but it has been done. I think of the journalist Ruth Gruber, who went to Korea and Vietnam to locate the families of TV newscaster Marjorie Margolies's adopted daughters.

Her success is recorded in the probing book on which she and Margolies collaborated, *They Came to Stay*.

Of course, most adoptive parents are not experienced investigative reporters and hesitate to make such a journey into unknown terrain. Still I would advise them to consider it where possible, for the more time that passes, the more difficult it will be for them to learn anything. When the children are older, adoptive parents might want to travel back with them to the country of their birth. This does not mean that the children will feel part of the original culture—they have been raised, after all, as Americans—but that they will have the opportunity to connect in some way with their origins.

Knowing Too Much

Sometimes adoptive parents tell me that they feel they know too much, things so negative that they would dread ever having to reveal them to their child.

A woman called to ask me: "How can I tell her she's illegitimate, that her mother was only fourteen?"

A father wrote me:

> What causes us particular pain for Audrey is that her natural mother, for all practical purposes, abandoned her. She was 17 or 18, adopted herself, lived in a kind of commune, and had no idea who the father was. Audrey was premature, seriously ill at birth. Her mother neglected her shamefully, keeping her in a dresser drawer, diapered her in rags, and never talked to her or played with her. At six months, when the social worker asked if she was really interested in keeping her, she answered no. We are told that at that time Audrey was listless, neither laughed, smiled, or cried. Our problem is, how much to tell her about all of this?

As we have already seen, Adoptees are able to pick up the anxiety that parents have in telling them about the past. There is no reason to burden a very young child with difficult information, but the parents should be guided by the child's need as to when to tell. If they are able to overcome their own revulsion, to accept what happened as the "shared fate" that David Kirk speaks of, the parents will be able to present the birth mother in a compassionate way, depicting her as someone who was unable to cope at that time, rather than as a rejecting figure. The child will learn to accept what happened as she accepts being too tall or too short because of those "other" parents, and will have a feeling of reality about the past.

One can never know *too* much about the past—if it is the truth. The information that parents have is usually secondhand, relayed as it is through a social worker or a lawyer. From what I have observed, adoptive parents would benefit from at least one meeting with the birth mother. It would give them a chance to empathize with her and understand their child's heritage.

Enid is now glad she met her son's mother when she picked him up at the hospital. The mother was a pretty woman in her twenties, separated from her husband. Her two other young children were being cared for by the grandmother, who refused to take in another one. Either the mother would have to return to her husband and care for all the children, or give up this baby. "I don't know who I am or where I'm going," she told Enid from her hospital bed. "I want to have time to find myself."

Enid reassured her that she would take loving care of her son. But after that day she blocked the memory of the scene from her mind. "I tried to forget her, so that I could make the baby mine," she said. "But now I realize that meeting her has given me a sense of reality about where my son comes from. It makes him real, with a real background."

Not Telling

There are still some parents who try to avoid the whole issue of *when* by not telling at all. I was reminded of this recently when a woman with a two-and-a-half-year-old boy told me, "I'm not going to tell my child—ever." Her rationale was that many birth mothers lie to their children about who their fathers are, and since no one can be positive of their parentage, why should she have to tell?

I know that such people sincerely believe that they can spare their children pain, but it is wishful thinking on their part. And no one, not even a parent, should have the right to tamper with a child's history.

But aside from the moral issue, we must ask if such secrets

can ever be kept. In the past, a married woman might disappear from the scene for a few months and come back with a bundle that she claimed as her own. I have heard of cases where women actually stuffed their skirts with pillows to make themselves look pregnant before bringing someone else's baby home from the hospital. Most people to this day trust the discretion of their friends and relatives not to talk. However, it is not so easy to impose those restrictions on children.

I think of the letter I received from a seventeen-year-old girl telling me how she found out about her adoption when she was in the fourth grade:

> One day I was across the street playing "kick the can" with a bunch of friends and one of them said, "Hey, I got a big secret to tell you that you're not supposed to know about." Of course, I wanted to know what it was, so then she said, "No, I better not tell you. It's sad. You'll leave home—you'll cry the rest of your life." And I said, "Well, tell me anyway." She goes: "You were adopted." Me: "So?" Her: "Your dad told my dad and my dad told my mom and my mom told me and now I'm telling you. You and your brother were adopted." Me: "So?" Her: "I just thought you'd like to know. Aren't you gonna cry?"

William Reynolds believes it is incredibly "naive" to think that children won't find out about their adoption. "It assumes that kids are dumb," he says, "that if you don't tell them, they don't know. Many adoptees tell me they always knew before anyone told them. It is typical of how little adults know about kids that they would try to get away with this."[5]

Of course, it is probable that some adopted people have gone through life, and to the grave, not knowing (or half-knowing) that they were not flesh of their parents' flesh. But in most cases, if they do not discover it in childhood, they will learn through some slip in the course of time, or while going through their deceased parents' papers.

One morning I got a phone call from a woman I shall call Harriet, who had seen me on a TV talk show. "I'm thirty-four," she blurted out, "and have just learned I'm adopted."

It seems that she had stumbled onto this alarming news a half-year before, when a neighbor from her hometown called to extend very belated condolences for her mother's death. In the course of reminiscing about her mother, the neighbor said: "Yes, she tried to have children so hard, and loved you so much."

Astonished at this statement, Harriet had managed to say, "You mean I didn't come from my mother?"

"Didn't you know?" the neighbor sputtered, and hung up in embarrassment.

"I didn't," Harriet told me. "I called my cousin, who said it wasn't the truth and that the family loved me. And then I called my adoptive father in Florida, and he said, 'Harriet, it's *not* true.'

"Well, I guess I had the need to believe them so I tried to forget about it, although it was always in the back of my mind. When I went south to visit my father and his new wife, Rose, later that year, she gave a luncheon for me. The subject of one of the women's adopted children came up, and a distant cousin of mine blurted out, 'Oh yes, Harriet is adopted too.'

"The conversation moved on to other subjects, but I sat there completely frozen. I didn't hear anything else that was said. When we got home, Rose said, 'Daddy never wanted you to know.'

" 'But why didn't they tell me?' I asked.

" 'They went through so much, I guess,' Rose said.

"That night I had the shakes and cried for hours. On the day I was leaving, Rose asked me if I wanted to talk to my father about it. 'He loves you,' she said. 'He remembers how hard your mother tried to have children. On her deathbed, she asked him never to tell you.'

"So I went into where he was sitting, and said, 'Look Daddy, I know.' He started to cry, and I tried to reassure him: 'Look, I love you—my feelings will never change.' "

But something has changed. Harriet finds herself obsessed with this knowledge. "I've had a wonderful life. I love my parents, but what do you do? Do you just forget about it?"

An aunt has told her: "Harriet, what does it matter? It's not the one who squeezed the baby through who is the mother, but the one who raises you." And her best friend keeps saying: "Hey, you are who you are! You're a wonderful mother and person."

But Harriet says to me, "I know no one can change me, I am the way I am. But when I found this out—I can't explain it—it was a shock. It hit my nervous system. It's in the back of my head. It won't leave. What do you do? Do you just forget it?"

She knew the answer just needed the sanction from someone who understood. And then she gave it words: "I can't forget it. I must know. If the woman is alive, I want to see her and meet her. If she doesn't want me, all right. I can understand. I'm a mother. I have my own life."

Finding out late seems to assure that the Adoptee will want to search for the truth. My friend Gordon Livingston, a psychiatrist and adoptive father, knows firsthand how one feels on learning as an adult. When he was thirty-eight, he was sitting with a cousin explaining the need to search of some Adoptees who had invited him as a professional to their meeting.

"What would you do if you were adopted?" his cousin asked.

When Gordon said, "I would start a search for my natural parents," the cousin replied, "Start looking."

Gordon did search, after confronting his adoptive father, now a widower. And though he understood that his father's reasons were those of love, he still felt a great deal of resentment toward him. "I think that understanding the need which produced the denial only partially alters the angry response," he told me. "I have had to struggle with a tremendous amount of rage at my adoptive parents for their misconstruction of the past. I've stopped apologizing to myself about this and accept it as a natural reaction to a real betrayal of trust. This is a long way from rejecting them as parents, but it is an important component to my feelings. My father has, needless to say, had a great deal of difficulty accepting or understanding this part of my response."

It took Gordon only three months to find his birth mother, since he had guidance in search techniques from his Adoptee contacts. "She proved to be a schoolteacher who never married, and never told anyone of her experience," he said. "For the first ten years after giving me up she taught children who were the same age as I would have been so that she could share vicariously in my development. Her open and relieved acceptance of my finding her, after breaking through her reserve, has been the best consequence of the whole experience."

What happens to one's identity when one learns late? Looking back, Gordon says that what jarred him most was that far from being the man he thought he was, secure in the knowledge of his heritage and his roots, he suddenly did not know anything about himself.

> Over the six years since then I have struggled in a number of ways to define what it means to be adopted, to have been given up by the persons who gave one life, to have no biological connections with the family that one grows up in. It is a different experience for both parent and child—this much I could feel. I could also see the energy that seems to go into denying that difference in many adopted families. Assertions by parents that one loves an adopted child just like one's biological children came increasingly to seem attempts at self-reassurance and denial, and were not consistent with my own experience as an adoptee.

By not telling, the adoptive parents hope to escape the consequences of the Adoption Game, but no one can do this. They are actually retreating from the most important area of parenting—helping the child master the truth about his reality. There is pain in life for everyone, and not to acknowledge it only lays the child open to being ambushed by revelations for which he will be unprepared. There is also the danger that the pressure of keeping such an unnatural secret over the years can erupt in ways beyond the parents' control, with devastating effects.

When Greg was seventeen, his younger brother, born to his parents late in life, threw his hi-fi set on the floor. Greg raised his arm to strike him, when his grandmother screamed: "Don't touch that child! He's theirs! You're not!" "It was like waking up one day after walking around with amnesia and realizing that what I thought was me wasn't. Everything that I thought was mine was suddenly not mine anymore. I was there by someone else's grace, but not rightfully there. I became an emotional basket case after that. A pathological liar, a cheat, a drug addict. It took years for me to sort things out, to shed my feelings of rejection."

Ellen had much the same experience. At the age of twenty-eight, she was standing at her father's deathbed in the hospital when he ordered her to get his clothes and take him home. While she was trying to explain that he needed more care than her mother could give, he became enraged and snapped, "She's not your mother! You were adopted, and you're no good, just like your real mother!"

A few hours later he had a massive stroke and died. For a while Ellen did not know which had devastated her more, her father's death or his revelation. She then developed a rare blood disease that was suspected of being fatal. It took years of analysis to purge her psyche, and perhaps her blood, for the disease gradually vanished as mysteriously as it had appeared. She is now in the process of searching: "As soon as I learned that things I thought were true, weren't, I wanted to know what was true."

Ellen, and others who were not told while growing up, must sort out all the false cues and signals they were given through childhood and adolescence to understand how this influenced what they have become. It is as if the center has fallen out of an existence which until then they had taken for granted.

What to Tell—The True Story

The more one examines the intense focus on when and how much to tell the child, the more one realizes that it has served to cover up the basic reality of the child's life—that he has been separated from the people to whom he was born. The wishful thinking on the part of many professionals that denying the child the truth of his heritage would help solidify his bond with the adoptive parents has been proven wrong. It is now time to consider a whole new way of approaching the adopted child.

It is time to break the taboo against the adopted knowing where they come from.

The whole subject of telling should be faced squarely. There is nothing parents can ever say that will erase the child's existential fate. It is not so much the timing of their disclosure as the way they present it. No matter what the age, the child will sense the parents' discomfort or ease with the topic. If they are tight and secretive, he will be too; if they are open and accepting, so will he. If they act as if it is a disaster area, he will regard it as one; if they act as if it is a natural condition, which they can accept and deal with, he will feel more at home in his own skin, and in their family.

It gets down to a basic attitude of honesty that should run through the parent/child relationship at all times. Children are aware when something is being withheld. There are indirect messages, such as family members never commenting on the child's

physical relatedness to others—like eyes resembling Aunt Lucy's
or a chin like Grandpa's—while making these casual associations
with each other. Blood-related people do not realize the fre-
quency of these biological references, but Adoptees do.

The Adoptees I spoke with did not underestimate the difficulty
of trying to help a child understand why he was adopted. Being
put up for adoption, for whatever reason, means being given up,
and being given up is synonymous with rejection. It is not a
"lucky" or a "happy" thing, as one of the latest of the chosen-baby
books would have us believe.[6] It is the primal reality of the
child's life, and if given a chance he can learn to accept it—just
as kids learn to accept that their parents are getting divorced or
that a loved one is terminally ill. Children would rather have the
difficult truth than the evasions they're given. By not speaking
candidly, parents begin a pattern of falseness in the relationship
that allows for future deceptions. Those lies, which seem to protect the child/parent relationship, will undermine the adult/
parent one.

A few child psychiatrists are coming to this view. In California, Barry Grundland perceives telling the child as a process
that should evolve in rhythm with his development. He sees the
child's very early questions as an attempt to absorb information
about himself and believes the parents should listen carefully
to what is being asked. Grundland says: "When the four-year-old
asks, 'Did I grow in your tummy?', you answer truthfully 'No,'
but you do not add whose tummy he grew in. When he is ready
to ask that question, he will, and that's when you deal with it."[7]

Grundland is the first one I've heard suggest that the parent
should not even use the word *adoption* at the beginning because
it is too abstract. He sees the term as a social symbol which the
child will not understand until he is able to think conceptually,
which occurs about the age of seven. It is then that the child
becomes aware that something unusual has happened to him and
will break his questions around adoption into their individual
parts—his birth, why he was separated, what happened to that
mother and father.

"It is important to get the child thinking in this process from
the beginning, absorbing the information as he goes along,"
Grundland told me. "Then there will not be a traumatic moment
of revelation at a later age."

I'm not sure the word *adoption* can or should be bypassed, as if you could get rid of the problem by getting rid of the word. But I do agree that this continual honesty over time will help the child have a sense of belonging with the adoptive parents, and the parents with the child, a bonding that has been sadly lacking in the guilt-ridden, secretive adoptive relationships of the past.

Putting this philosophy of openness into practice, we are replacing the inadequate chosen-baby story with open dialogue about what happened. Over the years the adoptive parents listen carefully to what it is the child is actually asking, and give the age-appropriate response. The answer to a three-year-old is not the same as the answer to a nine-year-old. As Jackie said, "The main thing is, if the child keeps asking questions, keep answering. Adoption is not so horrible if you can grow with it. The child can learn to take life for what it is, roll with it, and deal with it. You have to level or the kid will feel she's been had."

Of course, to be able to level, the adoptive parents must be able to accept the reality that they are not the biological parents. That as satisfying as their relationship is, it has points of difference from a natural family. They should be honest about their own inability to have a baby, about how they went about finding one. No more fake scenes of walking up and down rows of cribs until they spotted the perfect baby.

According to Jackie the *true* story, which she didn't hear until adulthood, was much more satisfying than the invented one. "The real story was beautiful—that they had waited a long time, a year, while being tested and accepted by the agency. The morning my mother was informed by the social worker that I was waiting to be picked up, she called my father at the store to come home immediately. And he *closed* the store—something he never did in all those years I was growing up. That was thrilling in itself, but she also transmitted to me how much they needed a baby, not just that the baby needed a home. The real story has heart and drama. The vibrations are good. It's as loving as the birth story that natural parents tell."

The actual details that the parents recount to the child will be determined by the individual circumstances, but even the murky area of why the child was given up can be handled straightforwardly. One should be careful to make it clear that the problem was not with the baby but with the relationship between the mother and father: because they were unable to make a home for the baby, they had to find someone who could.

Other difficult questions, such as why the parents have not come back for the child, should not be sloughed off, but explored thoroughly as just that—difficult questions. It might be wise for the parents to make clear that the adoption system prevents the birth parents from coming back, even if they wanted to.

If there has not been this kind of honest discourse in the family, there will be serious problems when the Adoptee reaches adolescence. Every week I come across the consequences of failed communication in letters from teenagers who have read my articles on adoption in *Seventeen* magazine and joined my Adoptee Pen Pal Club.[8] Their anguish reminds me that emotions on this subject are as charged now as they were when I was growing up. They write of feeling isolated in their adoptive families, unable to talk to their parents about the things that worry them. The very mention of adoption brings tears to the eyes of their adoptive mothers, just as it did to those of my mother's generation. Their questions reveal the same sense of loss and mystification that we felt: Who am I? Who are they? Why did they give me up?

One girl wrote: "I'm only fourteen, but I'm human too." And another: "I grew up knowing something was missing, like I had an empty spot, but I never could pinpoint what it was."

There are some who can verbalize it, like this sixteen-year-old:

> One night last year before I fell asleep, I suddenly thought to myself, "I wonder if my real mother ever thinks of me and wonders if I'm happy." That event triggered off the steady stream of thoughts and questions I have about my heritage. I consciously realized that more than anything I want to find my mother as soon as I can. I feel it will be easier for both of us when we are younger. I can't fool myself. I realize she probably won't welcome me with open arms into her life. She could even reject me straight out. But I feel as prepared as I'll ever be. I'll be satisfying a real need inside of me.

And this seventeen-year-old:

> I think that I have always wanted to know about my roots but pushed it out of my mind. I became aware of this about two years ago when my grandfather was visiting. We had one of those big family dinners and he kept talking about relatives that did great things. Everyone started to trace our ancestry.

It struck me then that I really needed to know about myself. I want to be able to tell my children and grandchildren about their ancestors. I don't want to leave my parents or go back to my natural parents. I just want to ask them a million questions.

Letters like these make me realize that even should records be opened to Adoptees when they reach legal age, it may be too late. Some kids need all the information about their heritage—their original name, the names of those other parents as well as their religious and ethnic background—at the beginning of adolescence, rather than at the end. And in some cases, much earlier. Phyllis Gurdin, a social worker who runs seminars with adoptive parents at Hofstra University in New York, told me about working with a mother who eventually told her very bright five-year-old everything. Both mother and child were relieved after that, but especially the mother, who was no longer tense when alone with her daughter, fearing the inevitable next question.

Most children will not be ready for *everything* at five, but whether overtly troubled or not, adolescents need the truth about themselves in order to separate out fact from fantasy while they are in these crucial years of development. Such information may be as essential to their psychological health as calcium to the bones of their bodies.

It is important to stress once again that the need to *know* is not the same as the need to *search*. As we have observed, Adoptees do not pack their things and rush out the door the minute they get a name and address—it takes time to move from one psychological stage to the next. In fact, being able to process the information gradually when young may take the obsessive intensity out of the whole subject. It may give young people time to integrate all those disparate parts of their identity into a workable whole. Later, when they have it all together, they can consider whether or not they want to meet those other parents.

Adoptive parents can help their children by returning to the agencies or professionals who arranged the adoption and requesting *all* missing information. By preparing in advance, they can give their children the feeling they are working on their side, not against them, that as parents they care about them in the deepest sense possible—which means having empathy for their needs.

25

Birth Mothers— Are They Baby Machines?

Now the other side to this question of origins is that the kinds of injuries that have been done to the child in the name of child welfare services have also been done to the parents and other relatives. The mother has been led to believe the kid is better off and has a better chance because she isn't part of it. So every time her urge to find her child surges up, she tells herself that it isn't fair to look for him, he's better off without her. . . . These people are the real moralists of our day. Very few people in any strata of life have the morality of parents who were forced to give up the child under duress and have voluntarily restrained themselves from fighting and saying, "I want to have that kid." They are the people who sacrifice in a way that most of us don't know how to sacrifice.
JOHN BROWN

Oh, to meet you once again! To pick up the thread that I left dangling so long ago, to weave it into my life, to finally emerge whole. Oh, the peace and wonder of it.
LEE CAMPBELL

Just as we have had to go back in time to understand where the adoptive parents were coming from, so must we go back with the birth mother. Until Adoptees have done this, they cannot come to terms with their feelings about her. Either they have managed to bury their resentment while growing up, or they have become increasingly bitter, like Gail, who wished she had been "an abortion": "I hated her because she dumped me. She shouldn't have had me if she was going to get rid of me."

Usually an Adoptee's emotions toward the mother are a compound of rage and resentment, love and forgiveness, but often one is not aware of this until after reunion, when all of one's repressed feelings come spilling out. As Trudy described it, "I got annoyed when all she talked about was why she gave me up and how she cried for years. I said, 'It wasn't exactly easy for me either.' I was amazed at how much anger I had."

It can come down to who suffered most.

When I met my mother she felt that I simply could not comprehend the trauma she had been through—that no one could. And in some sense she was right—no one but a birth mother who has been through the experience could possibly understand on the same visceral level. For even though we Adoptees try to empathize with our birth mother's dilemma at the time of our relinquishment, it is still hard for us to accept that any woman could give up her child, or that any clan could banish its offspring. It is only after getting to know a number of birth mothers as real people that we begin to perceive relinquishment not as a rejection but as the result of social and personal pressures that the young mother could not withstand.

Until recently it was almost impossible to meet these birth mothers, for they have always been the silent partners in the Adoption Game. I was reminded of this two years ago when I received a letter from a woman who signed herself Eva, explaining that if she used her full name her career would be destroyed. "Sorry to be so mysterious," she wrote, "but there can be no 'natural-mothers-who-gave-their-babies-up-for-adoption' liberation groups." She suggested that if I wanted to reach her, I run an ad in the Personal column of the *Times* any Wednesday: "To Eva, call me."

I never placed the ad, but I thought of Eva when I met Lee Campbell, a young, energetic woman who was starting an organization of birth mothers in Boston—CUB (for Concerned United Birthparents). It was to be a support system for both men and women who had surrendered children, as well as a political vehicle to get the records updated and open to the child at the age of majority.

Lee is now married and has two small boys. She tried for ten years to forget the baby she gave up as a frightened, unwed teenager. Now that she has awakened to her need to know what happened to her son, she has been awakening others. As I write this, CUB has just opened branches in three other cities and hopes to spread across the country.

"We're tired of being considered mere incubators or baby machines," Lee tells me. "And we're grateful to you Adoptees for waking us up. If you hadn't come out of the closet, we birth mothers would be in pain forever. I'd still be a zombie, sleepwalking, not letting anyone get close, not trusting anyone—not even my husband."

Trust is something birth mothers talk about a lot. They lost it with their babies.

Even now, when social mores are supposedly more relaxed, it still takes an act of courage and commitment to reveal one's identity. After an article on CUB came out in a Boston paper in the fall of 1977, Lee worried about how her husband's colleagues would react. She had to brace herself not to feel the old shame and panic that almost destroyed her as a teenager.

When I met Lee and some of the other CUB members, I felt I was peering through the veil to that forbidden side. I had entered the realm of the ghostly mysteries—who are our mothers?

The birth mothers I talked with cut across all segments of society, just as Adoptees do. In fact, studies show that there is virtually no evidence that unwed girls who gave up their babies for adoption have any special characteristics which distinguish them from girls who did not get pregnant. They were, for the most part, teenagers or young adults, trapped by their biology and ignorance of contraception at a time when abortion was illegal and dangerous.[1]

It was common to hear then of a girl's neurotic need to get attention, to give a "gift" to her mother—as if it were her head, not her body, that caused her condition. Not many professionals could concede as J. D. Pauker did that "Out-of-wedlock babies are a result of neither the stork nor a desire for an out-of-wedlock child, but rather the result of sexual intercourse."[2]

And yet, in spite of the emphasis on the psychological cause of pregnancy, there has been little follow-up on the aftermath. What happened to those young women who were pressured into giving up their babies? Doctors such as John Bowlby who have studied the effects of maternal deprivation on the human infant have not been concerned with the effects on the mother deprived of her baby, as if the maternal instinct is limited in duration, or just disappears with the child, as seems to happen with animals.

Amnesia was the prescription of the day. A healthy dose of this sleeping potion, taken at the moment of relinquishment, was guaranteed to last through the mother's lifetime. Today we call it numbing—this necessity to forget—and we know that a lot of other emotions are arrested along with the pain, such as the ability to love or to trust again.

"It was like an emotional abortion," a former social worker told me. "We told them to trust us, that we would do the right thing for the baby. It's wild when you think of it—why should they have trusted us?"

The women I met were trying to understand that very question. And how they could have let themselves accept that Faustian bargain with society: your virtue for your baby. How they could have believed they could infiltrate back into their old lives as if nothing had happened.

Living as if reborn, without a past, many became extremely religious, or pillars of the community, or devoted wives and den mothers. But always there was the fear that someone might see the scarlet letter burning red in the darkness within them, branding them as the sinners they really were. For although the bargain included forgiveness and forgetfulness, they knew it wasn't true: they bore a new sin for which they could not forgive themselves— giving up their babies.

It is these things that CUB members talk about at their meetings. Now that they are awake, they wear the scarlet letter openly for everyone to see, much as Hester, the adulteress in Hawthorne's novel, did a few hundred years before. Like her, they realize it is their passport into regions where other women dare not tread. Shame, despair, solitude—these were their teachers too, which made them strong.

They need this strength now, for once the past is relived, old wounds are opened, and the grief they had suppressed lies undiminished, waiting for them. Once again there is the shock of rejection from lovers and parents, as if this biological fact made them into something less than human; once again the sudden trauma of changing from the *everyday you* in the family and community into the *tainted you* who must be hidden or cast out.

This is how they describe it:

Connie, now a housewife with teenage children, was fourteen at the time. She had been going for two years with the nineteen-year-old father:

> I loved him as only children can love, expected to marry him and live happily ever after. He was surprised, but seemed pleased. I didn't tell my parents for six months for fear they would make me have an abortion. They were ANGRY. They would have preferred me to abort, but since that was impossible, adoption was the only alternative they could see.

Laurel, who has become a recluse, had just turned twenty-one:

> I was so afraid of their reaction that I had a male friend come with me. Years earlier, a very good friend of mine became pregnant and her father beat her up. Although my father had never raised a hand to me, I had much apprehension. When I told them, their very first concern was my health, that I hadn't been to a doctor. Their next concern was that no one should know, not even my older brother, who was away at college.

Gwen was in her early twenties and in love with a student she had been dating for some time:

> My mother was hysterical, no help at all. My father was very angry and called his parents, demanding that they make their son take responsibility. But they conveyed the old-world attitude that it was all my fault, that I was a slut, and that their son had no responsibility toward my bastard child. They had seemed so fond of me before—we had dinner with them almost every week. When marriage was refused, my parents saw adoption as the only alternative.

Iris had been living for a year in Italy when she became pregnant by a fellow student. She had just turned twenty. He wanted to marry her, but she fled home:

My parents were tremendously hurt at first. My mother, after the initial shock, was wonderfully supportive, but my father turned sullen, bitter, uncommunicative. He was more concerned with what I had done to him than with my welfare. He refused to discuss the baby—never asked afterward whether it was a boy or girl, or where it was.

Linda, at twenty-one, managed to carry her baby to term without her parents ever noticing she was pregnant:

I didn't want to believe I was pregnant. Not until I felt movement did I feel the sadness, the loneliness, the fear—but also a sense of life within me that I felt was very precious, and probably feeling the same sadness and sorrow—yet wanting to be born.

Cora, who was seventeen, had been going steady with the father for three years:

He was speechless when I told him, then he disappeared. My parents were very upset. Mother wept and said, "Now I'll never see you in a white gown."

The words Cora's mother spoke were the very ones used by a Japanese mother in Hiroshima when she saw her daughter disfigured beyond recognition by the atomic bomb. Being pregnant out of wedlock was a holocaust in our culture, one that threatened the well-ordered world of the girl's parents. Especially the mother's. Perceiving the daughter as an extension of her own body, she felt violated by this indiscretion. The illegitimate pregnancy acted as a self-accusation, as if she was to blame on some level. To relegitimize herself, her daughter, and her line, she had to take immediate radical action.

That action, in such cases where abortion was not possible, was to arrange for adoption. The baby was perceived as the enemy who had no rightful place on the family tree. Rather than the beloved grandchild who would perpetuate their line, the dark intruder would sully it. It threatened the mother's reputation and future prospects. It had to be exorcised.

Adoption is a form of exorcism.

Still, there was the problem of what to do with these daughters until their due date. The women I spoke with had been packed off to maternity homes, much in the spirit of those isolation huts provided by primitive societies to prevent menstruating women from contaminating the village. The community was concerned not so much with protecting the girls as with protecting itself from their negative influence.

The atmosphere in some of these maternity homes was much like reeducation camps: through individual counseling and group therapy the inmates learned to recognize the moral weakness that the baby growing within them represented. As a way of paying for room and board they were sent as domestics into "wage homes," or given work in the laundry and kitchen. In the process, everyone was stripped of whatever identity they had had as students or professional women, and reduced to "girls in trouble who had to learn a lesson." Lee Campbell, whose high-school sweetheart refused to marry her, recalls: "We felt worthless, degraded, useless before we arrived. Sometimes when a few of us relaxed together and actually laughed, I felt guilty. But it was the friendships we made that pulled us through."

Cora said:

Mother came to visit me once a week. The care was good and the personnel sympathetic, but I don't think I was really prepared for anything. I just kind of drifted along with what was happening. Deep inside I was hoping that the baby's father would come back and marry me, and everything would be all right. I still loved him very much.

Eva, who had sent me the anonymous letter, referred to her Catholic maternity home as her "alma mater":

I'm not Catholic, but I chose them over the Lutherans mainly because the Lutherans' way of helping was to farm you out as a hired girl, minus pay, of course. The staff went to great pains to protect the secrecy of the girls—ages thirteen through forty. False names and addresses were used. Often the girls, sweating it out in that scroungy town, wrote letters home from far-off exotic places. They were posted to a convent in the phony area from which they were mailed.

A journalist, who had signed herself into a home to prevent her elderly parents from learning of her condition, described it as something like a summer camp in that the experience was cut off from the rest of your life:

You lost your former self when you went into the Home, and you wondered, "Am I the person I was, or this person I am now living here?" I remember one night when the radio was playing "Sometimes I feel like a motherless child," everyone began to cry.

Labor and Delivery

When their time was up—"zero day" as it was called—the girls went alone into labor and the delivery room, either at the home or a nearby hospital. They went alone, without parents or anyone who cared at their side. It was the last stage of their journey into an exile from which they would emerge different people—mothers.

Iris, who had returned from Italy, was terrified:

I understood what was happening to me, but I've never felt more alone than when the aide from the maternity home left me at the hospital. It was the first time it occurred to me that women sometimes die in childbirth. I really panicked, fought the pain instead of going with it, and probably made things harder for myself.

Gwen, now in her thirties, feels bitter:

I had no preparation for labor, and was totally alone. I was left in a cold, bare room, and I could hear other women screaming as I screamed. I wanted to die, but I wanted my child to live. The nurses were sarcastic and unhelpful. I was finally wheeled into the delivery room and knocked out. I was terrified when I awoke from the anesthesia and asked to see my baby. A doctor, who had been informed I was not to see the baby, threatened to have me put into the state mental hospital "if I made any trouble." After that threat I stopped asking for anything. But I was still moved to the mental ward "for observation" twenty-four hours later.

Until she wrote me her anonymous letter, Eva had never shared this moment:

I was playing bridge with three other "pre-natals" (as we were called until that great day when we became "post-natals"), but my labor had already been going on for five hours. Every time a pain came, I would excuse myself (I tried to arrange it so that I was dummy) and lie down. On one of these trips I lay down and my water broke all over the bed. The nurse came in and screamed at me: "Don't you ever do that again!" "Have no fear, lady," I replied, and I never have. (It took me thirteen years to get up enough nerve to go to a gynecologist after the experience.) Well, I toddled over to the delivery room, never to make that three-no-trump contract, but rather to be delivered of a beautiful child (minus anesthesia, of course, so we'd remember the pain).

Cora remembers:

My water broke while I was asleep, and everything happened very fast after that. I was not in labor for very long. I really can't say what my first thoughts were or if I thought she looked like anyone. I can just remember opening the blanket and looking at her all over, noticing she had very little hair and she was very fair. I tried not to let myself feel anything because I knew what had to be. I saw her, held her, and fed her for the six days that I was in the hospital. I didn't see her again after I left.

Linda, whose parents still did not know, broke water around three o'clock in the morning:

I cleaned up the mess, and dressed, and paced the floor while I had labor pains till it seemed a decent hour to get up, get dressed, and tell my mom I was going to visit a friend for the day. I called my friend, and told her I was pregnant and about to deliver, and didn't know when or where or how. She immediately came home from work and rushed me to a hospital about thirty miles away. I looked so small, we had a hard time convincing the nurse I was going to have an actual birth, and not a miscarriage.

Some of the women had been advised by the social worker not to see their babies because it would only make relinquishment harder.

The journalist is now grateful that an intern read her chart wrong:

A voice at my feet asked, "Do you want to see your baby?"

I jerked my hands over my eyes. Didn't he know? It was supposed to be all clear.

He said, "Your baby is born. It's a girl. Don't you want to see her?" and I heard a tiny strange, hoarse little sound.

My hands flew away. My eyes opened. I did want to see my baby.

In the center of the blur there was a sharp vision. A beautiful, tiny baby, all white and clean. She hung from her heels, making that strange little sound again.

Within minutes she was handed to me. My baby seemed all big blue eyes, with a pretty face and blond hair, faintly red-blond.

I reached for her tiny hand. It clutched tightly around my little finger and would not let go. I was ecstatic, telling everyone what a delight she was. I had only six hospital days to be with my child, my whole lifetime to live with her in six days.

Surrender

Until now the actuality of the baby had not seemed real to many of the women—just an inconvenience that was forcing them to serve time. Quite a few changed their minds about giving up the babies once they saw them, but they were to learn that although *they* had changed, their parents and the social workers had not: there was still a stigma attached to an unwed mother keeping a baby.

Linda's parents came to the hospital as soon as her friend informed them she had given birth.

They were very kind and loving to me as they had always been. I had not seen the baby, but they told me it should be given away. Of course, my heart dropped at this point, but loving my parents as I did and not wanting to shame or harm them, I went along with their decision. When I saw my son later, I almost fell apart. My heart seemed as though it didn't want to work—and I fainted. For the next two days, I became as a child myself. The nurse brushed my hair. My parents forgave me, hugged me, loved me. When I left the hospital, I seemed to have left a part of me that no one could replace.

Phyllis, then a twenty-seven-year-old divorcée, still remembers the pain after twenty-five years:

My feelings changed as pregnancy progressed. I felt very protective of my unborn. I hated to have her come out. While she was inside me, she was mine. No one could get her then, and the way things were progressing outside, I wasn't so sure she would be mine very long. I had a social worker who was a nun. From the time a Catholic girl is very small, she is taught there is something special about "Sister." She demands unquestioning obedience. She is catered to, looking up to, god-like, mysterious, running around in a black and white costume like a giant Penguin, rattling with beads, eyes cast down, holy, awesome. Such a one you didn't cross. You were afraid. She had the idea I wasn't good enough for my own child, someone else could do better. So I surrendered her, but not in my heart. I just keep on loving her.

Eva never wavered in her decision at the time:

It was a most civilized action we took under very bad circumstances in giving our children to a legitimate agency. We did not leave them in a ladies' room or abandon them to a convent in the dead of night. At my Home they were kind in a condescending way, giving us messages from the adoptive parents like: "They love you very much." We were made to feel that we were doing the very best thing for our children. "Can you imagine anyone going through life illegitimate?" they would say. We solved that problem, and gave these children to what we were told were loving, religious homes. We went through hell to do it. I opted for a Catholic adoption because they had the process so streamlined. The priest who counseled me was also a notary public and, although I did not know it, probably a lawyer. The counseling at the thirty-day period was done with the papers already filled out and ready for signature. It didn't take more than ten minutes.

Foster Care

Those mothers who were adamant in their refusal to sign a relinquishment paper right away were permitted to put the baby "temporarily" into foster care—until they came to see the impossibility of their position. Which they did—sooner or later.

Iris, who had refused to marry the Italian student, was amazed at her own reaction:

After my daughter's birth, my feelings changed drastically and so suddenly that I thought I'd flipped out. What set it off, I think, was seeing her—and realizing she looked like me. I understood for the first time that I'd actually produced a child. I was tremendously proud of her. I'd planned all along to go back to graduate school right after her birth—and now the idea of writing research papers about some obscure poet seemed totally inane.

But she gave up after eight months:

Placing my daughter in foster care was mostly a stalling tactic and I think I knew it at the time. I was hoping, somewhat irrationally, that something would happen, change, allow me to keep her. Nothing did, of course. As the weeks went by the social worker's initial sympathy began to wear thin. The last session before surrender, she said that the baby wasn't being treated fairly. Either I should claim her or allow her to start living with an adoptive family. The idea that I was causing the baby to be hurt in any way was unbearable. I signed the next afternoon.

Nine years later, Gwen is still enraged about her foster-care attempt:

I deeply regret having tried it for a year. I might as well have surrendered him for adoption then because he was no longer mine emotionally. I was only allowed to visit him once a month at the agency. I was too scared and passive to ask for anything. I felt they were doing me a favor in letting me see my own child. I was never permitted to meet the foster parents. And all the while the social worker was counseling me to forget "my own selfish needs" and do what was best for the child. I was presented with a totally unrealistic picture of adoptive parents as incarnate gods, perfect parents handpicked by the agency to give my child everything I could not provide.

The event that precipitated my final signing was a visit to the lawyer to find out how to get my child out of foster care. He said I would have to prove in court that I was physically, emotionally, and financially able to care for my child—something I could not do. I would not have placed him in it if I had known I had to prove any of these things. As it was, I felt utterly beaten, defeated, worthless. I surrendered. I never heard from the agency again.

The Contract

The contract—also known as the surrender or relinquishment paper—was originally modeled after a property deed or bill of sale, especially in private adoptions.

The document below belongs to an Adoptee who has been searching unsuccessfully for years. Both of her birth parents signed it in the hospital in the presence of a notary public, but seem to have falsified their names and address. When contacted, the notary

said he cannot remember them because in those days he was
always at the hospital getting signatures on this form.

> The undersigned, residing at 562 Fox Street, Borough of
> Bronx, City of New York, does hereby transfer and set over
> unto _____ her right, possession and custody to a baby born
> to her on 9th day of March, 1937, at the _____ Hospital, in
> consideration of the sum of ONE ($1) DOLLAR and other
> good and valuable considerations, giving to the said _____
> the right to feed said child, clothe child and to apply to any
> Court at the end of six (6) months from the transfer hereto to
> adopt said child as her own.
>
> It is hereby acknowledged and stated that the within trans-
> fer is the free act and deed of the undersigned.
>
> IN WITNESS WHEREOF, the undersigned has hereto
> unto subscribed her name this 16th day of March, 1937.
>
> *Signature* _____

The Adoptee, who is a lawyer, pointed out that the sum of one
dollar (surely a bargain in these times, when black market babies
are going for as high as sixty thousand) was a legal convenience:
an amount had to be listed, but did not have to reflect the true
market value of the commodity.

Agency contracts vary from state to state, but in essence they are
all the same. The mother pledges that she will disappear from the
scene, and the agency promises to care for the child, or place it
for adoption. There is no mention of confidentiality in any of
them.

Connie had just turned fifteen when the social worker handed
her the pen for her signature: "I was terrified of that cold, old
bitch who really looked down on me. She had only one goal, and
that was to get me to sign. There were no alternatives offered. My
parents threatened to sign me away if I refused to release her for
adoption. I can remember reading it before I signed and freaking
out. I turned to my mother and asked her to read it, hoping I
suppose that it would make her relent."

> THIS CERTIFIES THAT I, _____, formerly known as
> _____ am the mother of a child named _____ born in
> _____, on _____, and that this child is indigent, destitute
> and homeless. Feeling that the welfare of the said child will
> be promoted by placing her in a good home, I do hereby vol-

untarily and unconditionally surrender her to the care and custody of _____ SERVICE, with the understanding that the agent of the said organization is to provide her with a home in the United States until she shall reach the age of twenty-one years, unless prevented from doing so by some physical or moral disease, by the gross misconduct of the child or by her leaving the place provided for her without the knowledge or consent of the _____ SERVICE, and I pledge myself not to interfere with the custody or management of the said child in any way, or encourage or allow anyone else to do so, and I hereby expressly authorize and empower the _____ SERVICE, to consent to the adoption of said child, in the same manner and without notice to me, as if I personally gave such consent at time of such adoption and do hereby myself consent to the said adoption.

Signature _____

Recalling the moment when she signed this form, Connie said, "I think I will never feel so impotent in my life as I did then. I was being treated as if I was not old enough to love my own child."

The unfairness of all the surrender papers in refusing to notify the birth mother as to her child's placement or state of health still rankles CUB members. Lee Campbell says there has never been a contract devised which is so biased against one party as the one involving transfer of a child's parentage:

> The birthparent has no options and, by implication, no feelings worthy of consideration. Her self-image is damaged severely at the most vulnerable time in her life. Feelings of worthlessness and guilt can remain within the core of her being for a lifetime. For in truth, a birthparent's feelings are not automatically obliterated upon her affixing a signature to a contract, however much society has been led to believe that.[3]

Linda Cannon Burgess, a former agency director who has come out for open records, professes mixed feelings during those long years of guiding young women's signatures to the contract, in her recent book *The Art of Adoption*:

> When the unmarried mother signs a relinquishment of parental rights for the child, the weight of the sober moment descends upon every witness to it. One can only react with silent reflection. I often found it necessary to allow myself several days of emotional adjustment between the sorrows of

the unmarried mother in surrendering her baby and the elation of the adopting parents in adopting him.

We must note here that while it takes the social workers perhaps several days to make the adjustment, it takes the birth mother a lifetime. Still, most birth mothers do not perceive the social workers as heartless—just the system. They know the workers were doing the job that society had assigned them—making legitimate the illegitimate. At that time there seemed no alternative.

The Catholic divorcée, who has been hospitalized several times since surrendering her child, expresses the way most women feel: "I don't hate any of the people that I consider did me wrong. Sister was doing what she had been trained to do, and she was a nice person. She just didn't know what she was doing, I don't think."

Court Appeal

Some birth mothers still try to get their babies back shortly after signing the surrender paper, as if once the cloud has lifted they realize with horror what they have done. However, once the baby has been placed in its adoptive home, few judges will order it returned to its mother. I think of nineteen-year-old Sandy, who gave up her baby at birth because of parental pressure, and then changed her mind one month later. With the help of a legal aid lawyer she went to court, but the judge ruled that the baby would be better off with its new adoptive parents than with a young unmarried mother who had only a clerical job to support them both.

Sandy was devastated by the decision, and dreaded returning to her apartment, which by now she had filled with stuffed toys and baby clothes. Shortly afterward, I received a card from her marked "Fort Jackson, S.C."

> HI,
> Sorry I haven't written sooner. As you can see, I've joined the Army. Hope to keep in touch, but right now I'm in boot camp, and I need all my energy.
> PRIVATE S. W.
>
> P.S. The baby was adopted in June. I entered the Army the next day.

My last communication from Sandy was from an airport phone booth. She had been discharged from the army because of an allergy to the sun, had become an alcoholic during the year of trying to live at home again, and was now on her way down south to a halfway house. "I asked the social worker for a picture of my baby just before I left," she told me as the operator warned that our three minutes were up. "She said she'd look into the possibility, but I doubt if I'll ever hear from her."

Depression

Part of the rage that birth mothers feel now is that no one warned them of the severity of the depression that would follow relinquishment. The social worker had said it would hurt for a while, and then they would forget, as if they had experienced nothing more serious than a nine-month stomachache. But as the divorcée points out: "The maternal instinct is very strong in women, and when people monkey with it, it causes trouble—all kinds of trouble."

Some of the mothers managed to repress sufficiently well to avoid the letdown. It was almost as if they had allowed themselves to be hypnotized into believing the baby belonged to someone else—the adoptive parents who were waiting for it. "Brainwashing" is the term Gwen used.

Cora, whose search for her daughter we will follow later, can't remember struggling as the others did:

> No alternative was ever suggested. No one mentioned foster care. I think the reason I didn't experience any deep depression at the time was that I became involved in a wonderful relationship with the man who was to become my husband. He was very good to me, even visited me in the maternity home, and helped bring me home from the hospital. The fact that he had been a friend of the baby's father didn't seem to make a difference. I was grateful to him, and didn't have time to dwell in the past.

Those who could not immediately master their emotions experienced a lot of pain. They found they could not go back to the life they had left behind because they had become different people in the process of becoming mothers. Since the "secret" was the one thing that had to be preserved out of the whole experience, many moved to other cities, or changed jobs, schools, and friends. But the feeling of worthlessness and despair continued. "Grief is an understatement," one told me. "It took months before I didn't break down daily and could think only fondly of my daughter."

Gwen recalls:

> They had won. I really surrendered in every sense of the word. I ceased to struggle. I almost ceased to exist. I never tried suicide directly, but I took chances while drunk or stoned, messing with drugs—things I would never have done before. Nobody who counseled me ever suggested that my depression was due to being separated from my child. I was even pressured by a psychiatrist to go out with other men long before I was ready for anything like that.

The recluse, who had also tried foster care unsuccessfully, found she could not "put it behind me" as she had been advised to do:

> For approximately four years I tried desperately to forget my daughter, but then I became almost frozen, unable to sleep, work, eat, or drink. I sought psychiatric help for a few months. I had been an administrative assistant in a department where three girls I supervised became pregnant. That depressed me. I got the flu and never left my parents' home after that. I think I'm punishing myself for everything—for giving her away. Each year that goes by I fantasize that I am the child at the age she becomes. Sometimes I act my age, but other times I may be ten or whatever age she is. I felt worthless until a year ago when I read about other birth mothers who felt like I do. Now I am trying to go out a little each week in the neighborhood.

The journalist, who never married, is still struggling to master her depression after seventeen years:

> "It" occurring some three weeks later and continuing with lessening intensity for some seven to thirteen years does not have an exact name. One psychiatrist calls it "panic"; it most fitted the descriptions I read in a book on grief reactions. There was something of slight amnesia for a while, since I could not remember what I had really been before—successful, community- and church-minded. "It" also included high blood pressure, anxiety attacks, headaches that made me check

for a brain tumor to be safe, excessive allergies followed by sinus infections, deep depression. One does not give up a child easily. I am a considerably different person from what I was before; such experiences do affect one's future course and, as Rodin says, the body is the chief recorder of an individual's history.

Last year she went back to college, taking courses in psychology to better understand what she had been through:

Perhaps any therapist should reread Freud's *Mourning and Melancholy* each time he deals with a surrendering mother. I did learn the difficulty in a woman's animal life of distinguishing between surrendering a child for adoption and feeling she has killed her child—since she has killed the child unto herself. One therapist actually told me I was behaving as if I had a dead child upstairs. I realize now the mother's need for a ritual burial, since the living relationship is dead to her. For a healthy woman to have to undergo this to satisfy a social system is a remnant of cruelty in our society.

The Second/First Child

Some women acted out in their grief by becoming pregnant almost immediately, as if to repossess the baby they had been forced to give up.

Connie, by now sixteen, did this:

I got pregnant with my second child ten months after I surrendered my first. I was still not married, but I was determined to keep *this* baby. I made plans to move in with a woman I had met at the maternity home, but before the baby was born, I married her father.

Gwen believes that being rejected by the first man she had loved, and being unable to keep the child "he had rejected," permanently destroyed any trust she had in men:

After I lost my child, I didn't care what happened to me. I became promiscuous. I didn't think I had a right to say no to anyone since I was so low. I was not sure who the father was until after I gave birth to my second son. I know now it was a subconscious attempt to replace my lost child. Of course, this never works. Nobody is ever a real replacement for anyone else. Natural mothers who do not realize this cause deep problems in their families. I spent two years as a welfare mother, and then married my present husband, by whom I had another son.

Birthdays

For everyone, birthdays were a particularly difficult time, no matter how hard they tried to repress everything. Gwen always makes a "symbolic" gesture of giving to some charity or to another child, because she cannot give anything to her son. They all spoke of having a hard time getting through the day, and wondering if the child was thinking of them. One woman said: "On his first birthday I even went out, bought a cake, and then ate it myself. I want so much to be able to send a gift to him. It hurts me to know he may be thinking I don't care, when I really do."

Fears and Fantasies

Everyone spoke of having intermittent fears and fantasies about her surrendered child over the years. Some worried that the chiid had been killed in Vietnam or had become a drug addict.

Gwen, whose son is now nine, said:

I feared he had suffered emotional damage from being kept in foster care a year. When the Karen Ann Quinlan story came out, I kept thinking of what I would do if that had been a boy my son's age.

Connie's daughter, only a few pounds when born, had gone into an incubator.

For many years I believed my child was dead or very ill. Every time I heard of a ten-year-old girl killed or injured, I wondered if it was my daughter. I still look at children on the street and wonder.

A Canadian woman wrote me:

I used to read the paper and torture myself about every boy his age mentioned in the news. There was a boy two years old struck and killed by a train in 1966, the year he was two. I phoned the agency and they told me it wasn't him, but I never forgot it, and to tell the truth, I didn't believe them. I couldn't trust them after what I had been through with them before.

Another woman, whose son is eighteen now, said:

> I used to watch boys who would be my son's age on the street.
> I have even followed cars down the street and written down
> license numbers when I believed my son was in that car. Some-
> times I try to think deeply and send him some kind of mental
> message that will let him know I am trying to reach him.

Hearing birth mothers talk of their lost children, it occurred
to me that they have given them the same mythic quality that
Adoptees project onto their lost parents. The phantom child is
always more golden than the actual one; its very absence makes it
more desirable, and more *there*. It must be a hard sibling for the
legitimate children to rival, being a creature of myth as it is.

Iris, who has three other children by now, says of that first
daughter:

> She is, of course, more beautiful, gifted, and special than any
> other child ever born. I think of her being very sensitive,
> mature beyond her years. I suppose that's because I'd like to
> think she's already questioning her adoption and wondering
> about me.

Iris has fun conjuring up situations in which she and her
daughter are reunited. All of them, she admits, are highly improbable, maudlin, and melodramatic:

> I've imagined teaching in my daughter's school and helping
> her with her term paper (on adoption, naturally). All the time,
> of course, I know who she is, but she doesn't know me until
> after we've become great friends, at which time she's thrilled
> at the discovery.
>
> I've also imagined her, as a teenager, rebelling against her
> very respectable, religious, middle-class parents and finding
> a kindred spirit in her agnostic, pacifist, pot-smoking mother.
>
> I imagine her, upon discovering her heritage, being fasci-
> nated with her ancestry, traveling to Italy to meet her father
> and to the Netherlands to meet her grandparents.

Reborn

Like the Adoptees, birth mothers seem to have their consciousness
raised by becoming involved with others who have been through
their experience. The awakening, with its resultant pain, is the

most difficult, for it is as if they are returning to that original anguish. I think of Laura Chester's "Pavanne for the Passing of a Child":

And then she took her child
and then she laid the child to rest
and then she laid the cover
on the child
and then she closed her heart.
And when she turned away
it made a breakfast of her.
It sucked   and made a vacant space inside her.

After the ordeal of trying to close her heart and to live as if her child were dead, the birth mother must now have the courage to open it. Once having done this, she can never return to that other numbed state of being—it is as if she, too, has been reborn.

"I'm more angry than depressed now," Iris says. "But I'm channeling my anger into constructive action, working with CUB for social and legislative change on the adoption issue."

Gwen has been living for this day. "I feel as if a part of me that has been dead has come alive again. I have begun to see some goals in life, instead of just drifting, to develop aspects of my personality that I repressed after losing my son. I see myself as a beautiful woman with a lot to offer, rather than as something that was thrown out."

26

Birth Mothers Who Search

I assure you
There are many ways to have a child.
I bastard mother
Promise you
There are many ways to be born.
They all come forth
In their own grace.
MURIEL RUKEYSER, "Life: The Answer"

Now that her feelings have been reawakened, the birth mother is overwhelmed by her need to know if her child is still alive. What does he look like? she wonders. What kind of people was she raised by? What kind of person has he or she become?

Using the underground tricks that they learn from Adoptees who have searched, many women manage to find the name and address of their child. At first it is exhilarating just to have that knowledge. It is proof that their child exists. They tuck the information away as fondly as one might a pair of baby shoes one was preserving for posterity. They believe they can wait until the child is eighteen, but the knowledge of where their child is grows in them as relentlessly as the fetus once did. What began as a casual quest for information now becomes an obsession to see the child—an obsession as strong as the one that seizes the Adoptee during the Search.

However, the birth mother has a dilemma not experienced

by the Adoptee. It was *she* who signed the baby away. And even though she may now feel that she was coerced into it by her family and social worker, she wonders if she is entitled to be the searcher. It is one thing to be searched for, another to search.

If the child is now an adult, the decision is somewhat easier. Although she may worry how she will be received, she feels she has a right to make contact. And, of course, when she does, the situation is reversed: it is the Adoptee who needs time to respond because he or she is the one taken by surprise, with no emotional preparation.

Usually those Adoptees who are already awakened are thrilled to be found. One woman who discovered her birth mother waiting at her house when she returned home from the office, said, "This is the first thing that has happened in my life that I did not have to work for." (She was to learn that she still had to work through her feelings about this woman, and the nature of the relationship, but she was spared those frustrating years of search.)

However, Adoptees who are unprepared emotionally have to struggle with the guilt toward their adoptive parents, whom they feel they are betraying, before they can respond to the birth mother's overtures. They must also come to terms with their deeply ambivalent feelings toward this woman who, for whatever reasons, did give them up. I have heard stories of birth mothers who were turned away by their grown children—especially by sons.

A twenty-six-year-old man, still living at home with his adoptive parents, told his mother on the phone: "You don't mean shit to me! Where were you when I needed you?" Only after she persisted with letters and phone calls did he agree to meet her just once, at which time he revealed that he had himself sired a child which had been put up for adoption. When they parted, he warned her never to contact him again—as if he knew the subject of adoption, his own and his child's, was to remain taboo until he was strong enough to deal with it. And now his birth mother is filled with more anguish—for the young woman and the baby her son abandoned. It seemed her own drama was once more being reenacted, the pollution spreading to future generations.

For the birth mother who spends years searching without success for an adult child, there is another kind of pain. Take the situation of the divorcée who paid money she could ill afford to a private detective, who came up with nothing. After that she worked two years as a housekeeper for a woman who kept promising to find her twenty-three-year-old daughter if she would stay on the job. But she was to learn that her employer was only using this as an excuse to keep her there.

"It has been a terrible emotional drain," she said. "People have gotten money and work from me without it doing any good. It has been like giving her up twice."

Birth mothers with minor children have even greater turmoil, for they are faced with what they see as a moral decision. "Do I have a right to make contact before the child is eighteen?" they keep asking themselves. "Do I have a right to threaten the adoptive parents, maybe disrupt the household?"

While they are trying to resolve their mixed feelings, they may drive past the child's house hoping for a glimpse of him, or they may look up her picture in the school yearbook. Some subscribe to the adoptive family's local newspaper, hoping for an announcement of the child's activities.

This vacillation between the desire to make contact and the fear they will be rejected by the child or his parents is also *similar* to that state of limbo the Adoptee goes through. They go back and forth over the question of whether it would be better for the child to know the truth of his origins when he is young enough to integrate it. In the meantime, they get relief in just viewing the child from a distance, or as one mother said, "just seeing his jeans waving on a clothesline in the breeze."

Iris felt much better after driving past her daughter's house:

Now that I've seen her, I feel I can wait. She was standing there in the front yard chewing gum, looking like any other little girl that age. Until then I had pictured her like a princess from a fairy tale, but seeing her with that gum made it all real. I was glad to have seen her, but sad that it has to be this way. I didn't want to take her home with me. I would just like to be a neighbor who could have a casual relationship. It would be so much saner.

Gwen has seen her son twice:

Once I drove by his house with a friend, and asked him for directions to his school. And another time I saw his Christmas play. The first thing I thought was—his front teeth have spaces just like mine did, and I'd like to tell his parents they'll grow together without braces. It was strange to see him—a mixture of regret and relief. I like the place where they live—a lower-middle-class suburb near the ocean and lakes. It looks like a fun, friendly place for a little boy to grow up.

Laurel, the recluse, was driven by her father past her daughter's house. Like so many parents who thought their daughters would forget, he wanted to make some amends.

My father was the person who did all the searching. He drove me and my mother through the whole neighborhood. It was some experience. I cried all the way home. The only concern my parents had was that I should not contact her until she is eighteen. She is only ten now.

I know many birth mothers who have had their children's addresses for years but are waiting patiently for that eighteenth birthday. Either they worry that their child might not be mature enough to handle their reappearance before then, or that the adoptive parents might turn the child against them if they made the move too early. However, it takes only a story like that of Karen Ann Quinlan or the Son of Sam to throw these women into a state of panic and undo the firmest resolution to wait. "Will our children end up like this?" they ask. "Would knowing the truth of their origins now make their growing up easier and save them from such a fate?"

Who can tell them yes or no? At the present time there are no "experts" to answer these questions. No research studies have been made on young children who have been contacted by birth parents, no statistics gathered on the state of their mental health after that. The adoption agencies turn a deaf ear, for they were never organized to handle the problem of phantom mothers who would materialize years later, agonizing over the fate of their children.

Not only do birth mothers fear for their children, they fear for themselves, as if they are racing death. What if they should be killed in a car crash before that reunion? What if something should happen to the child? Some have realistic cause for concern, like the woman who has been taking chemotherapy for lymphoma. "I have a right to know my eleven-year-old daughter before I die," she tells everyone who will listen, as if still trying to convince herself. "I am going to find her if it takes my last breath."

In the past, of course, birth mothers could never hope to see their children again, no matter what tragic circumstances befell them. Now, in an age when women's rights are being emphasized, they are able to speak out against what they consider a cruel injustice.

Listening to them, I am struck by their wistfulness. They do not talk of "snatching" the child away, but of merging with the parents, almost as if they want to be taken in by them too. They need their acceptance. It is as if only the adoptive parents can legitimatize them—give them the ultimate pardon. And although the rational side of them knows that society has deliberately polarized the two sets of parents, the irrational one envisions a large extended family, interchanging children, taking vacations together, with much of the casualness that exists in Polynesian societies where adoption is treated in a more open way.

The birth mothers dream of the adoptive parents having empathy for them, but it takes word of just one unsuccessful phone call to snap them back to reality. "How did you get this number?" is usually the first question they are asked. "How do you know this is your child?" "Why did you give him up?" "What do you want?" And always there is the ultimate question: "Why *now?*"

No matter how earnestly the birth mothers try to explain that they do not want to interfere with the parental relationship, that they only want to hear about the child, perhaps see a picture, that they are calling now because they have learned that their child might have the need to know he was given up out of love, not rejection, their words cannot penetrate the adoptive parents' defenses. They are told the child has no interest in them, is not asking questions, that they should wait until he is older. Often the adoptive parents will have their lawyer send the mother a letter warning her to cease and desist—in other words, to disappear.

When birth mothers hear of one negative experience after another, as those trying to make contact with the agency or family are rebuffed, they sometimes decide to wait until the adoptive parents may feel less threatened, even if that takes years. But there are others who become convinced they have no choice but to approach the children directly, and let them decide whether they want to include the parents.

What effect will a birth mother's sudden appearance have on an adolescent who is unprepared for it?

I find that even militant Adoptees have pulled back in alarm at this question, as if fearing the teenager within who yearned for light might have been blinded by it—as was Oedipus when he saw the forbidden. And yet one could postulate that if Oedipus had known the truth earlier, had Jocasta sought *him* out, the tragedy might have been averted.

We don't know about then—or now. We get back to the problem of not enough data. Older Adoptees who ponder this question were not stimulated by the media as are today's children. We must consider that they are in a different space from any we could have imagined, for they are not able to repress their feelings as easily as we could. I think again of Erik Erikson telling me that in periods of transition people must experiment. They must keep an eye on what is happening, and record it—that only time will tell how it will all work out.

With such thoughts in mind I interviewed Cora, whose earlier story we have followed, during the various stages of her search for her teenage daughter, Lisa. And then I was fortunate in being able to interview Lisa herself, and to learn how she perceived being found by Cora.

Cora and Lisa

Cora is now an attractive woman in her mid-thirties, with a house in the suburbs and three children by the man she married shortly after giving Lisa up. Although she experienced little depression at the time, she did wonder where and how her child was. She thought about Lisa on the child's birthday, and worried whenever she saw articles about children killed in accidents.

"I guess I always dreamed of finding her someday," Cora said, "even though I never spoke of it."

It seemed as if by chance that Cora came across a paperback book about an Adoptee's search for her mother. While she was reading the book, repressed feelings began to stir in her. She located an Adoptee group in her area and started attending their meetings. "It hurt me to hear how they had such a difficult time growing up, and how tortured they were not knowing about themselves. I didn't want to think of my daughter suffering that pain, becoming one of those sad young women all around me."

On her own, Cora managed to find her daughter's whereabouts. "At first I thought it would be enough just to know," she said, "but then I learned it is hard to have that information and not do anything about it. My daughter was only fifteen then, and I became very depressed that year. I cried a lot."

When Lisa turned sixteen, the pressure was too much for Cora. Fearing that the agency would not help her, she picked up the phone and called the adoptive mother directly.

"Her reaction was one of shock, but she was very kind and understanding toward me. I was feeling overwrought, and must have sounded very emotional and upset. She spoke to me for a long time, but her main point was that I should go back to the agency and ask to be referred for therapy."

Cora did this. For two months she tried to work out her feelings with a psychiatric social worker.

"This helped me to realize that the depression had been there all along, that I had suppressed it for sixteen years. I hadn't had a chance to mourn the loss of the boyfriend I loved, or the daughter I gave up. Now it was all surfacing."

Still, the therapist gave Cora the same message she had received sixteen years before—forget. Only now it was advice that her whole system rejected. She could not forget.

Knowing that it was fruitless to contact the adoptive mother again, and feeling that she should not contact Lisa until she was eighteen, Cora took an alternative measure. She mailed the adoption book she had read to Lisa at the summer camp she was attending. She was careful not to put a name or return address on the package. It was her silent message to her daughter that she was out there.

"Of course I worried that she wouldn't want to have anything to do with me, but I knew I would eventually contact her, no matter how it turned out. If I didn't, I would always wonder and never know. If it didn't go well, I felt I would have to accept it. But not knowing would be worse."

Cora was prepared to wait for Lisa's eighteenth birthday, but she couldn't resist the urge to see what her daughter looked like. She and her husband cruised past the apartment house occasionally, and once when they saw Lisa playing Frisbee with her friends, Cora sat in the car while he snapped pictures of the group. It seemed a harmless thing to do, and it made waiting bearable.

About a month before Lisa's eighteenth birthday, Cora was amazed to receive a letter from her. Her parents had obviously feared the birth mother's next move, and had taken the initiative by giving their daughter her address. Lisa's letter was friendly but worded with great caution. It said she had always wanted to search, but was not sure how she felt about a relationship. She included the number of her private phone.

Cora called immediately. Most of the time was spent planning a meeting—she was to park her car a block from Lisa's apartment at noon the following Saturday.

"That day was something I'll never forget. When I saw her coming toward the car, I got out and walked to meet her. We put our arms around each other and just stood there for a few seconds. Then we got into the car and talked for about two hours. I showed her pictures of her sisters and other relatives, and told her what had happened. She didn't ask many questions. She's quiet, like me. She seemed happy, in good shape. She said she knew the book was from me, and was glad that I looked her up."

Cora talked to Lisa a few times on the phone after that. Once, when Lisa was out, her mother answered it. "My first impulse was to hang up, and then I realized I didn't have to. 'This is Cora,' I said. 'I know,' she replied. 'You're her mother,' I told her. 'I can't be her mother. I just want to be a friend.' And then I added that I thought she did a terrific job, that if I couldn't have her, I was glad she did. 'I believe you mean that,' she said."

Lisa was busy preparing for college, but Cora saw her a few times that year. Once she came out to Cora's house and met her half-sisters, the youngest of whom had not been told who she was. Cora was not alarmed at Lisa's reserve with everyone, for she had learned from her Adoptee friends that such relationships take time.

"Lisa was friendly, but not too friendly," she recalled. "She talked casually, but never said what she was really feeling. She was guarded. Once I asked if her parents knew she was with me and she said, 'Yeah, I think so.' When I asked her how they felt about it, she said, 'I don't know. My mother was mad about something this morning, but I'm not sure if it was this, or that I hadn't cleaned my room.' I asked if her adoptive parents would like to meet me. 'Oh, no,' she said emphatically, 'they would never want to.' "

Cora has a sense of well-being now that she has been reunited with Lisa. "I feel free—as if a tremendous weight has been lifted. In fact, I'm feeling good about everything, and everybody. My husband has been very helpful and supporting. He was anxious to meet Lisa because he knew how much it meant to me. We're closer because of this."

But Cora feels that if she had it to do over again she would not have involved the adoptive parents. "Maybe Lisa wouldn't have wanted them to know. I put her in a position where she had no choice. It might have been better to let her decide."

The one thing that Cora has not yet told Lisa is that her father has no interest in seeing her. It was a difficult thing to do, but Cora contacted him at work and told him she had found their daughter. Married now, with young children, he obviously did not want to complicate his life. "I'll tell her someday," Cora said. "But in the meantime, I just want to enjoy our relationship."

Lisa

I met Lisa soon after the reunion. She showed no reluctance to share the experience with me.

"It feels good," she said with a shy grin when I asked her how it felt to be found by her birth mother. "It makes me feel different—lucky."

Lisa seemed as self-possessed as her mother had described her. She was cool, almost detached, as she told me that she had always known she was adopted. Her parents had told her early. "We're so glad we adopted you," they made a point of repeating over the years.

"I always thought about my mother while I was growing up," she said. "Even at six I used to ask every imaginable kind of question. When I got older I wanted to know what my mother looked like. I'm short, and I wondered if she was tall. As it turns out she's not, but my father is. I also worried about what diseases I might inherit, since my adoptive mother's family had diabetes."

Although she asked a lot of questions of her parents, Lisa did not share her private world with her friends. "I didn't tell anyone I was adopted. It wasn't any of their business. And I knew it was something different. In the first grade when I told the kids, it turned around on me. They used to make fun of me."

Lisa had been told that her parents were too poor to keep her, but she fantasized that her mother was someone very pretty who couldn't raise her because she was famous. Dual fantasies operated at the same time, and, we might speculate, were the reason she kept two sets of friends: the wealthy ones from the private school she attended, and the less privileged ones from the poor families on her city block.

When she was twelve, Lisa remembers getting into a big fight with her adoptive mother, a volatile, extroverted woman who always said what was on her mind.

" 'You're not my real mother!' I shouted at her. 'If I were with my real mother, things would be different!'

" 'That's a feeble excuse!' she shouted back. 'I used to say "If I were adopted, things would be different" to my mother too.'

"I guess even then I was fighting for my freedom," Lisa explained. "We used to quarrel all the time, but in some ways it was good. We got it all out."

When at sixteen Lisa insisted on knowing everything, her father took her to the adoption agency to talk to one of the social workers. "But I didn't want to hear all that crap they told me," she said. "They weren't really telling me anything. I knew I was being given the runaround."

It was shortly after the agency experience that Lisa received the mysterious book in the camp mail.

"I was really freaked out. I read the book right away. I got into trouble because this was a work camp, and I wouldn't do anything that day. I wouldn't even talk to anyone. Everyone was upset with me, but I didn't care. I guess I thought of it as a sign. My parents had given me articles to read on people who were searching, and even told me when there were TV shows on that subject, so I just guessed it must be *her*. Still I made a point of calling home and asking my parents if they had sent it. When they didn't know anything about it, I said, 'It must be from my mother then.' And my adoptive mother snapped: 'Don't get your hopes up.' "

Of course, Lisa had no way of knowing that her birth mother

had been in touch with her parents earlier that year and that news of the mysterious package would upset them. She felt really good about getting the book, even though she didn't have proof of its source. "I didn't change afterwards, but there's a difference when you *know* there's a person out there. She wasn't dead. But I thought I'd wait until I was eighteen before trying to find out more."

The next summer, when she was seventeen and going off to do museum work in another town, her parents made their own move. "We don't want you to get any more unsigned mail," they told her. "We know who your natural mother is. We have her address." They were trying to sound unthreatened, but they couldn't resist adding that her mother had been "spying" on the apartment house, and was sitting in a car in front of the building when Lisa came home from camp the past year. They said it was bad taste to have been hanging around like that, and Lisa understood how they felt.

"As they spoke, I remembered that two years before I was outside with some friends playing Frisbee when a man took pictures of us. He asked for my address to send them, and I said, 'If I give you mine, give me yours.' I thought that was pretty clever at the time. He did send the pictures, and I wrote a letter back thanking him. There was a woman sitting in the car, but I thought nothing of it.

"I was in shock after my parents told me everything. A million feelings were going through me. All I could think to do was run to my room and call my best friend in California. 'You won't believe this!' I shouted on the phone. 'Wow, listen to this. . . .'"

Still Lisa did not take her mother's address from her parents, even though they insisted on it. "So you won't be upset if she contacts you again," they said. When Lisa returned at the end of the summer, they asked if her mother had been in touch with her, or if she had written her.

"I said no to both, which was the truth. But I had thought of her all summer. And since my parents had pointedly told me the address was in a certain drawer anytime I wanted it, I finally did write a letter. But even then I didn't mail it. I needed more time to think."

Lisa waited six months before sending the letter. She was now almost eighteen. "I wrote that I was not looking for an ideal relationship, but I wanted to see what she looked like. I threw the cards on the table. I guess I was telling her that I wasn't going to reject her, but not to expect too much."

As we know, Cora called as soon as she received the letter. "We made plans to meet that Saturday, but I didn't tell anyone. It was *my* thing. I didn't want any encouragement from my adoptive parents. But I was very nervous—and curious."

Lisa said she felt "weird" when she saw her mother. "I thought she'd look like me. But she didn't look familiar, even though our eyes are alike. Her face is round, and mine is long and pointed. We just sat in the car and talked, and then her husband joined us, and the three of us talked. He said he had been my father's best friend when he was going with my mother. He was excited, kept saying things like 'She smokes a cigarette like him' or 'Her expression is like his.' We talked about everything, biological things, why I was put up for adoption, my school, my life."

Lisa learned that her father had disappeared after Cora got pregnant. She was told how eighteen years ago it was hard to keep a child when you weren't married. And she understood. When they parted, she agreed to meet again in a few weeks.

That evening Lisa told her adoptive parents where she had been. "They were upset that I hadn't told them I was going. I guess that's natural. I tried to reassure them. I said, 'Listen you guys, I'm not disowning you.'"

However, Lisa did not tell her parents the day she went to meet her half-sisters at her mother's house. "It was strange," she said. "We all sat stiffly around the table. I look a lot like the younger one. I think I'll get to know them gradually. I enjoy being with them, but I'm not trying to stick myself in a family. I don't feel I belong there. The only tie we have is a blood relationship. It's like a long-lost person is found. I know I'll keep in touch because Cora is a blood relation. It's a good feeling to have a blood relative."

Lisa has not told her adoptive brother, who is three years younger and has always had problems with discipline and school. "He's such a blabbermouth, he'd tell everyone I know," she said. But she added thoughtfully, "And it might make him feel bad to know I was sought out and he wasn't."

I noticed that "sought out" is the term she used for being found.

"My brother never talks about his adoption, or asks questions like I did. He just isn't ready. But age doesn't have anything to do with when you meet your mother. I think I would have been ready two years earlier. I had prepared myself. I thought about it thoroughly. A lot of kids say, 'Yeah, I would like to meet my mother,' but they don't think about the things that might happen. I knew I wasn't going to have a relationship. I've had a happy life. I used to be painfully shy and sensitive, but I've learned to overcome it. I'm very independent. I've always been my own person. I know who I am. Meeting my natural mother has only helped me to know myself biologically. I am myself."

Lisa felt that birth mothers of young children should wait, not "prowl" around their schools. "I would have felt freaked out if my mother had come up to me years ago. It's such a shock. And if you can't tell your adoptive parents, it sets up a conflict."

She seemed to be saying that if it could be done the right way, with the adoptive parents knowing, and if the Adoptee was thoughtful and prepared in advance, then it could be a good thing—being *"sought out."*

I asked how her adoptive parents were taking all this now.

"My father pretends it hasn't really happened. It's weird. And my mother says she does not want to meet Cora. I can understand. It's like coming face-to-face with your threat. But I keep telling her it is my life. It has nothing to do with how much I care about her and Dad. We've been together a long time, for eighteen years. I just don't tell her each time I meet them. It's not necessary. It would just keep hurting them. Like if someone has a defect, you don't keep talking about it—like 'you have a defect.' It's just something else that's happened. I'm not trying to be threatening to them."

Lisa is convinced that she would have searched if Cora hadn't found her first. "I think it's bad *not* to search," she said. "For biological reasons one should know. If a doctor asks if your family had cancer, you should be able to answer." She appreciates the risk Cora took—"I could easily have said I don't want to meet you."

Was it better to be sought after than to search?

She thought about this for a while. "It might be better to be sought out," she decided. "It's being magical. Being lucky. I guess

I am different now. I know I will make it as an actress. I know my mother, I've seen her. In my school there are other adopted kids, but I'm sure none of them were found. I'm more confident of myself now. I think my life is going to go well."

Lisa was already eighteen by the time her mother made contact. What happens when the children are even younger? It was to get further data on this that I followed up Connie's meeting with her fifteen-year-old daughter, Beth, and Julia and Jon's with their fourteen-year-old daughter, Debbie.

In both cases the birth parents had reached an obsessional stage where they could not turn back. And the adoptive parents were forced into the reunion process, because at some point they must have realized that not to participate would have endangered their relationship with their child. It would have meant being left out.

Connie and Beth

Connie, who had conceived Beth when she was fourteen, found herself thinking about her when her daughter reached that age. What was she like as a person? Did she ever wonder who her mother was? She returned to the agency and told the social worker that she would like to waive her right to confidentiality and put a letter to Beth in her file. She was informed that there was no way for her daughter's family to know about this unless they happened to contact the agency—something adoptive parents rarely do.

Hearing that an Adoptee group had just formed in her area, Connie went to a meeting. There she met other women like herself, who felt they had been forced to surrender their babies. A few of them had already begun searching for their whereabouts. It seemed impossible, but she was luckier than most. Within a few months she had Beth's adoptive name and address, but she was determined to wait until her daughter was eighteen before contacting her. "I can't be sure she knows she's adopted," she reasoned. "I wouldn't do anything to upset her at this stage of life."

Connie's daughter by her marriage was thrilled to learn she had an older sister. She kept urging her mother to write her. And

Connie found that though she wanted to forget Beth for the next few years, she was becoming obsessed with thoughts about her.

Eight months after she had located her daughter's address, Connie telephoned her, pretending to be a "roots" survey person for a national magazine that had carried an adoption article. The idea was to find out how she felt about not knowing her heritage. If possible, Connie wanted to learn if Beth had the need to meet her.

The ruse worked, but Beth didn't seem too interested in the subject. Loud music was blaring in the background. Connie, afraid to probe, asked a few general questions about heritage, but did not mention the subject of adoption. Reluctant to hang up, she asked Beth for the phone number of a teenage friend whom she might also contact for the survey.

It took Connie a few weeks to recover from the exhilaration of that conversation with Beth, but then she began brooding over the indignity of her position. "It was a shoddy thing for me to do," she said. "I shouldn't have to be talking to my daughter pretending to be someone else. I won't do it again. I'm going to wait until she's eighteen before making another move."

But a few months later, Connie picked up the phone as a roots survey person again. This time she called the friend whose number Beth had given her. She asked her if she knew any adopted people. "My best friend, Beth, is adopted," the girl said. "And does she want to know about her heritage?" Connie asked. "She always wonders about who her real parents were," came the reply. "Last year she asked the people she was living with to give her more information. But they didn't have any."

Connie was wild with joy after that call. She couldn't get over the friend referring to her daughter's adoptive parents as "the people she was living with." Now at last she knew Beth wanted to know about her. It convinced her that she had a right to enter her daughter's life. Certain that the agency wouldn't help, and afraid that the adoptive parents would resist her, she decided to call her directly. Beth would then have the choice of whether she wanted her parents to know.

Still, it took two months to muster up the courage. Then one afternoon Connie picked up the phone and called her daughter. "It was so easy dialing this time," she told me. "Such a normal, natural thing to do. I thought to myself, 'Why didn't I do this last year when I first got the number?' "

After some preparatory comments, Connie said, "This is your mother."

And Beth shrieked, "You're my mother? I can't believe it. I was just talking to my friend about you—only I didn't know it was you—saying I wanted to search for you someday. But I thought you were dead."

"I must have sounded like a voice from the grave," Connie told me. "I said I was very much alive, that she had a sister named Patty who wanted to see her. And I'd be glad to meet her parents if she wanted to share this with them."

Beth replied, "They have a right to know, because I'm so excited I won't be able to sleep for three days."

When Connie put down the phone her heart was pounding as if she had just robbed a bank or forged a check. She expected to hear from the authorities at any moment—the police, Beth's parents' lawyer, Beth's parents themselves, the social worker at her agency . . .

But she wasn't sorry she had done it. "It was too cruel a punishment, never knowing the end of your story," she said. "Now I know."

Although one might wish Connie had been able to have an intermediary to prepare her daughter's family for her sudden appearance, it seems to have worked out well for Beth. Two days after her phone call, Connie received a letter from her. She remembers feeling so faint when she saw the envelope in the post office that she had to run into her friend's delicatessen next door to sit down. The owner, who knew the story, hugged and kissed her, and then wept while stuffing the sausage, as she listened to Connie reading her daughter's words:

> I don't know where to start. I always wondered when walking down the street if the woman I'd pass was my mother. Thanks to you that wonder is gone, and the feeling I would never find you is gone, too. I was thinking all day and night about the things you said about always loving me, and it made me feel wanted for once. At one time I had a lot of problems. I thought no one cared. I once even tried to kill myself, then I realized that I never knew what tomorrow might bring.

"I've been going to a counselor about six months now, and she really helped me to straighten my head out. Most of the problem was me trying to find myself. I felt like I had an empty space, and I did until that day you called.

"My mother and father were surprised, and as shocked as I was. We are really closer now that I've found myself. My father said he would call you, but will tell me when he calls because it is about me. I hope he does but I know he's a stubborn man."

The rest of the letter was a description of her boyfriends and school activities.

"It was so mind-blowing to know she had my name and address," Connie told me. "And to see her handwriting—which was terrible!"

She could bring some humor to it all now. But she was serious about being sure she had done the right thing in contacting Beth. "I'm glad I did it, especially now that I've learned she was having problems. By the time she's sixteen or seventeen she won't have to work all of this out."

When they exchanged pictures, Beth wrote that it made her feel good, special, like she had another family. Yet Connie was aware of feeling depressed for a few days. "It was as if I were grieving for the baby I've been yearning for all this time. Babies don't write letters or have boyfriends."

Connie's mother had not wanted her to search for Beth, but now she was saying things like, "I hope I can see her before I die. After all, she's my granddaughter." At such moments Connie could not resist snapping back, "She wasn't your granddaughter then." Still she was glad that her mother wanted a copy of Beth's picture for her wallet, unlike her father, who said, "What can I do with it? I can't show it to anyone."

Connie knows that her mother feels guilty now. "I can forgive her," she said, "because she believed it was for the best at the time, that I would forget. But the child in me will never forgive her."

During the anxious period of waiting to hear from Beth's father, I received desperate calls from Connie: What did I think was going on in his mind? Were he and his wife seeking advice from the agency? Should she write and reassure them that she didn't want to take their daughter away? She didn't want to do this through Beth, for fear of using her as a battlefield. In the meantime, she kept rereading Beth's letters, especially the one that said, "I can hardly wait to see you in the flesh. I feel now that nothing is impossible."

Although the veil between life and death had separated them all those years, in reality Connie and Beth lived only a few hours apart. After a month had passed without a call from the adoptive father, Connie could stand it no longer. She picked up the phone once again and told Beth that she was coming in to shop in the large city between their two houses. Would she like to meet her there? Beth was excited by the idea, but wanted to ask her parents' permission. She called back shortly and said it was all right with them.

"I had three anxiety attacks on the way there," Connie told me. "I took my brother with me because even at thirty-one I couldn't have made it alone."

Beth must have felt the same way, for she arrived with her boyfriend. Later she said she was sure Connie would be late, and was surprised to see her waiting in the restaurant booth.

"I was amazed at how tall and striking she was," Connie recalls. "Her bone structure has an exotic cast. She's much slimmer than I ever was. I was wishing I had taken my diet more seriously, so she wouldn't be disappointed. It was awkward at first, but we laughed when we saw we each had a freckle at the tip of our nose. We didn't touch, but later when we were strolling through a park, we held onto each other crossing a narrow footbridge over the lake, because we each had a fear of heights. Our conversation was nothing special—just the things we liked to do. It seemed so natural. I alternated between feeling completely satisfied and cheated that I had been forced to give her up—but then she might not have been the same person if I had raised her. We hugged and kissed when we parted in the late afternoon. It was like letting air out of tires. 'This is the nicest day of my life,' she said. 'Let's do it again soon.'

"I gave her a tin of muffins I'd baked to give to her parents as a way of saying 'You were part of today.' I really appreciated their letting me see her alone the first time. Her father even gave her twenty dollars as she was leaving."

The next day Connie received an excited call from Beth that her parents were driving down to talk with her the next Saturday. They wanted to meet in a restaurant midway.

"I couldn't imagine what they'd say to me, but my daughter Patty was even more nervous than I was," Connie said. "Patty had started seeing a therapist shortly after I contacted Beth, and now she admitted that she was afraid that Beth would take me away from her, or that I would like Beth better. She even had a nightmare that Beth's father might come with a shotgun and shoot me, since Beth had written that he was a hunter. I had to assure her that my loyalties would always be with her, that nothing would change how I felt about her. And actually it's true—I have limits. I didn't want to take on too much."

Connie's husband was working that night so she took her brother with her to meet Beth's parents. They proved to be simple, straightforward people, genuinely concerned about their daughter's welfare. As soon as everyone had relaxed with a drink, they told Connie that their daughter had been so happy since first hearing from her that they would never take it away from her. In fact, they admitted, she had been a troubled, even angry kid until now. On her birthdays she often ran away, or stayed out overnight. Once in one of her uncontrollable rages she had put her fist through a glass window. In desperation they had put her into therapy.

Beth's mother did not appear threatened by Connie. "If I was adopted, I guess I'd want to know," she said. But she had taken no information from the agency except Connie's age and religion because, as she put it, it would have been "like having a fixed script."

Still both parents confessed to being shocked when Connie called. They said they would have felt less threatened if they had been contacted by the agency first. The only thing they asked of Connie was that she not get Beth too involved in "outside" activities such as adoption groups, because her school work was not too strong.

"I assured them they shouldn't worry," Connie said. "I told them that if there was ever anything out of line, to call or write me. We were feeling so good about each other by the end of the evening that they invited me to bring Patty and my husband to dinner at their house the following Sunday."

During that next week Connie was on the phone telling her

birth mother friends about this meeting with the parents. "My feelings toward them have really changed," she kept saying, as if she couldn't believe it herself. "They are real people. I can even call them Beth's parents without gagging. They've restored my faith in adoptive parents."

Dinner at Beth's house the next weekend was a real feast—baked scrod, fettuccine, blueberry tarts. Even Patty seemed to be enjoying herself, as if Beth was less threatening when seen in the context of her family life. "I could have been a neighbor or a distant aunt from Ohio the way we sat in the living room after dinner," Connie said. "But at one point when some of her friends dropped by, I heard Beth saying in the doorway, 'That's my real mother.'

"We spent a lot of time looking through old scrapbooks of Beth growing up, and her mother gave me a photo of her when she was three. I thought it was a sharing kind of thing. And I also thought how much Beth looked like both me and Patty at that age, but I didn't say so. It was a beautiful feeling to be sitting in that room with both my children. Once my eyes met Beth's, and we smiled. When we left that night, we all promised to get together soon, but I hope they'll let Beth come down alone to stay with us for a weekend. Patty wants that, too. She feels much better after our visit, especially after seeing Beth in her own house. I keep reminding her that right now it's like Hollywood—we're all fairy people—but after a while we'll be real. I'll be like an aunt or cousin, a relative who's always been there." There was a pause after this, as if she hadn't quite convinced herself. "But I also know I can never go away from Beth again. I can never reject her, not even by implication."

In her last letter Beth wrote that she would always feel special because her mother found her. Connie speculated. "Maybe kids who are acting out feel healed when contacted by us. Maybe searching redeems us."

Julia, Jon, and Debbie

It is still rare for the birth father to be involved with the Search, but when Julia first went to look for the daughter she had surrendered eleven years before, she had Jon with her. They were not married at the time of Debbie's birth and are not married now. They have always been, as they say, "independent, loyal friends," living together on and off over the years. Jon never wanted to be tied down, and certainly not when he learned that Julia had made a mistake about taking the birth-control pills. He still feels it was *her* mistake, and that there was no reason for him to change his lifestyle because of it. But, he admits, at that time the concept of a baby was unreal to him. It was only when he stood with Julia across the street from their child's house and saw a wonderful eleven-year-old girl climbing a tree in the yard that it became real, that he felt he was a father. That he wanted to meet her.

Julia was twenty-eight, Jon, thirty-one, when they first met. "I had high hopes of marriage then," Julia says, "but I was really frightened when I found out I was pregnant. I hid my predicament from everyone, feeling I would bring disgrace on my family, and that they would try to force Jon to marry me. Abortion was out since we were Catholic. And Jon was traveling in Europe. I told my mother that I was going to visit my sister for a few weeks in Seattle. I didn't tell her I was going to stay, for in those days, in traditional Italian families, even women of my age did not live outside their parents' home."

Julia got a job in Seattle, and her sister's doctor promised to arrange a private adoption. She told everyone at the office that her husband was finishing up his work in the Midwest and would join her later. When she had to leave work at the end of her sixth month, because of company policy, she managed to get through a baby shower, pretending to be thrilled with the lace dresses and bonnets, diapers and rattles.

It wasn't until her seventh month, while living alone in a bleak one-room, street-floor apartment, that Julia called Jon and told him her predicament. "I dared ask him the big question— would you marry me? I had no real hopes, but considered it an outside chance. He said no as gently as he could. He spoke from his heart. He was genuinely concerned for me and the baby, but feared he would become resentful if he had to take on family responsibilities. He was not coming from a rejection of me. He wanted to feel free, no harness, no corral."

Until now Julia was hoping she would not have to go through with the adoption plan. But knowing she could never return home to her mother with a baby, she consoled herself with the thought of her child growing up deeply wanted in a conventional family—one such as hers had been.

"I see now that the adoption process was a very stacked deck, still is," she says. "But I was too mixed up, embarrassed, and passive to even ask for counseling. I just knew that a state agency would be too remote and impersonal, and at least the doctor was telling me something about a few couples I could choose from."

During those last few months Julia had stayed hidden in her apartment so that no one would know her secret. The night she went into labor, the building superintendent and his wife, who lived below, heard her moaning and came up. She told them she had intestinal pains and asked to be taken to the hospital. Pretending to go along with her story, they got her there. She delivered Debbie the next morning, but because the doctor had advised her against seeing it, her baby was gone when she woke up. She had to content herself with descriptions that her sister gave when she came to take her back to the apartment.

"I couldn't go home to my parents, so I found another job," Julia said. "I told no one what I had been through, but I was really depressed. I felt I was a bad woman who had done a shameful thing. Not in having a baby, but in giving her up. I kept trying to hold onto the rationale that it was best for the baby, but my heart wouldn't accept what my head was saying. I didn't know why the pain wouldn't go away like everyone said it would. I felt so guilty. One day a kind of madness came over me. I closed all the windows in the kitchen, turned the gas jets on, and stuck my head in the oven. But I must have done something wrong, because after a while I was still conscious. I realized I didn't want to die after all. So I turned the jets off and opened the windows. I didn't tell anyone what I had done."

Six months later, when the time came to sign the adoption papers, the lawyer made a point of picking her up at the office and driving her to the courthouse. "I cried all the way back," she remembers. "He told me that if I had any questions I could always get in touch with him."

But all Julia wanted to do was forget. She moved back to the Midwest and, although her mother objected, took her own apartment. And continued seeing Jon. They never talked of the baby, but she found herself thinking about her constantly, and praying for her. She also began getting such severe migraine headaches that she went into therapy. "It helped me understand my heavy involvement with my mother, and to work out my guilt," she said. "I learned that I had given up the thing I had treasured most, but when I could face my own responsibility for what I had done, I felt better about it. I never imagined that I would go searching for Debbie."

On Debbie's tenth birthday, Julia and Jon found themselves talking about her, wondering what she was like. It was then that Julia confessed she had accidentally seen the name of the adoptive parents on the papers. "It's funny," she says, "I didn't know if I had a right to tell him the name. I had kept it to myself all this time."

The next year when they were passing through Seattle on a charter flight to the Far East, the plane was delayed for a few days. Jon surprised Julia by suggesting that they look in the phone book for the name she had seen. It was there. A short cab ride took them to the spot across the street where they saw her in the tree. That night, passing by once again, they glimpsed her silhouette in the window.

It was then that their obsession began. During the remaining days before the plane took off, they watched Debbie at her various activities, hung around the schoolyard where they took pictures of everyone, in order to get hers. They even managed to make friends with one of the teenage boys on her block. But still, they planned to wait until Debbie was eighteen before revealing who they were to anyone.

"Jon really changed after seeing Debbie. Before then he was always private, never shared his feelings with anyone. Detached, I guess you'd say. Now he became mellow, almost overnight. He couldn't talk about anything else all through the trip in the Far East."

When they returned to the Midwest, they began attending Adoptee meetings in their community and were moved by the vivid stories they heard of adult searches. What if their daughter had to go through the pain of not knowing her origins? They wanted to spare her. Updating her records seemed one solution. But how? Julia remembered that the nice lawyer who helped her at the time offered his services if she ever needed anything. She poured out her heart to him in a long letter, but there was no answer. A few months later she wrote again, this time to the adoptive parents, explaining that she and Jon were "good, decent folks" who did not want to steal their daughter away, but wanted to inform her about themselves, her grandparents, and "an assortment of other relatives."

> We are not national flags or ethnic cultures, but living, unique persons. Our stories are genuinely positive, undamaging, and acceptable. Personal dialogue is our way. We're recommending a preventive health strategy now in Debbie's early teens. It'll be a lot harder later. Debbie always owns herself, as we all do, and is old enough now to have some voice in her personal affairs. Why risk the possibility of Debbie's confusion about her genetic origins becoming a problem?

This time they got a formal reply from the lawyer, informing them that "when Debbie is sufficiently mature, she will be told more about you, and if she wishes to follow up the matter, then her adoptive parents will welcome that fact, and give her every assistance."

Julia and Jon became furious with the lawyer's rebuff, and what they considered a lack of consideration for them on the part of the adoptive parents. They changed their minds about waiting until Debbie was eighteen. They would fly out to Seattle that spring and contact her directly. They held to this plan, even though the adult Adoptees and birth parents in their group had cautioned them to think everything through carefully before taking any rash action.

I saw them shortly after they returned from the spring trip. Events had taken a turn that no one could have foreseen.

After checking into their motel, they began staking out Debbie's house again. There was no sign of her. For a few days they staggered their hours, and combed the schoolyard, but still they couldn't spot her. Finally they contacted the teenage boy on the block, whom they hardly recognized, he had grown so tall, only to learn that Debbie had been sent to boarding school in another part of the state.

That evening they looked up Julia's sister and her husband, Arthur, whom they had not seen for some years, and confided their plan to fly to Debbie's school over the weekend. Arthur was indignant: "What do you think you're doing?" he challenged them. "Do you want your child back?"

The morning they were to leave they received a call from

Arthur. He had phoned Debbie's parents and informed them what was about to happen. Now it was Julia and Jon's turn to be incensed. They remembered that this sister and her husband had given up their first child for adoption before they were married, and were obviously playing the good burghers now, on the side of law and order. There was no choice but to rethink their plans. Speculating that Debbie's parents might bring her home immediately, they stayed at the motel through the week. Then Julia phoned the adoptive home and asked to speak to Debbie. The father answered that she was away at school and asked who was calling. He seemed pleased to hear that it was Julia, almost as if he had been waiting. He suggested they all meet.

The lawyer, acting as mediator, sent over a list of conditions that they were to agree to in advance. They had to promise not to "spy" on the house anymore, not to contact Debbie again, and so on. Although they felt insulted by the innuendoes of the provisions, Julia and Jon agreed to everything in order not to jeopardize their meeting with their daughter.

The session with the parents was held at the courthouse—on long hard benches. Frances, the adoptive mother, was in an angry, aggressive mood. She declared that she would speak first, with no interruptions. For the next half-hour she complained that no one had considered her feelings. While Julia and Jon were traveling around the world having a good time, she was home doing dirty dishes and being a baby-sitter. Finally Julia touched her arm gently. "But you got the best part," she said, with tears in her eyes. At this both women began weeping, and the meeting went smoothly after that.

It was agreed that Debbie would come to the motel the next Saturday, but that she would be accompanied by her two older brothers—who were the adoptive parents' natural children.

Julia and Jon waited anxiously for that knock on the door. As Julia opened it, she spontaneously planted a kiss on Debbie's cheek, recalling at the same moment that Frances had warned her Debbie didn't like physical affection. "She let me do it, though," Julia said. "And she seemed excited to see the golden retriever we had brought with us on the plane. We explained that we had named it Debbie, after her. Then we all got into our rented car to go to the horse show which her brothers thought she would enjoy.

"Debbie piled into the back seat with me as if I were a casual friend, not the mother she'd never known. She had her baby album with her and showed me some of the pictures. I felt a pang at her surprise that I did not know about the birthmark on her neck. I couldn't bring myself to tell her that everyone had advised me not to see her. Anyway, we had a great day at the show, and had some ice cream together before we dropped them off. When we gave her our address, we didn't expect to see her again on that trip.

"We were feeling let down the next morning when there was a knock on our door. It was Debbie with a girlfriend. 'This is the dog I was telling you about,' were her first words as she proudly showed off her namesake to this girl. Then we talked about things in general, nothing really personal, for about an hour until they had to go. She was returning to school that afternoon. Before she left, I gave her the antique earrings I had brought with me, even though Frances had asked me not to when I mentioned them at the courthouse. 'She's too irresponsible now,' Frances had said. But I found myself doing it anyhow."

The next day Frances surprised them by phoning and suggesting a walk. Her husband had taken off on a fishing trip to get away from it all, and she was alone.

"We really had a relaxed afternoon with her, strolling along the pier and talking about everything," Julia recalled. "I apologized for giving Debbie the earrings. 'It's all right,' Frances replied quickly. 'Debbie gave them to me to keep for her.' "

Julia and Jon met with Frances once more before leaving, this time seeing more pictures of Debbie, and hearing anecdotes about her growing up. They learned that Debbie had been asking about them since she was five. At seven she was particularly persistent, but at nine Frances had deliberately turned her off the subject and she had not asked any questions since. "I didn't feel it was good for her to know anything more then," Frances explained. "That's one reason I was so upset to get your letter. I knew I would be lying if I said I didn't have any more information."

"We had a good feeling about things," Julia said. "Frances seemed to accept and trust us. She spoke about having gone into therapy when our letter arrived, about trying to work through her feelings so she won't be threatened. She wants to be able to tell her elderly mother who lives with them that Debbie met her birth parents, but she can't. I told her that I still haven't told my mother I had Debbie, let alone found her. Frances suggested that maybe she and Debbie could visit my mother's house together and break the news that way. It made us feel very close talking like this."

And yet.

They did not hear from Frances after they returned home. An invitation to Debbie to stop by on her way to Europe with her class that summer was turned down. And when Julia called the house to wish her bon voyage, Frances' first response was "Julia who?" Debbie's voice sounded much more restrained than it had been over the phone at school, when she had told them how happy she was to have seen them and had asked many questions about her other relatives. Now she was monosyllabic, as if already she was sensing the pulls between these two sets of parents.

There was not even a postcard from her during the trip, which worried them. In the fall they received a short note that she was now living at home, instead of returning to the boarding school.

It seemed that the adoptive parents were retrenching their position, keeping their daughter close by their side.

Not until October did Frances forward the Italian postcard which Debbie had mistakenly sent to the Seattle address three months before. There was no apology for the delay, just the line, "Thanks for keeping it low-key."

They understood the message, but still at Christmas they couldn't resist sending Debbie stacks of presents through a friend who reported that he found her composed, but noncommittal. However, Debbie did say that she and her mother were planning a trip to visit Julia and Jon the next summer.

"Will they really come? Can we continue to be her friend?" Julia wonders. She admits she'd like to be more than a friend since meeting Debbie, to be available emotionally as a mother, should her daughter ever need her.

"Why does it all have to be so heavy?" Jon keeps asking. "Why can't we be in her life when we want, traveling and having good times with her?"

Still they are restraining their impulse to call or write Debbie for a while. They don't want to put her under any pressure.

How will it all work out in the long run? As Erikson has told us, "Only time will tell." But for now we can say that no one was hurt, and Debbie, like Lisa and Beth, seems genuinely happy to have been sought out. Although her adoptive parents resisted for a while, they finally accepted the situation and could appreciate that Julia and Jon had not burst into their house, but had made the effort to contact them first. Their fears had proven worse than the reality.

Frances and Julia, the two mothers, really enjoyed each other during their walks, each empathizing with how the other felt. As Frances said: "We both love the same child." And even though Frances has obviously decided to slow things down for the present, one has the feeling that over the years everyone will find some way of accommodating, for the child's sake.

It is time to consider that some teenagers will be helped by knowing their birth parents while they are struggling to form their mature identity. That such an early meeting might alleviate their anxieties and self-doubts and save them from the confusion of those later years. As we have seen, adoptive and birth parents cease to fear each other once they have actually met as real people, although everyone realizes there will be some tensions until the newness of such situations wears off.

The question of whether these birth mothers have a right to reenter their children's lives is a murky but useless one. Once their need has become an obsession, they cannot stop. They, too, agonize that the timing of this need may not coincide with the child's, but how can they know as long as there is no intermediary to help them? Agencies are still unwilling to undertake the responsibility without a court order; religious and psychological counselors do not feel it is in their domain. The birth mother will remain in the impossible position of having to find her own hit-and-miss method of getting through to either parents or child until society recognizes that it is in the child's interests that her need be respected, and sets up authorized channels to assist her. The child can only be benefited by having the active participation of the adoptive parents in this reunion process: without it he will be burdened with yet another secret, and torn apart in a conflict over loyalties.

27

Adoptive Parents–
Are They
Baby-Sitters?

It would appear that adoptive parents need to be more
mature and psychologically aware than biological parents
because of the special obstacles they face. They need
to know more about themselves and to be capable of
empathizing with their child's position.
SOROSKY TEAM

A s we might expect, adoptive parents feel very anxious about
the birth mother's entrance into the search arena. They are
now faced with finding not only a workable strategy to cope
with their child's possible search but one to deal with the birth
mother's search as well. Like Lisa's parents, they can take the
offensive and act first by giving identifying information to their
child. Or like Debbie's, they can meet the nemesis straight on
and arrange a meeting among adults only. It is a big decision to
face the birth mothers—it makes them real. But adoptive parents
are learning they may have no choice. If a birth mother is determined to approach the child with or without their permission,
they may have to cooperate in order not to be excluded.

Of course, most birth mothers and fathers are not searching, but with every media story on the subject the adoptive parents' fear of losing their children is reinforced. They are catapulted back to the panic of that earlier childless state where things become polarized into either I have a child or I don't. Either I am a parent or a baby-sitter. Either/or.

Once again those earlier doubts are stimulated. Did they have a *legitimate* right to someone else's child? Are they impostors masquerading as authentic parents? Their own immortality is at stake if the child returns to that other family tree. They are overwhelmed with feelings of failure, separation, and loss.

I find that even the most hardy among them, those who had been determined to keep an open mind about reunion when their children were older, are now beginning to pull back in alarm.

Take Louise, whose daughter is now ten: "I have struggled for years around the issue of entitlement. When people say things like 'Are you still trying to have your own children?' and countless variations on this theme—which convey they don't think adoptive parents are real parents—that undermines the adoptive parents' feelings of legitimacy. I think some of the threatened feelings adoptive parents have stem from shaky feelings about their legitimacy as parents on the whole issue of 'Who are the *real* parents?' "

Louise has always tried to be honest with herself. A few years ago she and her husband started a small adoptive parent group, which held discussions on all the literature they could find. Louise said brave things like "When she is old enough to search, I hope I will be strong enough to help her."

She was thinking she had a lot of time—then. But now that her daughter is talking constantly about reunion with her *real* mother, Louise admits she does feel threatened. She's beginning to wonder if her talking so openly to her daughter over the past few years may not have had the effect of stimulating her into wanting to meet that mother. Now she's trying to put the lid on their discussions. "I did tell her some of my trepidations (since I don't want her to start repressing her feelings on my account), that though we love and support her and understand her need to search when she gets older, I personally do feel somewhat insecure and possessive about her and the search. She was very loving and reassuring when I told her that. It is very delicate—

I don't want her to feel guilty, but I think it is good for me to be more honest about my feelings than I was in the past."

Louise's fears are escalating with the escalation of birth mother activities. There is a large CUB group in her area, and it disturbs her to think her daughter's mother could be parked in front of the school, or even in front of their house. She's decided she does not like being part of a "social experiment." "I can't quite see the future of adoption as an extended-family situation in our culture. The point of view about being open about things is tempting, seems healthy, yet something in me says 'be cautious.' "

"What are you afraid of?" I ask Louise and other parents when we meet or correspond.

"That it will break up our family," Louise admits. She feels the birth mother who searches is unfair to both the child and the adoptive parents. "The child should have the choice of knowing or not knowing her birth parents. If the birth mother shows up, that takes away the choice."

It is this issue of *choice* that psychiatrists like Erik Erikson also worry about. They feel the child should make the decision about knowing, rather than either the adoptive or birth parent making it for him.

However, some adoptive parents rationalize that their fears are only for their children, rather than admitting that they also fear for themselves. As one father said: "I am really just worried about my son and daughter. I don't want them to be hurt."

For the adoptive parent, as for the Adoptee, it takes a long time to move from one psychological space to another—until one can cope with the full complexity of the emotions involved. One may think one will understand if the child ever talks about searching but feel devastated when it happens.

Many adoptive parents describe feeling angry before feeling threatened. One woman wrote:

> My eleven-year-old daughter has brought up four or five times this year her desire to know her *other parents*. My initial reaction was one of anger at her curiosity. I could see no reason, because we have always enjoyed a special closeness. I asked myself how we could not be enough. My next reaction was fear that her curiosity would somehow threaten our relationship.

When anger turns to fear, adoptive parents express it like this:

I fear I'll lose my children. That I'm not lovable. It's very scary.

You devote your whole life to them, and all of a sudden they're saying "Where's the mother who had me in her stomach for nine months?"

We've got our own family, and I hate to think of a whole other family getting involved, I guess. There could be half-brothers and sisters.

We fear separation. He might reject us.

Much of the adoptive parents' anxiety centers around that phantom birth mother whom, until now, they have been able to dismiss *as if* dead. She has been frozen in time for them, as for the Adoptee, and strangely enough they, too, fantasize about her—as if she is some eternally young Lucy in the sky with diamonds—rather than a mortal being like themselves, on whom the years have taken their toll. Although they have been protesting, too much, that they are the *real* parents, they often slip into the term *real* for her, exposing momentarily their darkest fear—that blood may after all be thicker than water:

What frightens me is that there'll be this real relationship that's recognized when our children meet those biological parents. Instant recognition I guess you'd call it.

My fantasy is that she's young and beautiful. It's scary. She'll steal them away.

They'll have things in common, the same attitudes. And then our relationship will be grafted onto that relationship.

Many parents try to delay the whole issue of the birth mother's identity by saying they'll wait to deal with it until the child is mature enough. And when is that? Some of them feel that eighteen, the legal age for everyone else, is too soon. A few suggest twenty-five as the earliest possible age. And, as we've seen, some believe the Adoptee could never be old enough. We must ask whether the adoptive parents, with their own bias, can judge when their child is ready, if they themselves are not; and if they have a moral or legal right to make that decision for a person who is considered by law to be enough of an adult to vote and to die for his country in war.

John Gregory Dunne, a writer married to the novelist Joan
Didion, expressed their fears about their eleven-year-old daughter, Quintana, quite articulately in an *Esquire* magazine article.
He admitted that although it was never an effort to say she was
adopted, they are aware "that sometime in the not too distant
future we face a moment that only those of us who are adoptive
parents will ever have to face—our daughter's decision to search
or not to search for her natural parents."

But while insisting that he sees his daughter's possible search
for roots as an adventure, like life itself, with the possibility that
it will be both painful and enriching, he adds: "We would prefer
she wait to make this decision until the Sturm and Drang of
adolescence is over."

Like the others, Dunne is resistant to the fact that adoption
adds much of the Sturm and Drang to their child's adolescence.
He does not understand the innate wisdom of his little daughter,
whom he quotes anecdotally: "I once asked her what she would
do if she met her natural mother. 'I'd put one arm around Mom,'
she said, 'and one arm around my other mommy, and I'd say
"Hello, mommies." ' "[1]

We are reminded here that the young Adoptee, unlike the older
one, is not fully aware of how polarized the two sets of parents
are supposed to be. She wishes to do what comes naturally, which
in this case is to be friendly with both. The child seems to be
able to accept that duality, to reject the either/or.

We saw Lisa calling her parents from camp, asking if they
had sent the book, although something in her knew they hadn't;
and Debbie giving Julia's earrings to her adoptive mother to
hold; and Beth wanting to share the excitement over the call
from Connie with her adoptive parents. In just such a spirit,
how nice it would be if adoptive parents and birth parents could
link arms when the need arises and say "Hi, child!"

Still, in sober reflection, we must ask if it is possible, given
the strict taboos of the past, for these two sets of parents to link
arms in the near future. We must ask if the Adoption Game can
change radically all at once—or if it will take years for the par-
ticipants to be able to approach each other in a spirit of recon-
ciliation and confidence, rather than hostility and fear.

For now, there is the danger that the adoptive parents may lose
the self-confidence that everyone needs to be a good parent, and

collapse under the pressure. The mother of two young girls confessed to me, "I can't handle this. I'm beginning to feel I haven't got it in me to help my children grow into integrated people." However, after passing through this panic stage, and discussing her fears openly with groups of adult Adoptees and with other adoptive parents, she called to say she felt freer, that she was no longer in fear of what her kids will ask next.

She was on her way to becoming a *real* parent.

It is at the time when the adoptive parents feel most threatened and vulnerable that they must experience a kind of rebirth, not unlike the Adoptees', after they have accepted the limitations of rootedness along with its joys. The adoptive parents will regain their confidence when they understand that their problems with their children are special, but not insurmountable; that part of the process of raising adopted children is to give them the freedom to seek their origins, and to sanction the special identity that will develop out of this.

I am beginning to hear from some parents who are actively involved with their children in the Search. One mother of a fifteen-year-old wrote:

> I think you have to know your own child, how sincere she is. Whether she's asking out of a fit of anger or really wants to know. If it's weighing on her mind day in and day out, it's sincere. Then she would search at whatever age. She won't outgrow this feeling. A lot of my whole family thinks I'm nuts to be doing this. "Do you really know what you are doing?" they ask. I do. And I try to prepare her for it.

Another adoptive mother approached me after a workshop to tell me that she knew the identity of her six-year-old son's birth mother, and had been keeping track of her whereabouts in case he ever wanted to meet her. Still, she worried about the possibility that he would be rejected, and wondered how she could learn the birth mother's attitude without revealing her own identity. I suggested that she have the lawyer who arranged the adoption ask the birth mother if she would like to update her own file and have periodic news of her son's development. In this way she could find out how the birth mother felt about her son, and prepare him realistically for the future.

We see that, as adoptive parents gain confidence in themselves, a whole new concept of parenting will develop—one in which the parent does not have to claim "exclusive" rights and absolute loyalty at all times. The tie that binds parent and child becomes one of the heart, which is the only tie that holds.

An eighteen-year-old, whose parents helped her search, sent them this telegram during her reunion:

DEAR MOM AND DAD YOU ARE THE ONLY PARENTS I'LL EVER KNOW AND HAVE—NO ONE COULD TAKE YOUR PLACE

YOUR DAUGHTER ALWAYS AND FOREVER

28

The Right to Know

We have been concerned until now with the psychological complexities of the Adoption Game, not the legal ones. However, the former cannot be relieved until the law decrees a change. And this will not happen until the legislators and adoption professionals (many of whom are adoptive parents) understand that for adoption to survive as a legitimate institution, it must be transfused with new imagery and language and new concepts of human dignity both for children and adults.

Already there is a strong trend in our society toward candor. Under the new Freedom of Information Act, citizens have a right to request the files kept on them by government agencies. In the same spirit, consumers have a right to inspect credit-company reports, students have a right to their university files, and the dying patient has the right to expect truth from the doctor.

But as yet there is no such freedom for the adopted. Their records remain sealed by state law and court order, with a criminal penalty attached to any violation. And this obtains in spite of the fact that there is nothing in most state statutes that suggests there was an intent to cut the child off from knowledge of his birthright. Rather, the original purpose was to protect the privacy of the adoptive and birth families from the prying eyes of the community, and the child from the stigma of illegitimacy.[1] The very vagueness of the law on this crucial point of the child's eventual knowledge makes us feel that Adoptees were not meant to be deprived of their heritage, that this interpretation was pushed through at a later time by interested parties who were aware of the judicial ambiguities.

Confidentiality from Whom?

At present, proponents of the sealed records view their opening as a threat to the institution of adoption, charging that women will not give up their children in the future without the guarantee of secrecy. They also claim that birth mothers were promised "eternal anonymity" and could have their lives traumatically disrupted by the appearance of the child they have never publicly acknowledged.

They have managed to make the issue into an adversary situation, pitting the right of the adult Adoptee to know against the right of the birth mother to confidentiality. But a close look at the lobby groups reveals that it is the conservative adoption agencies and the adoptive parents, not the birth mothers, who are struggling to keep the records closed. The adoption agencies are more afraid of losing their business, and the adoptive parents of losing their children, than the birth mothers are afraid of being found. Those young mothers were given no choice about the issue of confidentiality at the time of relinquishment—it was forced on them as adoption policy.[2] The strange truth of the matter is that in some states they *never* had confidentiality—their names were on the court papers that were handed over to the adoptive parents when the adoption was finalized. An arrangement, it might be added, that was never reciprocal: the birth mother has never been entitled to a legal document of any kind (not even the birth certificate) to show for her baby.

John Brown found that the birth parents he worked with continued to wonder and worry about the status of their children. He believes that very few parents would deny their relinquished child the right to know them if they understood that child's need. As for the few who would still wish anonymity, he states emphatically that no one should have either the moral or legal right to remain anonymous to the child they brought into the world.[3]

Recent polls in this country show that the majority of birth mothers favor open records,[4] but this will not happen until society recognizes that the right of the child takes precedence over the right of any dissenting adult. Especially when that child had no say or legal representation in the adoption transaction. William Reynolds, who is himself an adoptive father, feels that the agencies and the law are really protecting the adoptive parents' need for exclusive possession of the child—the "our very own baby" syndrome.[5] And Norman Paul states emphatically, "Kids—all kids— whether adopted or children of divorced or deceased parents, have a right to know their origins. They should not be penalized for the way they have been conceived. The issue here is the child's right to know his own history."[6]

The Backlash

We have now the paradox of things getting both better and worse in the adoption world. The media has given sympathetic coverage to the search phenomenon, and many adoption agencies are now disclosing all nonidentifying information to adult Adoptees who return, rather than treating them as candidates for a back ward. There are social workers who have come out publicly on the side of open records, and some agencies have quietly been helping Adoptees in the Search.

However, the inevitable backlash that comes with any movement for change is also happening under the guise of reform. While it appears encouraging that state legislatures are debating the issue of open records, it is discouraging that they are recommending it for future adoptions, not past ones. Some states are even plugging up the few loopholes around "good cause"—the ability to get records on grounds of psychological need—by adding the requirement that the court must furnish the written consent of *both* birth parents before the Adoptee's petition can be considered.[7] This is rather mind-boggling when we remember the incredible difficulty of the Search even with the mother's maiden name. As proposed, the court would appoint a guardian to accomplish the task within a given time, and to represent the birth parents' interests should they prove missing or deceased.[8] The court would also be guided by the opinion of a social worker assigned to do mandatory interviewing with the Adoptee to determine his or her fitness for such information. (And who, we might well ask, pays the costs for this elaborate scheme? The Adoptee, on all counts.)

Improbable as it seems, proposals to give the power of consent to those invisible parents who had been legally written out of the child's life are looked upon in some circles as the perfect compromise solution. These "experts" miss the point made earlier, that all children have a right to knowledge of their parentage, and no parent has the right to keep that truth from them. Furthermore, Adoptees consider any system that forces them to use intermediaries in the Search and undergo mandatory counseling an indignity, in that it removes their own autonomy.

Rather than forego their principles and submit to the emotional and financial strain of pleading for their birthright, I would encourage Adoptees to join groups that are bringing suit in the federal courts to secure the records on constitutional grounds—such as Yesterday's Children has done in Illinois and ALMA has done in New York.[9] And I would advise individual Adoptees to continue their search in the underground until they can get their records through the courts with no strings attached.

New Forms

Of course, even when the records are eventually open to Adoptees at the legal age, the emotional problems we have been discussing will not automatically disappear. The law can set boundaries, but it cannot legislate what happens in the human heart. It cannot take away an Adoptee's need to know the truth while growing up; it cannot take away a birth mother's obsessive need to see her young child; it cannot take away the adoptive parents' fear that they will lose their child.

The law can set the course for healthy attitudes in the future, but it cannot rule away the confusions left in the wake of the old system.

At present, there is no place for anyone in the adoption circle to turn for counseling, other than those financially ailing adoption agencies which, because of the baby shortage, would like nothing better than to get state funding for this role as a way of staying in business. However, this would mean resurrecting Mrs. Barker—and how can she, who has had no insight into the psychological problems of the past, suddenly qualify as an "expert"?

A growing number of professionals are going on record that society must create "new forms" to deal with the changes that are already taking place in the adoption field. New agencies must be established and newly trained workers must build up a new tradition.

We need a new generation of social workers who are aware that all children separated from their birth families will have some trace of the adoption syndrome—whether they come from Asia, South America, or the ghettos of this country; workers who, because of their empathy with these children, will not give them to people who will feel threatened by their need to know their heritage.

We need agencies that would make it a policy to update medical and social history on the birth parents and child, and to share that information with any of the parties that request it.

We need agencies that would explore the concept of open adoption, the newest frontier in the adoption world—an arrangement where the birth mother gives up her baby with the understanding that she will receive periodic information about its development and have occasional visiting rights. Annette Baran, of the Sorosky team, believes that the possibility of such flexible terms would encourage young women, who might otherwise have abortions, or give their children to the black market, to use the licensed agencies.[10] It would, in other words, make adoption more acceptable to young mothers than it is now.

The ground rules would have to be worked out carefully in advance, but it is possible that with a new attitude toward parenthood—one in which adoptive parents do not possess the child, but rather guide its development to maturity as best they can (which is all any parent can do)—this kind of openness would prove more healthy and satisfying for all three parties than does the closed system we have now.

Open Placement

How open is open? That is the question, and at present there is no one answer. It runs the spectrum from birth parents and adoptive parents having an initial meeting with no follow-up, to an exchange of correspondence to update each others' lives, to a relationship of some kind during or after the child-rearing years.

Open placement is not as radical as it sounds when one remembers that in private placements of the past, birth mothers and adoptive parents often knew each other, and no harm ever came to anyone as a result. The problem with private placement—no matter how responsible the legal go-betweens—is that there are as yet no state regulations on keeping vital family information for the child. And private placement will continue to be plagued with black marketeers and newspaper advertisers who offer big money until adoption agencies become more flexible in their practice.

It is happening. The Adoptees' push for open records is influencing the trend to open placement.

Margaret Gilling began thinking about it eight years ago, when frustrated adult Adoptees returned to her agency in Green Bay, Wisconsin, with questions about their origins and the circumstances of their surrender. She noticed the same despair in birth mothers who came back with inquiries about the babies they had relinquished, and was surprised when adoptive parents, in response to her questions, spoke of their frustrations at being unable to answer their children's questions. She decided that if the pain of everyone in the adoption triangle was the result of the secrecy her agency had practiced in the past, it was time to make changes for the future.

Gilling and her co-workers now hold eight three-hour group meetings with prospective adoptive parents to help them understand how knowing their baby's mother and background will enable them to answer their child's questions in the future. At the same time, they are counseling pregnant young women (and even a few birth fathers) as to the value of meeting the people who will become the baby's parents.

At first Gilling let the adoptive parents who still felt threatened retain their anonymity even after meeting the birth mothers, but now she is encouraging a mutual exchange of identities. They are free to make their own informal arrangements as to the amount of correspondence to be exchanged and if and when they will have contact over the years.

The outcome has been positive so far because basic trust has been established. The adoptive parents still have the privacy they need, and the birth mothers find it easier to cope with their loss by getting updated reports about the child.

As for the Adoptee, social workers like James Gritter, whose agency "took the plunge from the rear end to the front end" three years ago in Traverse City, Michigan, believes the child will be the winner.

There are risks and gambles, to be sure, as with any social reform, but the expectations are that the Adoptee will be spared the negative consequences of "genealogical bewilderment" when there are no murky secrets shrouding the past, and will be freer to develop a close bond with the adoptive parents when the relationship is founded on openness and honesty.

Legacy

Tolkien tells us that all fairy tales must have recovery and consolation at the end. The evildoer is punished and the hero's universe put into order. But in the adoption story there is no evil to be punished—for there is no villain. All the characters thought they were acting in "the best interest" of the baby at the time of adoption. And that baby, the hero of our story, cannot have the order completely restored. His or her fate cannot be changed. The past can be recaptured, but not rewritten.

No one knows this better than those of us who have taken the mythic journey through Search and Reunion. But we also know that the basic assumptions of the system in which all the characters are trapped can be reordered if the laws are rewritten. The hero can at least be given the right to his heritage, which is, in effect, the right to reality.

In the meantime, we assure those who seek us out that the Search is a vital and necessary stage for those who would find themselves. We say this with certainty, albeit in measured tones. The experience has taught us to think more subtly, not to look for quick and easy solutions. We have learned to look at all of life as complex, mysterious, unresolved. To regard our adoptive parents and birth parents with compassion.

We tell those just setting out that we have affirmed the right to know. That we have taken control of our lives, although like all people we will never be able to control them completely. That we have upheld the right to truth as opposed to deception, autonomy as opposed to manipulation, in human relations.

And perhaps this is all the adopted and nonadopted can ever ask of themselves, or of life.

Epilogue

"Nothing ever ends, it only changes," an Adoptee told me the other day. I know that. I have said it in many ways in this book. But I have to learn it each day anew.

Four years have passed since I began research on this project. I ask myself how things have changed during this period. And then I ask everyone else.

"But you've changed, B.J.," a birth mother tells me.

I am taken by surprise. I have been writing about others for so long, I have forgotten to observe myself, the medium through which I have been filtering my data, and have forgotten that others may have been observing me.

"How have I changed?" I am intrigued.

"You seem more relaxed now. Less angry."

"Was I angry?" I ask genuinely, for a moment thrown back to the Good Adoptee who was so out of touch with her rage as a child that she still has trouble acknowledging that bottled emotion whenever it spills forth as irony, sarcasm, or wit.

"You seem more comfortable with things now than that woman who wrote *Twice Born*. In fact, your book for teenagers, *I'm Still Me*, was downright mellow."

Yes, she is right, I decide. How strange I hadn't noticed. I am calm about this subject most of the time, no longer argumentative when I meet someone who doesn't agree. I am strategic, rather than emotional, in my responses. I am even philosophic, able to accept that it may take a few more years for society and the courts to catch up with our perceptions.

And yet, I have my lapses.

In the past few years the adoption field has been thrust into the national political arena. The action, once exclusively limited to state legislatures, is beginning to move into the marble halls of the congressmen and senators on Capitol Hill.

When the Federal Model State Advisory Panel, appointed by the Carter Administration to revise adoption law for the benefit of special-needs children, came up with a recommendation for open records in 1980, it seemed that the dream of adult Adoptees who had grown up in the old system had finally come true.

At last the adoption specialists—a panel made up of social workers, lawyers, judges, adoptive parents, and even a token Adoptee and birth mother—had determined that at the age of majority the Adoptee "may inspect the original record that contains the names of his birth parents," and "is most capable of defining what is in his own welfare." It instructed the adoption agencies not only to give adult Adoptees identifying information, but to act as a go-between for birth parents who requested contact with their adult children.

In probing, the panel had discovered that the present adoption system was like a listing ship that needed a complete overhaul. Repair one leak and another would spring up. There was no choice but to re-evaluate the whole adoption law structure with the philosophy that any innovations that benefited all Adoptees couldn't help but benefit the special-needs ones also.

Of course, a Model State Act is not mandatory in any state legislature. It is just that—a model to follow. But archconservatives in the field of adoption, like the Edna Gladney Home in Fort Worth, Texas, thought even the possibility of open records alarming enough to raise big money for a lobbying organization, The National Committee for Adoption. Its stated goal was to knock out the open record provision of the Act.

The National Committee for Adoption (The NCFA) would more appropriately be called the National Committee Against Changing the Old Adoption Game. It had no trouble convincing archconservative senators like John Tower of Texas and Jeremiah Denton of Alabama to oppose open records. It started a mail campaign, and public commentary received by the Commission showed a preponderance of opposition to reform coming from Texas and Ohio.

On October 8, 1981, the final Model State Adoption Act approved by Health and Human Services Secretary Richard

Schweiker was published in the Federal Register in a truncated version—the original seventy-seven pages reduced to a mere seventeen. The conservatives, riding the crest of the right wing mood of the government, had managed to eliminate not only open records but other progressive revisions as well.

It was a blow. But take heart, I tell my fellow Adoptees. The fact that a national commission of adoption experts recommended open records means that its time has come. We must spread the word to the state legislators and everyone concerned. No one can turn back the tide of history, as reactionary forces have always tried to do as they seek for some "golden past" that never was. And no one can rewrite history—those volumes that have been written in the last decades on the psychological damage caused by the sealed records system remain a testimony to our cause.

Earlier I wrote that there were no villains in the adoption story—and that was true in the past, before all the research was in. But now I wonder as I see the archconservatives—the Moral Majority of the adoption field—willfully ignoring the alarming data on the old system as they push for federal and state projects (like the Adolescent Family Life Bill) that would restore maternity homes built on the foundations of shame and secrecy, and hire our old social worker friend, Mrs. Barker, to deliver her canned message that adoption is "a more positive option" than keeping your baby in the family. The hope of the conservatives is that the government's penchant for cutting off aid and support systems for dependent families will underline such a message. More babies for the baby market, more business for the agencies.

What would life be without its paradoxes? The politicizing of the adoption field has energized the progressive forces in the adoption movement to act. Adoptee groups across the country, until now just a loose network, have joined with birth parent groups, forward-looking adoption agencies, and individual adoptive parents, lawyers, doctors, and judges to form the American Adoption Congress. Its purpose is to educate the country as to the need for open records and greater openness in adoption practice.

The AAC, which came into being in Washington, D.C., in 1979, attempts to meet the needs of everyone in the adoption circle. It offers legal and medical referral services, a national reunion registry, and a newsletter, while also serving as a watchdog on legislative activity.

As long as the various states continue to offer half measure alternatives to open records, such as intermediary services and restrictive reunion registries (like the NCFA's proposed reunion-proof registry, which would necessitate the birth father's signature before the Adoptee and birth mother could meet), the AAC will continue to offer the necessary skills and support for its individual members.

The ultimate goal, then, is open records in every state of the union, and Canada, which is also represented in the AAC. Ideally, open records would be supplemented by a federally supervised reunion registry, such as the one Senator Carl Levin has been attempting to get passed (the Adoption Identification Act), for many Adoptees and birth parents do not even know in which states their records are kept. A well-publicized national registry would update names and addresses that had become obsolete under seal, sparing those who wish to find each other years of difficult search.

It is endlessly fascinating, this journey of the adopted through the Dark Wood, but consuming in its demands. As a writer I am aware that I must go on to other subjects, and I have. But I know now that some part of me will always be involved in the struggle, and that I will never, in my writing, or my life, be able to escape from the theme of adoption. Whether in fantasy or reality, it haunts us all, the adopted and nonadopted alike. It is a metaphor for the human condition, sending us forth on that mythic quest that will prove that we are bonded to the world, and to each other —and in the process, reveal to us who we are.

Rights and Responsibilities for Everyone in the Adoption Circle

I keep coming back to this issue of rights and responsibilities, for we cannot speak of one without the other. Whether bound by blood or social ties, by an adoption or marriage contract, there are unwritten moral laws for the way we relate to one another in society.

Now, while everyone is groping toward a new vision, it seems a good idea to reexamine the stresses in the adoption circle and to consider what we can do to mitigate some of them.

To this end I have drafted a preliminary list of our rights and responsibilities to each other.

I am aware of the pitfalls of such an undertaking: that everything will come out drastically oversimplified. It could be said that issues of the heart cannot be listed in such a pragmatic, utilitarian way. But having acknowledged many of the complexities involved in the preceding pages, I am presuming to do so.

I wanted to see what it would all look like, laid out bare like this, even knowing that under the best of circumstances it cannot solve all the problems. The human condition is far too complex for such illusions.

This is a small list, an optimist's list, a visionary's list, but I hope that others will shape and expand it over the years. Make it a working list.

Psychologically, this list affirms the need for an adoption system, but one that is more flexible and more humane. It also assumes that people can change.

Legally, it is predicated on the concept of open birth and adoption records for those parties directly concerned.

Practically, it is dependent on certain innovations—such as the establishment of a central bureau in each state where all adoption records can be kept and updated over the years. This would be, in effect, a uniform repository system that would not be subject to the ephemeral fortunes of adoption agencies or legal agents. Ideally, such a bureau could also be responsible for maintaining a reunion registry for those wishing to find each other, and an intermediary service for those requesting it.

Realistically, this list will take some time to happen.

However, we do not have to wait for everything suggested here to come to pass to relate to each other with empathy and honesty, which is, after all, the right and responsibility of all people who truly care for one another.

Adoptees have the right:

To know they are adopted.

To a birth certificate that has not been amended.

To knowledge of their origins—the name they were given at birth, their ethnic and religious background, the complete medical and social history of their birth families.

To open and honest communication with their adoptive parents.

To updated medical and social history on the birth parents and their respective families.

To legal access to their adoption and birth records.

To personal contact with each birth parent.

To live without guilt toward either set of parents when they explore questions about their heritage.

Adoptees have the responsibility:

To treat their adoptive parents as their "real" parents.
To help their adoptive parents understand their need to know their heritage.
To contact their birth parents in a discreet way that will not invade their privacy.
To be considerate of the birth parents after contact.
To be considerate of the adoptive parents during their Search and Reunion period.

Adoptive parents have the right:

To be regarded by the child and society as the "real" parents.
To raise the child according to their social and religious background, even when it differs from that of the birth family.
To expect the birth parents to respect the privacy and integrity of their family unit, and to make contact through them or an intermediary rather than through a minor child.
To full information about their child at the time of adoption, and updated information on the birth parents over the years.

Adoptive parents have the responsibility:

To tell the child that he or she is adopted and to keep communication channels open after that.
To obtain all the information they can in writing about the child's background at the time of adoption.
To have empathy for the child's need for knowledge about his heritage and to help him integrate it over the years.
To avoid inflicting feelings of indebtedness or guilt on the child.
To give the social worker or legal agent updated material on the child's development should the birth parents request it.
To request updated information on the birth parents over the years.
To acknowledge the possibility that the child may need to search for and meet the birth parents.

To have some kind of communication with a birth parent who has made contact either directly or through an intermediary.

To inform an Adoptee of such contact.

To avoid going through black marketeers to find a child, and to be certain the child's records are not falsified.

To explore open placement at the time of adoption.

To lobby in their state legislature for open records.

Birth parents have the right:

To privacy from the public, but not from their own child.

To put their own requirements into an adoption contract.

To waive their option of confidentiality at the time of adoption, or at any time afterward.

To explore *open* adoption.

To updated information about the child's development while it is growing up in the adoptive family.

To determine the time and place for meeting with a child who has searched for them in such a way that will preserve their privacy.

To contact a child who has reached adulthood.

Birth parents have the responsibility:

To put their child's needs before their own.

To give their child to licensed agencies or certified agents rather than black marketeers.

To supply the agency or legal go-between with a complete medical and social history and to update this over the years.

To balance their right to information about the child with respect for the adoptive family.

To find some way to contact the adoptive parents of a minor child, either directly or through an intermediary, rather than approaching the child.

To meet with their child if they are contacted, and to reveal any relevant information, especially the identity of the other birth parent, siblings, or half-siblings.

To lobby in their state legislature for open records.

Social workers and legal agents have the right:

To arrange legal adoptions.

To receive reasonable fees for their professional services.

To expect state legislators to clear up the present ambiguities in the adoption statutes.

Social workers and legal agents have the responsibility:

To examine their own attitudes about adoption and to be trained in the psychology of the Adoptee, the adoptive parents, and the birth parents.

To choose adoptive parents who are able to understand the psychological needs of the adopted child.

To keep legal fees reasonable, and to itemize costs.

To have legal counsel representing the child at the time of the adoption procedures.

To consider the needs of all parties while writing the adoption contract.

To place twins and, if possible, siblings in the same family.

To get a full medical and social history from both birth parents, as well as their authentic names and addresses.

To give all information in writing to the adoptive parents.

To give updated material to all parties on request.

To treat Adoptees who contact them with courtesy, consideration, and honesty.

To act as an intermediary for any party requesting this service.

To get a full medical and social history on children of inter-country adoptions.

To lobby for controls on black market adoptions.

To lobby in state legislatures for open adoption records.

To help medical schools and schools of social work to devise courses on the adoption syndrome and the psychological complexity of the adoption circle.

To explore the advantages of open placement.

The Adoption Resource Network

The groups listed below are in the vanguard of the adoption reform movement. Most of them offer membership to everyone in the adoption circle, and give much needed sanction and support to those suffering from the injustices of the closed adoption system. The majority belong to the American Adoption Congress (AAC), the national umbrella organization of Adoptees, birth parents, adoptive parents, adoption agencies, and individual professionals dedicated to opening records and making a more humane adoption system. Write to the AAC (under District of Columbia) for complete listings of groups and open-placement agencies, medical and legal referrals, speakers, legislative updates, and the newsletter. Be sure to sign up with the AAC's national reunion registry: the "Soundex Register."

ADOPTEE GROUPS

Alabama

Adoption Study Project
1250 Lake Forest Circle
Birmingham, AL 35244

Arizona

SEARCH
P.O. Box 1432
Litchfield Park, AZ 85340

California

Adoptees, Birth Parents' Assoc.
P.O. Box 33
Camarillo, CA 93011

Central Coast Adoption Support Group
P.O. Box 1937
Santa Maria, CA 93455

PACER
860 Bryant St.
Palo Alto, CA 94301

Search Finders
P.O. Box 2374
Santa Clara, CA 95051

Triadoption Library
7571 Westminster Blvd.
Westminster, CA 92683

Colorado

Adoptees in Search
P.O. Box 27294
Denver, CO 80227

Orphan Voyage (Nat. HQ)
c/o Jean Paton
Cedaredge, CO 81413

Connecticut

Adoptees Search Connection
1203 Hill St.
Suffield, CT 06078

District of Columbia

American Adoption Congress (AAC)
P.O. Box 23641 (Nat. HQ)
Washington, D.C. 20024
(Write for info, speakers, referrals)

Florida

Adoption Associates
9320 S.W. 170th St.
Miami, FL 33157

OASIS (Nat. HQ)
P.O. Box 53-761
Miami Shores, FL 33153

Orphan Voyage
13906 Pepperell Drive
Tampa, FL 33624

Georgia

Roots and Wings
Box 32
Tucker, GA 30084

Hawaii

Adoption Support Group
Box 8377
Honolulu, HI 96815

Illinois

Search Research
P.O. Box 48
Chicago Ridge, IL 60415

Truth Seekers in Adoption
Box 286
Roscoe, IL 61073

Yesterday's Children
P.O. Box 1554
Evanston, IL 60204

Indiana

SEARCH
P.O. Box 1202
Elkhart, IN 46515

Search for Tomorrow
P.O. Box 441
New Haven, IN 46774

Iowa

The Adoptive Experience
1105 Fremont
Des Moines, IA 50316

Kentucky

Searching
P.O. Box 7722
Louisville, KY 40207

Louisiana

Adoptee's Birthright Comm.
P.O. Box 65327
Baton Rouge, LA 70896

Maine

Orphan Voyage
10 Forest St.
Dexter, ME 04930

Maryland

Adoptees in Search (AIS)
P.O. Box 41016
Bethesda, MD 20014

Adoption Connection Exchange
5502 Southberd Rd.
Baltimore, MD 21209

Massachusetts

The Adoption Connection
11 Peabody Square, Rm. 1
Peabody, MA 01960

Cape Assoc. for Truth in Adoption
Box 606
Woods Hole, MA 02543

Michigan

Adoption Identity Movement
P.O. Box 20092
Detroit, MI 48220

Roots and Reunions
P.O. Box 1409
L'Anse, MI 49946

Minnesota

Leaf
23247 Lofton Court North
Scandia, MN 55073

Link
1700 West 76th St. #1C
Minneapolis, MN 55423

Missouri

Adult Adoptees
Box 15225
Kansas City, MO 54106

Montana

Search
Box 214
Melville, MT 59055

Nebraska

Midwest Adoption Triad
P.O. Box 37262
Omaha, NB 68137

OPEN A.R.M.S. Mag.
Box 1522
North Platte, NB 69101

Nevada

Southern Nevada Adoptees
P.O. Box 18432–34
Las Vegas, NV 89114

New Jersey

Adoption Triangle Ministry
Box 156
Oaklyn, NJ 08107

New Mexico

Operation Identity
13101 Blackstone Rd. NE
Albuquerque, NM 87111

New York

Adoptees Information Service
19 Marion Ave.
Mount Vernon, NY 10552

The Adoption Circle
3 Townhouse Circle #2A
Great Neck, NY 11021

ALMA (Nat. HQ)
P.O. Box 154
Washington Bridge Station
New York, NY 10033

AIM   Always in Me
Box 454
Orchard Park, NY 14127

The Right to Know
Box 52
Old Westbury, L.I., NY 11586

North Carolina

Adoptees Together
Rt. 1 Box 30-B-5
Climax, NC 27233

Ohio

Adoptees Search Rights (Nat. HQ)
P.O. Box 8713
Toledo, OH 43623

Chosen Children
311 Spring Brook Blvd.
Dayton, OH 45405

Reunite
Box 694
Reynoldsburg, OH 43068

Oklahoma

Adoptees As Adults
8220 N.W. 114th St.
Oklahoma City, OK 73132

Oregon

Adoptive Rights
P.O. Box 1332
Beaverton, OR 97075

SOAR
1076 Queens Branch Road
Rogue River, OR 97537

Pennsylvania

Adoption Forum
6808 Ridge Ave. (Rear)
Philadelphia, PA 19128

Pittsburgh Adoption Lifeline
P.O. Box 52
Gibsonia, PA 15044

Rhode Island

Parents & Adoptees Liberty Movement
861 Mitchell's Lane
Middletown, RI 02840

South Carolina

Adoptees & Birth Parents in Search
Box 1000
West Columbia, SC 29171

Tennessee

The Right to Know
P.O. Box 34334
Memphis, TN 38134

Texas

The Right to Know
P.O. Box 1409
Grand Prairie, TX 75050

Searchline
725 Burkwood
Irving, TX 75062

Utah

Adoption Identity
Box 8124
Salt Lake City, UT 84108

Virginia

Adoptees & Natural Parents
15 Caribbean Ave.
Virginia Beach, VA 23451

Washington

Washington Adoptees Rights Movement
15749 NE 4th, Room 12
Bellevue, WA 98008

West Virginia

The Lost Children
312 8th Ave.
St. Albans, WV 25177

Wisconsin

Adoption Info & Direction
P.O. Box 3397
Madison, WI 53704

Australia

JIGSAW (Nat. HQ)
P.O. Box 33
Cannington, 6107, Australia
450-2052

Canada

Parent Finders (Nat. HQ)
120 Eglinton Ave. East
Toronto, Ontario M4P1E2

BIRTH PARENT GROUPS

**Concerned United Birth
    Parents (CUB) (Nat. HQ)**
P.O. Box 573
Milford, MA 01757

Origins
Box 105
Oakhurst, NJ 07755

INFORMATION FOR TEENAGERS

Adopted Teen Connection
P.O. Box 16567
Phoenix, AZ 85011
(formerly Betty Jean Lifton
TEEN PEN PAL CLUB)

AAC REUNION REGISTRY

"Soundex Register"
P.O. Box 2312
Carson City, NV 89701

OPEN PLACEMENT ADOPTION AGENCIES

Catholic Social Services
P.O. Box 38
Green Bay, WI 54305
414-437-6541

**Community, Family & Children
    Services**
1000 Hastings Street
Traverse City, MI 49684
616-947-8110

Lutheran Social Service
615 Elm St. at McCullough
San Antonio, TX 78202
512-227-8142

Vista Del Mar Child-Care Services
3200 Motor Ave.
Los Angeles, CA 90034
714-836-1223

Acknowledgments

In the process of my research for this book over the past few years, many people have entered and enriched my life—Adoptees, adoptive parents, and birth parents—all generously sharing their story. They are too numerous to name, but each offered up his or her deeply personal feelings with the hope that it would somehow contribute knowledge to the much-neglected field of adoption. Their faith in me that I would transmute their history into a communication to the professional and lay world has been a responsibility that has been with me throughout this book.

Many of the insights that I had from my own adoption experience were further developed because of two incredible years of weekly rapping with a very special group of psychologically aware Adoptees, the majority of whom were professional people. Aphrodite Clamar, Linda Traum, and Julie Frankel became like sisters in the process. Others, each close in a special way, were Naomi Roepe, Carol Rettig, Doris Bertocci, Peter Gros, Alice Olick, Jeramie Hansen, and Leon Levy.

I am also indebted to Geoffrey Nusbaum, a fellow Adoptee who shared his own ideas with me during long walks in Central Park, as did Gordon Livingston, by long-distance phone and letters, and Michael Haag, through long taped conversations sent back and forth from one coast to the other.

In Philadelphia, which houses not only the Liberty Bell but also a group that is valiantly working for liberating Adoptees (Adoption Forum), my thanks to Penny Partridge and Debbie Steinberg. To Patricia Hirsekorn, and her husband, Jerry, who shared their personal lives and their professional skills as librarians, which meant digging out esoteric articles and out-of-print books, my eternal gratitude.

I have never met Jean Paton (a condition I hope to remedy soon), but all Adoptees eventually become aware that twenty years ago she was the very first to call attention to the unfairness of the Adoption Game, through her writing and lecturing. It isn't easy now, but it was much more difficult then, and progress in this field must be traced to her. I refer most Adoptees who write me to her group, Orphan Voyage, in Cedaredge, Colorado, because I know she is sitting up there on her mountaintop personally answering their letters, referring them to the proper sources, and at the same time preparing her invaluable quarterly newsletter.

Another very special Adoptee is Margaret Lawrence, who for years has been gathering psychological material through her Adoption Study Project and has generously guided those Adoptees who have been fortunate enough to find their way to her telephone number or her door. Along with Donna Cullom, another dedicated leader, Margaret founded Yesterday's Children, which is one of the most active of the Adoptee groups.

Among birth mothers, Lee Campbell allowed me to share the birth pangs of CUB, as well as her own in giving up her son. Joanne MacDonald gave me baked muffins as well as her deepest secrets. Mary Ann Cohen gave me her poems, and her friendship, both of which I treasure.

To Rene Baumel, for her skills as a professional researcher as well as her sensitivity as an adoptive parent, I am deeply grateful. Because of her taped interviews with her circle of adoptive parents in the Middle West, I was able to get much more in-depth material than if they had filled out my questionnaire individually. I am also grateful to Mary Ross, Sarah de Ris, and Jan McLean for their intimate communication with me about adoptive parenting.

Among social workers who have taught me that there are exceptions to Mrs. Barker, I am grateful to Annette Baran, whose warmth, enthusiasm, and intelligence have given me great hope for the field, and to Reuben Pannor, her colleague; Phyllis Gurdin, who has been a dedicated pioneer on the East Coast with her adoption seminars; and Linda Burgess, who has always been ready to give friendship and assistance to those of us Adoptees who were not her babies.

Among psychological professionals, I want to express my admiration for Erik Erikson, who very generously does not run away when he sees me coming toward him during summers on the Cape; Marshall Schecter, for his continuing involvement in the adoption field at the side of his wife, Anne, who is an Adoptee; Arthur Sorosky, whose invaluable research is bringing the adoption field out of the Dark Ages; William Reynolds, whose professional skills and human approach are throwing light into much-needed areas; Norman Paul, for his deep concern with helping Adoptees achieve intergenerational continuity; and Ellen Kenniston, for her very valuable insights as psychologist and friend, on the sands of Wellfleet over the years. My gratitude to Gertrud Mainzer for her tireless skills as a professional and as a friend; my thanks to Judith Bernstein, and Eleanor Munro for listening, reading, and sharing; my admiration as a poet and a woman for Muriel Rukeyser, a birth mother who kept her child, who taught me the importance of scaling prison gates from within and without.

I would like to thank Ellyn Polshek, who edited this book with warmth and care; Joyce Johnson, who helped give birth to *Twice Born*, whose resonances could not help permeating this present undertaking; Berenice Hoffman, who was always there as agent and friend; Caroline Shookhoff, whose skill and intelligence with the final typing gave an aura of security to the bundle in her care; Karen Preissler and Sandra Lugo, for their sustenance throughout; and Carol Kirschner and Catherine Huntington, for being there always.

And I must add my husband, Robert Jay Lifton, who has somehow survived twenty-five years of marriage to a searching adoptee, and in the process always gave his warm emotional support and his invaluable perceptions, along with a wonderful sense of humor that always manages to illuminate everything.

Finally I come back again to those hundreds of people whose names and stories fill my file and my heart, all of whom are helping to make the dignity of the adopted person possible.

Notes and Sources

PART ONE—LOST

1. On Being Adopted

1. Betty Jean Lifton, *Twice Born: Memoirs of an Adopted Daughter* (New York: McGraw-Hill, 1975 [paperback—New York: Penguin Books, 1977]).

2. Messages from the Underground

1. Joseph and Julia Quinlan with Phyllis Battelle, *Karen Ann: The Quinlans Tell Their Story* (New York: Doubleday, 1977), p. 328.

3. The Adoption Game

1. For a thought-provoking survey of adoption history, see Mary Kathleen Benet, *The Politics of Adoption* (New York: The Free Press, 1976), pp. 22–118.
2. In re *Adoption of Bryant* v. *Kurtz*, 134 Ind. App. 480, 487, 189 N. E. 2nd 593, 597 (1963). Commenting on this statute in "Recognizing the Needs of Adopted Persons: A Proposal to Amend the Illinois Adoption Act," *Loyola University Law Journal* 6:49 (1975): 49–70, Stephen A. Gorman points out that having to consider his natural parents dead for "legal and practical purposes" is an unnecessary mockery of the child's very existence. "It is as though the state has decided that the child was never genealogically a part of anyone. It is biologically and historically impossible to graft one person onto the family tree of another."
3. C. L. Gaylord's article, "The Adoptive Child's Right to Know," *Case & Comment* 81 (1976), has eloquence as well as clarity in discussing the psychological implications in the legal aspects of adoption. As he says, "The adopted child who seeks the door to its past will find it shut and if it tries to open it, will find it locked" (p. 38).
4. Gaylord, "Adoptive Child's Right," p. 38.
5. For a fascinating insight into the mentality of the social welfare field in the mid-nineteenth century, read the book of the man who originated the "orphan trains" to rid New York of delinquent street children who were a threat to the middle class. Charles Loring Brace, *The Dangerous Classes of New York and Twenty Years of Work among Them* (New York: Wynkoop and Hallenbeck, 1880). Brace founded the Children's Aid Society, an adoption agency still in existence. Also see the novel

289

based on the fate of the children shipped out on the trains: James Magnuson and Dorothea Petrie, *Orphan Train* (New York: The Dial Press, 1978).

6. There are many books on the history of social welfare, but I particularly liked Walter Trattner, *From Poor Law to Welfare State* (New York: The Free Press, 1974).
7. This idea was brought to my attention by an adoptive mother, Ann Putzel, in her unpublished paper, "Adoption and the Sealed Record Statutes: An Historical Perspective" (1977).
8. Florence Clothier, M.D., "The Psychology of the Adopted Child," *Mental Hygiene* 27 (April 1943): 222–30.
9. Personal interview, 1977. Margaret Mead feels strongly that the Adoptee's need to connect with the past is culturally determined, rather than influenced by a biological need, as I had suggested to her.
10. George Macdonald, "Baby," in *A Child's Book of Poetry*, selected by Arthur Malcolm (New York: J. H. Sears & Co., 1927), p. 29.

4. The Chosen Baby

1. Although I prefer the term *natural,* I am using *birth* mother in this book in order to avoid an unimportant controversy over what I consider an unimportant issue. Also, birth mother has the advantage of acknowledging that someone did give birth to the Adoptee.
2. John L. Brown, "Rootedness," a talk given to a meeting of Browndale regional directors and printed in *Involvement: The Family Resource Magazine* 6 (May–June 1974). Reprints can be obtained upon request from Box 19, Station P, Toronto, Ontario, Canada.
3. Valentina P. Wasson, *The Chosen Baby* (Philadelphia and New York: J. B. Lippincott, 1939). In 1977 this book was reissued and updated with splashy new illustrations rather than new ideas. Florence Rondell and Ruth Michaels, *The Family That Grew* (New York: Crown, 1951). This volume comes in a set with *The Adoptive Family: Book I—You and Your Child, A Guide for Adoptive Parents*. It is a compendium of misguided information, such as that the child has no real kinship with his biological parents since he has never known them, and that it is all right to tell a young child his parents are dead because "a well-loved child, secure in his parents' affections, is not easily damaged."

5. The Adoptee as Mythic Hero

1. Susan Farber, Ph. D., "Sex Differences in the Expression of Adoption Ideas: Observations of Adoptees from Birth through Latency," *American Journal of Orthopsychiatry* 47 (October 1977): 639.
2. Lydia Jackson, "Unsuccessful Adoptions: A Study of 40 Cases Who Attended a Child Guidance Clinic," *British Journal of Medical Psychology* 41 (1968): 389–98. Jackson uses the term "unsuccessful" to mean cases where an adopted child was referred to the child guidance clinic or brought there by his parents on account of seriously disturbed interpersonal relationships.

6. The Adoptee as Double

1. For an unusual account of twins who were reunited with each other as adults, see Bard Lindeman, *The Twins Who Found Each Other* (New York: William Morrow, 1969).

8. Adolescent Baggage

1. Florence Clothier, M.D., "The Psychology of the Adopted Child," *Mental Hygiene* 27 (April 1943): 222.
2. Marshall Schecter, "Observations on Adopted Children," *A. M. A. Archives of General Psychiatry* 3 (July 1960): 21–32.
3. Talk at Adoption Forum, an Adoptee group in Philadelphia, 1978.
4. Marshall D. Schecter, M.D., et al., "Emotional Problems in the Adoptee," *Archives of General Psychiatry* 10 (February 1964): 109–18.
5. See James J. Lawton, Jr., M.D., and Seymour Z. Gross, M.A., "Review of Psychiatric Literature on Adopted Children," *Archives of General Psychiatry* 11 (December 1964): 635–44; D. R. Offord, M.D., J. F. Aponte, M.A., and L. A. Cross, "Presenting Symptomatology in Adopted Children," *Archives of General Psychiatry* 20 (January 1969): 110–16; N. M. Simon and A. G. Senturia, "Adoption and Psychiatric Illness," *American Journal of Psychiatry* 122 (February 1966): 858–67.
6. Alexina M. McWhinnie, "The Adopted Child in Adolescence," in *Adolescence: Psychological Perspectives,* eds. Gerald Caplan and Serge Lebovici (New York: Basic Books, 1969). See also McWhinnie, *Adopted Children and How They Grow Up* (London: Routledge and Kegan Paul, 1967).
7. J. Triseliotis, *In Search of Origins: The Experiences of Adopted People* (London: Routledge and Kegan Paul, 1973).
8. Lynn Cunningham et al., "Studies of Adoptees from Psychiatrically Disturbed Biological Parents: Psychiatric Conditions in Childhood and Adolescence," *British Journal of Psychiatry* 126 (1975): 534–49. Also, Remi J. Cadoret et al., "Studies of Adoptees from Psychiatrically Disturbed Biologic Parents, II: Temperament, Hyperactive, Antisocial, and Developmental Variables," *The Journal of Pediatrics* 87 (August 1975): 301–6.
9. Raymond R. Crowe, M.D., "The Adopted Offspring of Women Criminal Offenders: A Study of Their Arrest Records," *Archives of General Psychiatry* 27 (November 1972): 600–603.
10. For a good summary of differing opinions on the mental health of adopted children, see Arthur D. Sorosky, Annette Baran, and Reuben Pannor, *The Adoption Triangle: The Effects of the Sealed Record on Adoptees, Birth Parents, and Adoptive Parents* (New York: Anchor Press/Doubleday, 1978), pp. 87–103. Also, the report by Marshall Schecter, "Psychoanalytic Theory as It Relates to Adoption," American Psychoanalytic Association, New York, Fall 1966.
11. See Povl W. Toussieng, M.D., "Thoughts Regarding the Etiology of Psychological Difficulties in Adopted Children," *Child Welfare* 41 (February 1962): 59–71; Marshall Schecter, "About Adoptive Parents," in *Parenthood: Its Psychology and Psychopathology,* eds. E. J. Anthony and T. Benedek (Boston: Little Brown, 1970), pp. 353–71; Lydia

Jackson, "Unsuccessful Adoptions: A Study of 40 Cases Who Attended a Child Guidance Clinic," *British Journal of Medical Psychology* 41 (1968): 389–98; L. W. Sontag, "Effect of Maternal Emotions on Fetal Development," in *Psychosomatic Obstetrics, Gynecology, and Endocrinology,* ed. W. S. Kroger (Springfield, Ill.: Charles C Thomas, 1962).

12. Barney Greenspan and Elizabeth J. Fleming, "The Effect of Adoption on Adolescent Development" (Paper delivered at American Orthopsychiatric Association, March 1975).

13. A. D. Sorosky, A. Baran, and R. Pannor, "Adoption and the Adolescent: An Overview," in *Adolescent Psychiatry,* eds. S. C. Feinstein and P. Giovacchini, vol. 5 (New York: J. Jason Aronson, 1977), pp. 54–72.

14. E. Wellisch, "Children without Genealogy—A problem of adoption," *Mental Health* 13 (1952): 41–42. All subsequent Wellisch references in this section are to this letter.

15. H. J. Sants, "Genealogical Bewilderment in Children with Substitute Parents," *British Journal of Medical Psychology* 37 (1964): 133–41. All subsequent Sants references in this section are to this article.

16. Max Frisk, "Identity Problems and Confused Conceptions of the Genetic Ego in Adopted Children during Adolescence," *Acta Paedopsychiatrica* 31 (1964): 6–12.

17. Erik H. Erikson, *Toys and Reasons: Stages in the Ritualization of Experience* (New York: Norton, 1977), p. 76.

18. Personal communication, Summer 1977.

19. Norman Garbo, *To Love Again* (New York: McGraw-Hill, 1977), p. 31. Garbo has edited the tapes of an anonymous psychiatrist who poured out his feelings about adoption, among other subjects, as he was dying.

20. Talk at Adoption Forum, 1978.

21. See their book on this research, cited in note 13 of this chapter, above.

9. Good Adoptee—Bad Adoptee

1. See Margaret Lawrence, "Inside, Looking Out of Adoption" (Paper presented at the Eighty-fourth Annual Convention of the American Psychological Association, Washington, D.C., September 4, 1976). Lawrence makes the point that there is a "slave psychology" in the adopted child because he must submit to the will of his parents as a reflection of his gratitude for what they have done for him.

2. See Jules Glenn, "The Adoption Theme in Edward Albee's *Tiny Alice* and *The American Dream,*" *The Psychoanalytic Study of the Child* 29 (1974): 424–28.

10. The Adoptee as Adult

1. Sigmund Freud, "Some Character-Types Met with in Psycho-Analytic Work, I: The 'Exceptions'," *The Standard Edition of the Complete Psychological Works of Sigmund Freud,* ed. James Strachey, vol. 14 (London: Hogarth Press and the Institute of Psycho-Analysis, 1957), pp. 311–15.

2. William F. Reynolds, Cathy Levey, and Mark F. Eisnitz, "Adoptees' Personality Characteristics and Self-Ratings of Adoptive Family Life" (Paper presented at the annual meeting of the American Psychological Association, San Francisco, August 1977), pp. 10–11.

3. Norman Paul, "On a Child's Need for a Sense of Intergenerational Continuity: The Need to Know One's Roots" (Paper prepared for the G. A. P. Committee on the Family, November 1973).
4. Erik H. Erikson, *Childhood and Society* (New York: Norton, 1963), pp. 266–68.

PART TWO—FOUND

11. Waking Up from the Great Sleep

1. Erik H. Erikson, *Toys and Reasons: Stages in the Ritualization of Experience* (New York: Norton, 1977), p. 54.

12. Who Searches?

1. William F. Reynolds et al., "Personality Factors Differentiating Searching and Nonsearching Adoptees" (Paper presented at the Eighty-fourth Annual Convention of the American Psychological Association, Washington, D.C., September 4, 1976).
2. Personal communication, 1976.
3. Margaret Lawrence, "Inside, Looking Out of Adoption" (Paper presented at the Eighty-fourth Annual Convention of the American Psychological Association, Washington, D. C., September 4, 1976).
4. E. J. LeShan, "Should Adoptees Search for Their 'Real' Parents?," *Woman's Day* (March 1977).

13. The Decision to Search

1. Ernest Becker, *The Denial of Death* (New York: The Free Press, 1973), p. 21.
2. A. D. Sorosky, Annette Baran, and Reuben Pannor, *The Adoption Triangle: The Effects of the Sealed Record on Adoptees, Birth Parents, and Adoptive Parents* (New York: Anchor Press/Doubleday, 1978), p. 156.

14. Stages of the Search

1. A. D. Sorosky, Annette Baran, and Reuben Pannor, *The Adoption Triangle: The Effects of the Sealed Record on Adoptees, Birth Parents, and Adoptive Parents* (New York: Anchor Press/Doubleday, 1978), p. 220.
2. I am referring here facetiously to Mrs. Barker, the social worker in Albee's play *The American Dream* (New York: New American Library, Signet, 1959). See Chapter 9, Good Adoptee—Bad Adoptee.

15. Varieties of Reunion Experience

1. E. Mansell Pattison, "The Myth of Death in the Family," *The American Journal of Psychiatry* 133 (June 1976): 674–78.

16. The Journey after Reunion

1. Ernest Becker, *The Denial of Death* (New York: The Free Press, 1973), p. 271.
2. Erik H. Erikson, *Toys and Reasons: Stages in the Ritualization of Experience* (New York: Norton, 1977), p. 50.
3. T. S. Eliot, *The Confidential Clerk* (New York: Harcourt, Brace & World, A Harvest Book, 1954), p. 145.
4. Personal communication, 1977.

17. Father—The Mini-Search

1. Elizabeth Herzog, "Some Notes about Unmarried Fathers," *Child Welfare* 45 (April 1966): 194–97; Also see R. Pannor, F. Massarik, and B. W. Evans, *The Unmarried Father* (New York: Springer, 1971).
2. This is known as *Stanley* v. *Illinois*, 405 U.S. 645 (1972). In 1978 the United States Supreme Court ruled that, to maintain his rights, an unwed father must show interest in the child.

20. Aftermath: The Restless Pulse

1. Ernest Becker, *The Denial of Death* (New York: The Free Press, 1973), p. 266.
2. Lionel Tiger, *Optimism: The Biology of Hope* (New York: Simon & Schuster, forthcoming).
3. Edward Lear, "Calico Pie," from *The Complete Nonsense of Edward Lear* (London: Faber and Faber, 1952), pp. 78–80.

PART THREE—ROOTS AND WINGS

23. The Chosen Parents

1. Rael Jean Isaac, *Adopting a Child Today* (New York: Harper & Row, 1965), pp. 6–24.
2. Barbara Kohlsaat and Adelaide M. Johnson, "Some Suggestions for Practice in Infant Adoption," *Social Casework* (March 1954): 93.
3. John L. Brown, "Rootedness," *Involvement: The Family Resource Magazine* 6 (May–June 1974).
4. David Kirk, *Shared Fate* (New York: The Free Press, 1964), pp. 59–74.

24. Telling the Child

1. Robert Knight, "Some Problems Involved in Selecting and Rearing Adopted Children," Bulletin, The Menninger Clinic, vol. V (1941): pp. 65–74.
2. Herbert Weider, "On Being Told of Adoption," *The Psychoanalytic Quarterly* 46 (1977): 1–22.
3. Thomas A. Harris, *I'm OK—You're OK* (New York: Avon, 1973), pp. 194–95.

4. Personal communication, 1977.
5. Personal communication, 1977.
6. See Carole Livingston, *"Why Was I Adopted?"* (Secaucus, New Jersey: Lyle Stuart, 1978). The author is obviously aware of the difficulty of her task, which she should be, but her tone is condescending and her spirits so alarmingly false that you wouldn't have to be adopted to know there was a snow job going on. Although touching on some of the important questions, this book coyly manages to evade rather than squarely confront the answers, leaving the child with little more than the old hackneyed message —only in this version instead of being "special," he is "lucky."
7. Personal communication, May 1978.
8. Betty Jean Lifton, "My Search for My Roots," *Seventeen* (March 1977), and "Why Adoptees Search for Their Parents," *Seventeen* (October 1977). The Adoptee Pen Pal Club began in 1977 under the auspices of *Seventeen* magazine. Its growing membership now comprises about two hundred teenagers representing almost every state in the union.

25. Birth Mothers—Are They Baby Machines?

1. Prudence Mors Rains, *Becoming an Unwed Mother* (Chicago and New York: Aldine, 1971), p. 4. See also Leontine Young, *Out of Wedlock* (New York: McGraw-Hill, 1954), pp. 1–18.
2. J. D. Pauker, "Girls Pregnant Out of Wedlock," in *Double Jeopardy, The Triple Crisis, Illegitimacy Today* (New York: National Council on Illegitimacy, 1969), pp. 47–67.
3. Concerned United Birthparents brochure.
4. Laura Chester, "Pavanne for the Passing of a Child," after the music of Ravel, in *50 Contemporary Poets*, ed. Alberta T. Turner (New York: David McKay, 1977), pp. 70–73.

27. Adoptive Parents—Are They Baby-Sitters?

1. John Gregory Dunne, "Quintana," *Esquire* (June 1977): 8.

28. The Right To Know

1. See "Report Concerning Disclosure of Adoption Records to an Adopted Child at Age 21," prepared by the Commission Staff of New York State Senator Joseph R. Pisani, Chairman, Temporary State Commission on Child Welfare, March 1976, pp. 6–13. See also Mary Ann Jones, *The Sealed Record Controversy: Report of a Survey of Agency Policy, Practice, and Opinion* (New York: Child Welfare League of America). Jones points out that the Child Welfare League's standards do not address the specific issue of whether an Adoptee, upon becoming an adult, should have the right of access to any or all information about his or her natural parents, including their identity.
2. Jones, *Sealed Record Controversy*, p. 29.
3. John L. Brown, "Rootedness," *Involvement:The Family Resource Magazine* 6 (May–June 1974).
4. See "The Changing Face of Adoption" (Report of Research Project, Children's Home Society of California, March 1977). Write: 3100 West

Adams Boulevard, Los Angeles, Calif., 90018. See also Arthur D. Sorosky, Annette Baran, and Reuben Pannor, *The Adoption Triangle: The Effects of the Sealed Record on Adoptees, Birth Parents, and Adoptive Parents* (New York: Anchor Press/Doubleday, 1978).

5. Personal communication, 1977.

6. See Betty Jean Lifton, "The Search," *The New York Times Magazine,* January 25, 1976, pp. 15–22.

7. It is interesting to note that Connecticut, whose probate court adoption records were open until 1974, felt compelled to move into the Dark Ages on October 1, 1977, with its new law, Public Act No. 77-246, entitled "An Act Concerning the Availability and Confidentiality of Information Concerning Adoption. . . ."

8. Gertrud Mainzer, a New York lawyer who has obtained Adoptees' records on "good cause" in the past, spoke to me about the Catch-22 aspect of this. "If I had asked the judge to search for my client's birth parents in the past, he would have thought I was crazy. But he's the one who insists on searching for them now, although all my clients want are the records." She also makes the intriguing point that it may be illegal for the court to appoint a guardian for those birth parents, since they had already surrendered their rights to the child before adoption proceedings. Having removed them from legal responsibility, how can the court defend representing them now?

9. Yesterday's Children, an Adoptee activist group, filed in the United States District Court on February 5, 1975, seeking declaratory and injunctive relief for violations of their rights secured by the First, Fifth, Ninth, and Fourteenth Amendments to the United States Constitution. After they lost on jurisdictional grounds, the plaintiffs appealed to the United States Supreme Court, which, in declining to review the case in June 1978, upheld the lower federal court decision that the state courts should make such a determination. Submitted by Patrick Murphy, 33 North La Salle Avenue, Chicago, Ill. 60602.

   ALMA filed in the United States District Court for the Southern District of New York in 1977, contending that statutory enactments of New York State and New York City deprive them of the most fundamental of all human and constitutional rights, the right to be, in the whole sense, a "person," and thus the subject of all other rights. The complaint states that discriminations against Adoptees "not only violate the Equal Protection clause of the Fourteenth Amendment, but also abridge fundamental 'liberty' protected by the Due Process clause of that Amendment." It also violates the Thirteenth Amendment, "by imposing one of the historic badges and incidents of African slavery upon a discrete, insular and politically powerless minority; the 2% of the adult population who are adult adoptees." Submitted by Cyril Means, Jr., New York Law School, 57 Worth Street, New York, N. Y. 10013.

   For a most lucid analysis of the legal problems around the sealed record, see Stephen A. Gorman, "Recognizing the Needs of Adopted Persons: A Proposal to Amend the Illinois Adoption Act," *Loyola University Law Journal* 6 (1975): 49.

10. Annette Baran et al., "Open Adoption," *Social Work* 21 (1976): 97–100. See also Sorosky, Baran, and Pannor, *The Adoption Triangle*, pp. 207–214.

Index

Adolescents, 43–53; and genealogical bewilderment, 47–53;
and identity, 43, 45; maladjustments of, 43–45, 47; and
parents, 43, 46–47; searched
by birth mother, 233, 255
Adoptee, adolescent, *see* Adolescents; adult, *see* Adult, adoptee as; bad, 57–61; double life
of, 8; and genealogical bewilderment, 47–48; good, 55–57;
good vs. bad, 54, 61; responsibilities of, 276; rights of, 275–
276; search groups, 280–282
Adoptee Pen Pal Club, 205
Adopting a Child Today (Rael
Jean Isaac), 184–185
Adoption Forum, 283
"Adoption Game," 11, 12–18;
and adolescents, 44; "as if,"
15; circle, 14; early adoptions,
12–13; fraudulent birth certificate, 18; rules of, 13; triangle,

13; "veil between living and
dead," 15–18
Adoption Research Project, 47
Adoptive parents, and adolescents, 43, 46–47; as baby-sitters,
256–262; and birth parents,
259, 260; chosen, 183; double
life of, 8; and doubts and confusions of adoptee, 59; fears
of, 260–262; fraud on, 185;
how viewed, 185–186; and
phantom birth mother, 259;
reaction to birth mother's
search, 256–257, 258; reaction
to child's search, 257–258;
and records, 264; responsibilities of, 276–277; and reunion,
180–181; rights of, 276; and
search, 92–93, 94, 178–182,
206; and social worker, 184–
185; stresses of, 186–187; telling adoptee, 178–180; and
Twice Born, 7

Campbell, Lee, 207, 208–209, 213, 220, 284
Chester, Laura, "Pavanne for the Passing of a Child," 227
"Chosen" baby, 19–20
Chosen Baby, The (Valentina Wasson), 21
Chosen-baby stories, 22–27; and adolescents, 43; and adoptee as survivor, 39–40; as distortion of reality, 22; and fantasies, 30; reaction to, 23
Chosen parents, 183
Clothier, Florence, 17, 29, 44
Concerned United Birthparents (CUB), 209, 284
Confusion, 43, 59
CUB (Concerned United Birthparents), 209, 284

Dahlberg, Edward, *Because I Was Flesh*, 153
Denial, 56
Depression, 43–44, 64
Didion, Joan, 260
Dostoevsky, Fyodor, 34
"Double bind," 188
Double life, 8, 34–38
Doubts, 59
Dunne, John Gregory, 260

Earthly Possessions (Anne Tyler), 28, 29
Eiseley, Loren, 172; *The Unexpected Universe*, 86
Eliot, T. S., 147
Emma (Jane Austen), 164
"Emptiness," 65
Erikson, Erik, on adoptees as "new species," 62; on aftermath of reunion, 151; on aftermath of search, 173; on alienation, 51; on child's choice to know about past, 58; on intimacy, 66; on searching, 7, 72; on transition periods, 233, 255

"Family romance," 28–29
Family That Grew, The (Florence Rondell and Ruth Michaels), 21
Fantasies (of origins), 28–33; categories of, 30; children's, 30; during search, 97–99; effect on aftermath of reunion, 142–143; "family romance," 28–29; girls vs. boys, 30; negative, 33; "poor parent," 32–33; studies of, 30–32; treating, 33; of twins, 36–38
Farber, Susan, 30
Father, search for, 152–161; acceptance of adoptee, 154–156; ambivalent father, 160–161; concerned father, 158–159; denial by father, 157–158; macho father, 156–157; missing father, 159–160; and his name, 153
Fears, 59, 64, 95, 96–97
Forgiveness, in aftermath of reunion, 151–152
Fragility, 169
Fraud on adoptive parents, 185
Fraudulent birth certificate, 18
Freedom of Information Act, 263
Freud, Sigmund, 28, 62–63, 164
Frisk, Max, 50–51

Game, adoption, *see* "Adoption Game"
Gaylord, C. L., 15
Gays, 67
Genealogical bewilderment, and adolescents, 47–53; and alienation, 51–53; and "body im-

My guess is
that The shift,
from open (ancient?)
adoption to closed
is recent. Wrapped by
adoptive P's who
wanted secure relationships
+ were allowed to
close off the other channel —
in part because illistimate
birth mothers have no clout.
(If poor, giving up is a
rich, nice family, no real
the child — see the Willows)